AMERICAN
TASTE

OTHER BOOKS BY JAMES VILLAS:

Villas at Table
James Villas' Country Cooking
The Town & Country Cookbook
The French Country Kitchen
My Mother's Southern Cooking
The Great American Stewpot

AMERICAN TASTE

A CELEBRATION
OF GASTRONOMY
COAST-TO-COAST

by James Villas

LYONS & BURFORD, PUBLISHERS

First published by Arbor House Publishing Company
Printed in the United States of America

Parts of some chapters in this book appeared originally in
Town & Country, Esquire, TWA Ambassador, and *Bon Appétit.*

1 3 5 7 9 10 8 6 4 2

Villas, James.
    American taste: a celebration of gastronomy coast-to-coast/
by James Villas.
        p.   cm.—(The cook's classic library)
    Originally published: New York: Arbor House, c1982.
    Includes index.
    ISBN 1-55821-572-7 (pbk.)
    1. Gastronomy.   2. Cookery, American.   I. Title.   II. Series.
TX633.V54   1997
641.5973—dc21   96-29570
                                                          CIP

CONTENTS

FOREWORD
BY JAMES BEARD

THERE ARE many people who love to read cookbooks, and many more who love to read about food. James Villas's book is definitely an addition to the literature of gastronomy.

Over the years there have been brilliant writers who were not so much great cooks as reporters of their times who wrote on culinary topics. As long ago as Roman times, Ausonius wrote spectacularly about the vineyards of the Rhine. Brillat-Savarin's reportage on his adventures on both sides of the Atlantic became classics, as did Dumas's great *Dictionary*. Maurice des Ombioux and Père Androuet and the great books of Carème were all part of this tradition in France.

In recent years in England, Elizabeth David has written beautiful prose, as have Jane Grigson, George Ellwanger, and Morton Shand. I've liked Ian Campbell on wine, Alan Davidson on fish, and Quenton Crewe's criticism of restaurants that leads him into discussions on the history of food.

In America, we have few commentators who have written gloriously about gastronomy: perhaps they were too busy building a cuisine for America. Among those we could mention are Eliza Leslie, who wrote amusing and acute commentaries on *la cuisine française;* Catherine Beecher and Harriet Beecher Stowe; and, in the mid-nineteenth century, Theodore Child. We have been producing hundreds and hundreds of cookbooks, but as yet, except for M. F. K. Fisher, we haven't yet produced a single extraordinary commentator on food and gastronomy.

Now James Villas, who has been writing about food with great delight and disdain for some years, and who has become nationally known as a commentator on our times, has seen fit to give us a book of his opinions. Jim is a man of stature. He travels widely, he has a keen eye and a keener palate, he knows the arts and the times, and has many interests, which make him all the sharper when he writes about food.

His treatise on Bourbon is extraordinary and knowing. In my memory, which goes back quite a few years, I don't recall anyone else ever coming near his account of this truly American liquor.

He writes an amusingly prejudiced splurge on the barbecue of North Carolina, being a loyal and patriotic fan of barbecue as practised in his home state.

He writes wonderfully about soup. I have great sympathy for his treatment of this subject. Soup can be something between weak broth and dishwater in some cases and will have guts and exquisite taste and texture in another. Anyone who has tasted the tripe soup one finds at The Coach House in New York, or the lobster bisque at Lutéce, or a gazpacho at a roadside restaurant in California, knows of the glories of soup.

I was amused by his treatise on caviar, which is slightly snob, completely revealing, and educational in the nicest possible way. And I enjoyed his idealization of breakfast. His almost gluttonous appreciation of fine bread baking in the mornings is so much to my taste that it made me feel I could live on breakfast alone. I have never been one to feel that breakfast should have a narrow-minded menu. A good slice of cold roast beef, a breakfast steak, or a fresh bit of chicken are all delights in the morning. And I remember a marvelous breakfast in England that consisted of romaine and watercress gathered fresh from the garden, dressed with vinaigrette, and eaten with crisp toast that we dipped into the vinaigrette instead of buttering it. Now that we're being preached to about small breakfasts, miserable glasses of juice, and dry toast, I found it a joy to wallow in Villas's lore of the great days when people weren't afraid to indulge themselves in beautiful eggs, fish, ham, bacon, sausages, tea, coffee, and wondrous marmalades.

Then, James Villas should be listened to when he writes about restaurant service. This chapter alone makes the book a gem. It recounts the author's experiences as a captain in one of America's most glamorous and successful restaurants. He performed the tasks there unknown to the others on the staff, and his sometimes sad account is unique in the annals of gastronomic writing. I have always felt that few people know how to be guests in a fine restaurant, just as I am certain that very few people know how to order from a wine list or how to tip. When I read this chapter, I laughed with it and I suffered with it.

This is a book to enjoy if you like to read one man's opinions. It is, after all, his book, and they are his opinions, and you are free to agree or disagree as you like. At any rate, it's exceedingly good reading, it contains a lot of profitable information, and there is all through it something to make us savor the thought of good food, good living, and the joys of the good life. It led me to the kitchen to busy myself reproducing some of the goodies therein. It's a delicious volume!

⌐····INTRODUCTION····⌐

WHILE EVERY effort has been made to interpret and analyze the complex evolution of American cookery, no one captures the truth of the matter more succinctly than our most distinguished spokesman, James Beard. "What interests me," says the author of *The New James Beard,* "is how the quality of cooking in this country can be followed from a period of simplicity and function to one of goodness and bounty, then to an age of elaboration and excess, back again to functional (and, for the most part, mediocre) eating. Finally, we hope, we are now in another epoch of gastronomic excellence."

For those of us who devote our lives to serious eating, it sometimes seems nothing less than absurd to refer to "gastronomic excellence" in a country where millions are nourished on junk food, frozen TV dinners, stale produce, and charred steak. Yet I am convinced there is no nation on earth that has a more exciting culinary potential than ours. For the first time in our history, gastronomy is being recognized as an art worthy of the same respect and personal involvement as any other, and for the first time we have thousands of devoted native professionals fully capable of interpreting that art on many levels. Who can fail to be impressed with the growing consumer interest in good kitchen appliances and speciality food shops, with the almost staggering number of cookbooks and wine manuals on the market, with all the cooking schools and food societies sprouting like mushrooms coast-to-coast, with all the young people who are changing careers to open new restaurants, and with a large segment of the public's ever-increasing dining sophistication?

To discuss gastronomy in America is by no means the same as discussing American cookery since, unfortunately, far too many so-called gourmets (professionals and amateurs alike) still refuse to equate any sort of culinary refinement with our native fare; they are blindly convinced that all Americans are hopelessly addicted to a steady diet of hot dogs, tuna salad, and hamburgers and that no dish is worthy of serious appraisal that does not have at least a slight foreign accent. None other, for example, than the restaurant critic for a major newspaper had the temerity a few years back to write: "There definitely is such a thing as American cuisine. I think of fried chicken, baked ham, turkey, of course, and angel food cake, apple pie, and ice cream." Period. Add to this the pernicious influence of Madison Avenue, and who can wonder why the noted French gastronomic critics Henri Gault and Christian Millau strike so hard: "From ketchup to cake mix," they comment, "from Jello to peanut butter, from Coke to orangeade without oranges, this is a veritable autopsy of the American stomach seen in the TV ads which dictate to millions of families the menu of the day."

Contrary to what the odious messages on the Tube might imply, there are indeed numerous regional styles of cooking that are nobly American and that, it seems to me, anyone seriously interested in fine food should make a proud and concerted effort to exploit to the fullest. Merely a quick glance at our prodigious regional bounty suffices to illustrate what can be accomplished in the hands of inventive and talented cooks: fresh fruits and vegetables year-round from California, Florida, Texas, and Hawaii; the finest beef in the world from the Midwest, as well as a bountiful variety of wheat, corn, wild mushrooms, dairy products, and freshwater fish; moose, elk, venison, ruffed grouse, partridge, and pheasant from the Rocky Mountain states; fresh salmon, halibut, Dungeness crabs, razor clams, tiny Olympia oysters, and a profusion of wild berries from the Pacific Northwest; reindeer, Arctic char, fiddlehead ferns, and rosehips from Alaska; milk-fed veal from New Jersey, and pure maple syrup from New England; and from the overly blessed Southeast and Gulf states, wild turkey, cured hams and sausages, turtles, crawfish, and dozens of varieties of shrimp, crab, saltwater fish, corn, peas, greens, rice, and nuts. The list seems endless, and when you add to all this the fact that California now produces wines of such quality that even the French are rushing to buy acreage, that such luxury items as fresh sturgeon caviar and homemade goat cheeses are currently being produced on a national basis, and that our Culinary Institute of America in Hyde Park, New York is offering extensive training in creative American cookery, there can be no doubt that we are in the position to develop one of the finest cuisines in the world.

Testimonies to this potential have come not only from well-known authorities such as M. F. K. Fisher, James Beard, Evan Jones, Louis Szathmáry in Chicago, Craig Claiborne, and even Julia Child, but also from a number of restaurants that have already managed to elevate American cookery to new and distinguished heights. In New York, I refer to the venerable Coach House, The River Café, The Four Seasons, and Windows on the World. In Kansas City, I refer to the American Restaurant at Crown Center, with its applejack chicken with chestnuts, Plymouth clam pie, Montana elk with lingonberries, and Sugarbush Mountain maple mousse. In New Orleans, I refer to how a young, creative Cajun, Paul Prudhomme, is adding new dimensions to New Orleans cookery with the flourless gumbo, eggplant with powdered sugar, and coconut beer-battered shrimp served at his K-Paul's restaurant, and to the never-ending innovations carried out in the kitchen of Commander's Palace. In Chicago, I refer to a talented American head chef named Mike Beck who, inspired by the legendary Jovan Trboyevic, transcends the language of the menu at Le Perroquet by creating dishes with ingredients and flavors that can only be termed American. And in San Francisco, I refer to Alice Waters gradually but painlessly leaving the Gallic shadows at Chez Panisse, with her fresh goat-cheese soufflé, her grilled pork loin with crookneck squash, and her scallops with Walla Walla onions.

It has taken more than three centuries to approach what might be considered a stylized form of cooking in this country, and no doubt it will take a few more decades before culinary experimentation results in formal codification of certain dishes and cooking techniques. Over the years American cookery has been shaped by hundreds of influences: early French, English, and Dutch colonization; the black influence in the South; the pioneer tradition in the West; not to mention the immigration of Central Europeans to New Jersey, Pennsylvania, and the upper Midwest, of Greeks to Florida, of Portuguese to Cape Cod, of Armenians and Italians to California, of Basque sheepherders to Idaho, and of Russians, Poles, Jews, and Puerto Ricans to New York. Together these human infusions have created the most complex melting pot in history, perhaps depriving America so far of a readily definable cuisine but providing the ingredients and seasonings for what could evolve into a spectacular dish. Today what we are witnessing in the way of experimental cooking and fine dining is unprecedented in this nation, and it will indeed be curious to see what happens after more and more regional dishes are translated from one area to the next, after the motors burn out of the first food processors, and after all the novelty of ducks with rose petals and sweetbreads with raspberries has brought about sufficient ennui.

Naturally we can rest assured that McDonald's and Kentucky Fried Chicken will continue heavy trading on the big board, that more fields and orchards will be torn up for commercial and housing development to reduce further our valuable supply of fresh produce, and that the less inspired, less bold restaurateurs will continue to highlight their "continental" menus with shrimp scampi, steak Diane, chicken cordon bleu, and *fettuccine Alfredo.* But, on a more positive level, let us say that the pathfinders will recognize the same needs and directions at this stage of our gastronomic evolution as those suggested in Beard's new cookbook: lighter food and fewer items on the plate; fresh vegetables (preferably braised) served as a first course and more grains featured as a main course; meat used as a seasoning in the creation of new dishes; greater use of root vegetables and variety meats; a rediscovery of raw foods; and a much more serious endeavor to match American ingredients with the foods of such hitherto neglected cuisines as Spanish, Mexican, Peruvian, Thai, and Moroccan.

I have hopes that in the near future new millions will experience the taste of genuine Carolina pork barbecue, golden caviar from the whitefish of Lake Superior, buster crabs from Louisiana, Maine blueberry honey, Jack Daniel's sour mash whiskey, Liederkranz cheese, and a California Late Harvest Zinfandel. I hope that after having learned all we can from the chefs of other countries, we can let them stay at home and then staff our kitchens with many well-trained native talents. And I hope that the new breed of chefs will learn how to turn out as fine a loaf of sourdough bread as a piece of puff pastry, a grits soufflé as delicate as *crostini di polenta,* and a Creole seafood gumbo as aromatic as *bouillabaisse.*

In this book I purport to portray the multifaceted, ever-evolving hedonistic lifestyle of one hungry American for whom all wanderings are measured in terms of the next meal. This is not a cookbook, although recipes are included when—and only when—they serve to illustrate or reinforce a particular topic. Rather, it reflects an approach to gustatory adventure in America, a suggested means whereby those who, like myself, love to nourish themselves well can begin to really develop and improve their own taste in all things pertaining to food and drink. Some cookbooks are important as basic tools, to be sure, but the time has come for Americans to devote their attention to aspects of our gastronomy other than how to prepare flounder, chicken breasts, and chocolate cake a hundred different ways. Presently, the market is glutted with every type of cookbook imaginable, very few of which are destined to become classics. Often I am asked which ones I could not do without, and the list is short, simple, and virtually unchanging: *Joy of Cooking, Larousse Gastronomique,* Julia Child's two-volume *Mastering the Classic Art of French Cooking,* Marcella Hazan's *Classic Italian Cooking,* and *More Italian Cooking, The Doubleday Cookbook,* James Beard's *American Cookery,* Evan Jones's *American Food: The Gastronomic Story,* Craig Claiborne's *New York Times Cookbook,* and Time-Life's *Foods of the World* series. Most other volumes in my vast culinary library pale by comparison with these steadfast companions.

Over the past three centuries American cookery has indeed undergone a strange but understandable evolution, and now with the melting pot lowered below simmer, we are finally in the position to begin skimming off the fat, analyzing closely the ingredients, and transforming chaos into order. Already our culinary heritage has given us much we can be proud of, and this book is an attempt to celebrate that tradition. But this very legacy demands that within the realm of our experience we act boldly, expand what knowledge we have acquired, use our imagination, and create something truly superior that we can all our own. "Cuisine is the reflection of a culture," to quote once again those two influential French mavericks of all things gustatory, Gault and Millau, "and it would be absolutely abnormal for Americans to allow foreigners the exclusivity of nourishing them. The more American cooks there are, the more the gastronomic level of the country will rise. America has her architects, her painters, her musicians. In the name of what should she not also have her own cuisine? The new young chefs we have encountered have worked in the finest restaurants of Europe and studied one recipe after another. Thanks to them, we can now hope that a new style of cooking will emerge which will not be a copy of ours and will one day be a mode of expression that is authentically American."

WHISTLING DIXIE

UNDERSTANDING FRIED CHICKEN

●●●●●●●●●●●●●●●●●●●●●●●●●●●●●●●●●●●●●●●

WHEN IT comes to fried chicken, let's not beat around the bush for one second. To know about fried chicken you have to have been weaned and reared on it in the South. Period. The French know absolutely nothing about it, and Yankees very little. Craig Claiborne knows plenty. He's from Mississippi. And to set the record straight before bringing on regional and possibly national rage over the correct preparation of this classic dish, let me emphasize the fact that I'm a Southerner, born, bred, and chicken-fried for all times. Now, I don't know exactly why we Southerners love and eat at least ten times more fried chicken than anyone else, but we do and always have and always will. Maybe we have a hidden craw in our throats or oversize pulley bones or . . . oh, I don't know what we have, and it doesn't matter. What does matter is that we take our fried chicken very seriously, having singled it out years ago as not only the most important staple worthy of heated and complex debate but also as the dish that non-Southerners have never really had any knack for. Others just plain don't *understand* fried chicken, and, to tell the truth, there are lots of Southerners who don't know as much as they think they know. Naturally everybody is convinced he or she can cook or identify great fried chicken as well as any ornery reb (including all the fancy cookbook writers), but the truth remains that once you've eaten real chicken fried by an expert chicken fryer in the South . . . there are simply no grounds for contest.

As far as I'm concerned, all debate over how to prepare fried chicken has ended forever, for recently I fried up exactly 21½ chickens (or 215 pieces) using every imaginable technique, piece of equipment, and type of oil for the sole purpose of establishing once and for all the right way to fix great fried chicken. In a minute I'll tell you what's wrong with most of the Kentucky fried, Maryland fried, oven-fried, deep-fried, Creole fried, and all those other classified varieties of Southern fried chicken people like to go on about. But first *my* chicken, which I call simply Fried Chicken and which I guarantee will start you lapping:

Equipment (*no substitutes*)

> A sharp chef's or butcher's knife 12- to 13-inches long
> A large wooden cutting board
> A small stockpot half-filled with water (for chicken soup)
> A large glass salad bowl
> A heavy 12″ cast-iron skillet with lid
> Long-handled tweezer tongs
> 1 roll paper towels
> 2 brown paper bags
> 1 empty coffee can
> A serving platter
> A wire whisk
> A home fire extinguisher

Ingredients (*to serve 4*)

> 3 cups whole milk
> ½ fresh lemon
> 1½ lbs. (3 cups) top-quality shortening
> 4 Tb. rendered bacon grease
> 1 freshly killed 3½–4 lb. chicken
> 1½ cups plus 2 Tb. flour
> 3 tsp. salt
> Freshly ground black pepper

To Prepare Chicken for Frying:

Remove giblets and drop with neck in stockpot. (This is for a good chicken soup to be eaten at another time.) Cut off and pull out any undesirable fat at neck and tail. Placing whole chicken in center of cutting board (breast-side up, neck toward you), grab leg on left firmly, pull outward and down toward board, and begin slashing down through skin toward thigh joint, keeping knife close to thigh. Crack back thigh joint as far as possible, find joint with fingers, then cut straight through to remove (taking care not to pull skin from breast). Turn bird around and repeat procedure on other thigh. To separate thigh from leg, grasp one end in each hand, pull against tension of joint, find joint, and sever.

Follow same procedure to remove wings. Cut off wing tips and add to stockpot.

To remove pulley bone (or wishbone to non-Southerners), find protruding knob toward neck end of breast, trace with fingers to locate small indentation just forward of knob, slash horizontally downward across indentation, then begin cutting carefully away from indentation and downward toward neck till forked pulley-bone piece is fully severed. Turn chicken back-side up, locate two hidden small pinbones on either side below neck toward middle of back, and cut through skin to expose ends of bones. Put two fingers of each hand into neck cavity and separate breast from back by pulling forcefully till the two pry apart. (If necessary, sever stubborn tendons and skin with knife.) Cut the back in half, reserving lower portion (tail end) for frying, and tossing upper portion (rib cage) into stockpot. Place breast skin-side down, ram tip of knife down through center cartilage, and cut breast in half. (Hint: Level the cutting edge of knife along cartilage, then slam blade through with heel of hand.)

Rinse the ten pieces of chicken thoroughly under cold running water, dry with paper towels, and salt and pepper lightly. Pour milk into bowl, squeeze lemon into milk, add chicken to soak, cover, and refrigerate at least two hours and preferably overnight.

To Fry Chicken:

Remove chicken from refrigerator and allow to return to room temperature (about 70°). While melting the 1½ pounds of shortening over high heat to measure ½ inch in skillet, pour flour, remaining salt, and pepper to taste and drop into paper bag. Remove dark pieces of chicken from milk, drain each momentarily over bowl, drop in paper bag, shake vigorously to coat. Add bacon grease to skillet. When small bubbles appear on surface, reduce heat slightly. Remove dark pieces of chicken from bag one by one, shake off excess flour, and, using tongs, lower gently into fat, skin-side down. Quickly repeat all procedures with white pieces; reserve milk, arrange chicken in skillet so it cooks evenly, reduce heat to medium, and cover. Fry exactly 17 minutes. Lower heat, turn pieces with tongs, and fry 17 minutes longer uncovered. With paper towels wipe grease continuously from exposed surfaces as it spatters. Chicken should be almost mahogany brown.

Drain thoroughly on second brown paper bag, transfer to serving platter *without* reheating in oven, and serve hot or at room temperature with any of the following items: mashed potatoes and cream gravy*, potato salad, green beans, turnip greens, sliced homegrown tomatoes, stewed okra, fresh corn bread, iced tea, beer, homemade peach ice cream, or watermelon.

*To Make Cream Gravy:

Discard in coffee can all but one tablespoon fat from skillet, making sure not to pour off brown drippings. Over high heat, add two remaining tablespoons flour to fat and stir constantly with wire whisk till roux browns. Gradually pour 1¾ cups reserved milk from bowl and continue stirring till gravy comes to a boil, thickens slightly, and is smooth. Reduce heat, simmer two minutes, and check salt and pepper seasoning. Serve in gravy boat.

Now that's the right way, the only way, to deal with fried chicken. Crisp, juicy on the inside, full of flavor—not greasy and sloppy, fabulous. Of course one reason my recipe works so well is that it's full of important subtleties that are rarely indicated in cookbooks but that help to make the difference between impeccable fried chicken and all the junk served up everywhere today. And just to illustrate this point, I cite a recipe for "Perfect Fried Chicken" that once appeared in a popular woman's magazine:

1. Rinse cut-up 2½- to 3-lb. broiler-fryer and pat dry.
2. Pour 1 in. vegetable oil in skillet, heat to 375°. Combine ½ cup flour, 2 tsp. salt, dash of pepper in a bag. Coat a few pieces at a time.
3. Preheat oven to 250°. Place paper towels in shallow baking pan.
4. Fry thighs and drumsticks, turning occasionally, for 12 minutes until golden. Pierce with fork to see if juices run clear. Remove to baking pan and place in heated oven. Fry remaining pieces for 7 or 8 minutes. Serves 4.

Snap! That's it. A real quickie. Fast fried chicken that promises to be perfect. Bull! It tastes like hell, and if you don't believe me, try it yourself. The pitfalls of the recipe are staggering but typical. First of all, nobody in his right mind fries a skinny 2½-pound chicken for four people, not unless everyone's on some absurd diet or enjoys sucking bones. Second, the recipe takes for granted that you're going to buy a plastic-wrapped chicken so hacked up and splintered by a meat cleaver that blood from the bones saturates the package. What help is offered if the chicken you happen to have on hand is whole or only partially cut up? Third, what type of skillet, and what size, for heaven's sake? If the pan's too light the chicken will burn on the bottom, and if you pour one full inch of oil in an eight-inch skillet you'll end up with deep-fried chicken. And as for sticking forks in seared chicken to release those delicious juices, or putting fried chicken in the oven to get it disgustingly soggy, or serving a half-raw thick breast that's cooked only seven or eight minutes—well, I refuse to get overheated.

Without question, the most important secret to any great fried chicken is the quality of the chicken itself, and without question, most of the 3 billion pullets marketed annually in the United States have about as much flavor as tennis balls. After all, what can you expect of battery birds whose feet never touch the dirty earth, whose diet includes weight-building fats, fish flours, and factory-fresh chemicals, and whose life expectancy is a pitiful seven weeks? Tastelessness, that's what, the same disgraceful tastelessness that characterizes the eggs we're forced to consume. How many people in this country remember the rich flavor of a good old barnyard chicken, now a nearly extinct species that once pecked around the yard for a good fifteen weeks, digested plenty of barley-and-milk mash, bran, grain, and beer, got big and fat, and never sent one solitary soul to the hospital with contamination? I remember, and how I pity the millions who, blissfully unconscious of what they missed and sadly addicted to fast-food chicken, will never taste a truly luscious piece of fried chicken unless they're first shown how to get their hands on a real chicken. Of course, what you see in supermarkets are technically real chickens fit for consumption, but anyone who's sunk teeth into a gorgeous, plump barnyard beauty (not to mention an inimitable French *poularde de Bresse*) would agree that to compare the scrawny, bland, mass-produced bird with the one God intended us to eat is almost ludicrous.

I originally intended to discuss how to raise, kill, draw, and prepare your own chickens. Then I came to my senses and faced the reality that unless you were brought up wringing chickens' necks, bleeding them, searching for the craws where food is stored, and pulling out their innards with your hands—well, it can be a pretty nauseating mess that makes you gag if you're not used to it. Besides, there's really no need to slaughter your own chickens, not, that is, if you're willing to take time and make the effort to locate either a good chicken raiser who feeds and exercises his chickens properly (on terra firma) or a reliable merchant who gets his chickens fresh from the farm. They do exist, still, be their number ever so dwindling. If you live in a rural area, simply get to know a farmer who raises chickens, start buying eggs from him, and then tell him you'll pay him any amount to kill and prepare for you a nice 3½- to 4-pound pullet. He will, and probably with pride. If you're in a large city, the fastest method is to study the Yellow Pages of the phone book, search under "Poultry—Retail" for the words "Fresh Poultry and Eggs" or "Custom Poultry" or "Strictly Kosher Poultry," and proceed from there. Even in huge metropolitan centers, it's not as hard as you think to find a nice barnyard chicken.

Next in importance to the quality of the fowl is the cutting-up procedure, a subject rarely even touched upon in cookbooks. I suppose most cooks just don't like to be bothered cutting up their own chickens, but again, if you're determined to have the best possible, you must get into the habit of buying only whole chickens and doing the job yourself (my mother literally will not cook a bird she hasn't dismembered herself). And the reasons are logical. First, as any fried chicken expert knows, the way commercial birds are rapidly hacked apart in supermarkets today, it's a wonder people aren't dead from swallowing splintered bones (a possibility Southerners have feared for generations). Second, unless care is taken to separate parts at the joints and cut evenly through the skin, you end up with bloody pieces of chicken with half the flavorful skin ripped off. Third, the only way on God's green earth to get ten pieces from a chicken (including the lower back and pulley bone) is to cut them yourself. Why the back portion and pulley bone? I'll tell you why. Not only does the former contain that delectable morsel of meat known only to Southerners as the "oyster," but by cutting away the tender pulley-bone piece, you reduce the size of the two breasts and thus allow for greater flexibility of space in the skillet. Besides, eating fried chicken is just not eating fried chicken without the age-old ceremony of two chicken eaters pulling on the pulley bone for good luck (the one with the long end getting to make the wish).

From this point on, arguments over fixing fried chicken become hotly outrageous, and since I don't care to defend every step of what I'm inalterably and forevermore convinced is the fail-proof recipe, I'll explain, one-two-three, only the most essential features while occasionally making reference to all those other varieties of fried chicken I mentioned.

The Skillet: I can't overemphasize the importance of frying chicken in a heavy cast-iron skillet that's well seasoned and black as tar from long use. All expert chicken fryers agree. Not only does cast iron heat slowly, evenly, and maintain heat well (all of which are essential when shallow-frying many pieces); it also yields gravy-making drippings like no other cookware. If you don't own this skillet, buy one (at a hardware store), wash it thoroughly, rub the bottom and sides with unsalted oil, and heat it slowly in the oven at 275° F for at least one hour to season it. I find enameled cast iron a weak substitute.

Seasoning and Batter: Real fried chicken should be seasoned with nothing more than salt, fresh pepper, a touch of lemon juice, and a few tablespoons of bacon grease added to the cooking fat. Some people like to add paprika, cayenne, and anything else they can sprinkle on; others dump on soy sauce and Worcestershire; and Creole fried chicken can contain anything from garlic to thyme to Tabasco. All of these are unacceptable if what you're looking for is classic fried chicken.

One reason Maryland fried chicken (which even Escoffier included in his cookbook, *Ma Cuisine,* with, mind you, a béchamel sauce!) never seems to be quite crisp enough on the outside is that it's not coated with a well-seasoned batter before frying. (The other reason is that people glop gravy all over the chicken—which is wrong—instead of pouring it in the center of a mound of mashed potatoes—which is right.) Lots of recipes for Kentucky fried chicken indicate an egg-milk (or egg-cream) batter, while in the Deep South it's not unusual to find chicken dipped in buttermilk before flouring. The first possibility is out of the question since the egg absorbs too much grease. The second, I must say, makes for pretty good eating if you don't mind a slightly sweet taste to your chicken. Overall, I still prefer a seasoned whole-milk batter, and I'm absolutely convinced that soaking the chicken for at least a few hours before dredging not only allows the seasoning to penetrate the meat to the bone but also gives it a nice, moist texture.

Cooking Oil: This is the area in which most people really make a mess of things, either out of ignorance or carelessness or cheapness or just plain laziness. Cookbook writers, in particular, almost consistently offer you the option of lard or shortening, or lard or vegetable oil. That's sloppy teaching. The one and only thing to use is a bland, high-grade shortening (Crisco is best) that holds up well over intense heat. Lard, which is animal fat, not only breaks down quickly but also overwhelms the natural flavor of the chicken (it's great for quickly cooked French fried potatoes but not for slowly cooked chicken). Bottled corn oil stinks, literally, and even the odor of hot vegetable oil makes me nauseated. Now, I don't know why those very, very healthy polyunsaturates smell and taste so bad, but they do, and I wouldn't drop even a wing in a single ounce. Nor would I ever consider frying chicken in peanut or olive oil, both of which are too heavy in flavor. As for adding butter to the shortening (as even some Southerners do), I'm also against that, for the simple reason that it makes the chicken taste like some fancy, rich French dish. Classic fried chicken is neither fancy nor rich, and this is why butter-basted oven-fried chicken is not fried chicken. Don't get me wrong about butter, not for one minute, for I normally use it for everything but bathing. Butter is great for soothing grease-spatter skin burns, but chicken sautéed in butter is soft and golden on the outside, while true fried chicken is so crisp and brown it crumbles almost like a croissant when bitten into. Both are superlative, but the two just aren't kin.

Frying: The first rule in frying chicken is never to allow more than ½ inch of grease in the skillet. If you add any more, you'll end up with deep-fried chicken, or something that resembles the atrocities served at greasy spoons. The same principle explains why, contrary to what the books say, the pieces should be arranged fairly close to one another, allowing the bottoms to brown without the grease bubbling too far up the sides. Whether or not to cover the skillet has always been a major point of debate, and I suspect the true reason many people keep a lid on throughout the process is to keep grease from spattering all over God's creation—which is, of course, stupid. After frying my 21½ chickens, I concluded that covering the skillet during the first seventeen minutes helps the upper sides of the pieces to retain moisture, which is later sealed in when you turn the chicken. During the next seventeen minutes, the lid should be removed so the upper browned portion absorbs no more moisture and remains crisp on the outside. Never turn fried chicken more than once, never, and don't fiddle with the drumsticks. They'll cook properly without being rolled all around. Please note that my frying time is for a chicken three and a half pounds or larger. if your bird is smaller (which it really shouldn't be), you'll have to reduce the time.

The Paper Bag: Nothing in heaven or on earth (not even a sponge or Kleenex) absorbs chicken grease like a brown paper bag. Again, I don't know exactly why this is true, but if you don't have a paper bag on hand, forget about frying chicken till you do. Paper towels just don't do the job. Still again I don't know why, but I do know when you pick up a piece of fried chicken that's been draining on paper towels, the chicken is, for some reason, still greasy on the bottom. Some experts use the same bag for both dredging and draining, and sometimes that works just fine. But flour tends to sneak through the folds of most paper bags, so unless you don't mind a little white dust on your chicken (I do), it's a good idea to have a clean bag for draining.

Now, if you think I take my fried chicken a little too seriously, you haven't seen anything till you attend the National Chicken Cooking Contest held annually in early summer at different locations throughout the country. Created in 1949, the festival has a Poultry Princess; vintage motorcar displays; a flea market; a ten-feet-by-eight-inch skillet that fries up 7½ tons of chicken; 10,000 chicken-loving contestants cooking for cash prizes amounting to over $25,000; and big-name judges who are chosen from among the nation's top newspaper, magazine, and television food editors. It's a big to-do. Of course, I personally have no intention whatsoever of ever entering any chicken contest that's not made up exclusively of Southerners, and of course, you understand my principle. This, however, should not necessarily affect your now going to the National and showing the multitudes what real fried chicken is all about. A few years back, a young lady irreverently dipped some chicken in oil flavored with soy sauce, rolled in it crushed chow mein noodles, fried it up, and walked away with top honors and a few grand for her Cock-a-Noodle-Do. Without doubt, she was a sweetheart of a gal, but you know, the people who judged that fried chicken need help.

CREOLE, CAJUN,
CHOCTAW . . .

●●●●●●●●●●●●●●●●●●●●●●●●●●●●●●●●

"HONEY, HOW 'bout another Sazerac?" insisted Ella Brennan, tearing off a small piece of hot garlic bread. "I've always said there's no finer drink in New Awl-uns. So very refreshing. Especially on a hot day like this when it takes every ounce of strength you can drum up just to catch a deep breath. But that last one they poured you was a double. And since I don't consider that sort of trick to be in very good taste or in the best of anybody's interests, I'm gonna speak with my captain this very minute."

While New Orleans's grande dame of gastronomy conversed with the cowering captain on the impropriety of allowing any waiter to serve, without fair warning, a double whiskey laced with Pernod and spiked with both Peychaud and Angostura bitters, I glanced around the ornately decorated room which was once the parlor of a Victorian mansion but, in more recent years, has served as the main dining salon of Commander's Palace. Although I was raised elsewhere in the South, I, like so many others who appreciate New Orleans's special culinary offerings, had been to the restaurant many times. Little had been changed since I was there last, and as I studied the room's stately furnishings, the smartly dressed clientele enjoying a leisurely lunch, and the intriguing aromas of classic Creole-Cajun dishes being served, strong emotional memories were evoked. Here, as a child, I had tasted my first gumbo, that sublimely spicy soup-stew with shrimp, okra, and rice. Years later, a couple of Sybaritic college friends and I drove hundreds of miles just to eat our way through the restaurants of New Orleans, and in the verdant garden-patio of Commander's Palace I was introduced to soft-shell turtle stew, baked oysters Bienville, and creamy crab meat Imperial. In the years that followed I must have tasted every dish turned out by the kitchen, from the rich turtle soup to former chef Paul Prudhomme's inimitable pompano with fat buster crabs to filet mignon debris to a more recent dessert creation consisting of two beignets (New Orleans–style doughnuts) baked with an apricot sauce. In other words, I felt at home, the only curious difference being that sitting at my table was Ella Brennan who, for as long as I could remember, had run the famous Brennan's Restaurant over on Royal Street in the French Quarter along with the rest of her family.

"Well, honey, I'll tell you about it," she explained, sipping from her glass of Corton-Charlemagne and nodding her approval of the wine. "As you know, my brother Owen opened the place on Royal back in 'forty-six, and we all worked our heads off making that restaurant into what it became and still is. Well, by the time the nephews had grown up and were able to take on some of the responsibility, I, my two brothers Dick and John, and sister Adelaide were all eager to start all over again and accomplish somewhere else what we'd done at Brennan's. Guess we wanted more excitement and a new challenge. When Commander's went up for sale, we grabbed it, not only because it suited our business purposes but also because it's located right here in the Garden District, just three blocks, mind you, from my and Adelaide's big ole white house. Look, here come your buster crabs, and, honey, you must wait till you taste those!"

I had little doubt when I arrived that the crabs, as well as the other dishes that made up my Corinthian lunch, would be superb. But what impressed me most was that here an entire generation, formerly associated with one famous institution, had now moved to another with the intention of not only carrying on a brilliant culinary tradition but eventually transcending it. On the other hand, the more I thought about how so many of the city's legendary restaurants have for generations remained self-contained family enterprises, the more I realized that this phenomenon was really quite normal. Antoine's, Galatoire's, Corrine Dunbar's, Chez Helene, Bon Ton, Arnaud's, Le Ruth's, the Caribbean Room—some very old restaurants, some relatively new, some superlative, some disappointing, but all are family establishments that have contributed so much over the years to making New Orleans what many connoisseurs consider to be the gastronomic capital of America.

Sadly enough, however, there are millions of Americans and foreigners who have never visited New Orleans, much less the surrounding bayou country of southern Louisiana where many of the city's superlative dishes originate. Even sadder is the fact that many of those who do venture down for Mardi Gras or the Sugar Bowl game are either misinformed about the city's exciting culinary attractions or totally discouraged by the enormous crowds that inundate the restaurants. Frankly stated, trying to dine out in New Orleans during any of the festival periods is nothing less than a nightmare for those mainly interested in food—a demoralizing experience involving long lines, indifferent service, jacked-up prices, and, often, modified menus.

Since New Orleanians are fiercely proud of their culinary heritage, it pays the curious visitor to have at least an elementary knowledge of Creole and Cajun cooking. What, first of all, is the difference between Creole and Cajun? Or, as some locals might suggest, is there really any difference at all? Is it true the Creole kitchens aspire to haute cuisine with their delicate blends, various sauces, and subtle combinations of ingredients, while Cajun kitchens serve down-to-earth food prepared in huge iron pots and heavily spiced (as at K-Paul's or Bon Ton)? Does the Creole cook attribute more importance than the Cajun to starting most dishes with a roux of oil or butter and flour, and which of them makes greater use of rice? These and hundreds of similar questions have been debated in and around New Orleans for generations or, more precisely, ever since the two cultures developed independently in southern Louisiana more than two hundred years ago.

The first group of settlers in this area were Frenchmen, high-born and low, followed by Spaniards and West Indians. Then in various waves came French nobles escaping political persecution, Germans, Italians, Scots, Irish, and Africans. But the dominant influences in the community remained essentially French, not only as to customs and manners but also in regard to cooking. Eschewing, however, the highly stylized cuisine of the French aristocracy in favor of savory bourgeois dishes, the Creoles (French and Spanish families who came before 1803) were quick to take advantage of the natural resources that surrounded them. They were particularly lavish in their use of seafood from the Gulf, lakes, and streams as well as the vegetables which grew so rapidly in the vast rich farmlands that stretched on all sides of the city. From the Choctaw Indians they learned of filé, a fragrant powder made from the young leaves of sassasfras that many cooks still consider indispensable as a thickening for soups and stews. From trade with the West Indies, Mexico, and Cuba came new herbs and spices, sugarcane, bitters, and innumerable tropical fruits and vegetables hitherto unknown to the European settlers. And above all, from Africa came the Negro cooks, without whom the various techniques of the new culinary form would never have evolved as they did. Indeed, because of them Creole cookery has come to be what it is, and today most of the best cooking in New Orleans is still done by blacks.

In the eighteenth century another group of settlers arrived in southern Louisiana—but under altogether different circumstances. They, too, were of French origin but for nearly a century had been living in what is now Nova Scotia (then known as Acadia). When the English won Canada, the Acadians, who refused to swear allegiance to the Crown, were gradually driven out and left to wander in search of an area in the New World where they could settle. Finally, in the swamps and marshes west of New Orleans they found a new home and became, in local dialect, Cajuns (a corruption of the word *Acadians*). They, of course, had retained many basic principles of French peasant cookery, but also they began to develop more imaginative dishes based on the varied fauna and flora indigenous to the area. Eventually, exchanging experimental ideas with Creole cooks with whom they came in contact, they perfected ways of preparing food which to this day are virtually impossible (or at least, very impractical) to reproduce outside New Orleans and the surrounding bayou country.

Staple Creole and Cajun dishes naturally differ from each other, but in a way that still defies explicit definition. Essentially these differences are negligible. Gumbo (the original African word for okra), for example—that most subtly balanced of soup-stews which pretentious gourmets somewhat derisively refer to as "poor-man's *bouillabaisse*"—is generally considered to be Creole, but one of the finest I ever tasted was prepared by a Cajun. On the other hand, it's often said that nobody can turn out an authentic crawfish bisque like a Cajun, but I still say the one that remains most firmly fixed among my many delicious memories was served by a New Orleans lady who must have been at least seventh-generation Creole. Redfish stuffed with crab meat, *daube glacée*, jambalaya, red beans and rice, oyster bisque, turtle stew, tomatoes and okra, crab cakes—all are found in restaurants throughout New Orleans and all should be classified simply as good ole southern Louisiana specialities. Some people might prefer to say that Creole cookery comprises more elements of classic French cuisine while Cajun tends towards more basic but spicier dishes, but whatever the distinctions, it's for sure that these wonderful dishes add a significant dimension to the cooking of America.

SHRIMP REMOULADE

½   cup Creole mustard (available in speciality food shops)
½   cup prepared mustard
½   cup catsup
¼   cup white vinegar
¼   cup horseradish
¼   cup Worcestershire sauce
3   Tb. paprika
2   cups finely minced celery
1½   cups minced green onion
⅓   cup oil
5   eggs, lightly beaten
1   bunch parsley, minced
4   bay leaves
1   lemon, seeded and diced
2   Tb. garlic powder
1   Tb. salt
1   tsp. Tabasco
   Juice of 1 lemon
36   large unpeeled raw shrimp, deveined
   Well-chilled shredded iceburg lettuce

Combine first 7 ingredients in a blender or food processor and mix well. Add remaining ingredients except shrimp and lettuce and blend thoroughly. Cover and chill several hours or overnight. About 2 hours before serving, peel shrimp and place in a shallow dish. Cover generously with some of the sauce and marinate until serving time. Line individual serving plates with small amounts of shredded lettuce and top each with 6 shrimp plus a little extra sauce. SERVES 6.

Eggplant Soup

8   Tb. butter
¾   cup diced onions
¾   cup diced celery
2   cups diced eggplant
¾   cup peeled and diced potatotes
½   tsp. curry powder
    Pinch thyme
    Pinch basil
2   cups chicken stock
1   cup heavy cream

In a large, heavy skillet sauté in butter the onions, celery, eggplant, and potatoes about 5 or 10 minutes over medium heat. Add curry powder, thyme, and basil and continue cooking till potatoes start to stick to bottom of skillet. Add chicken stock and bring to the boil. Reduce heat and simmer till the starch from the eggplant and potatoes thickens the stock. When soup is thickened, remove from heat and stir in whipping cream. SERVES 4–6.

Gumbo Ya Ya

1   5-lb. chicken, cut into 10 pieces
      Salt
      Cayenne pepper
      Garlic powder
2½   cups flour
1   cup oil
2   cups chopped onion
2   cups chopped green pepper
1½   cups chopped celery
6   cups chicken stock
1   lb. andouille sausage or kielbasa, diced
1½   tsp. minced fresh garlic
      Salt and freshly ground pepper to taste
      Steamed white rice

On a baking pan arrange chicken pieces, season evenly with salt, cayenne, and garlic powder, and let stand 30 minutes at room temperature. Combine chicken pieces and flour in a large paper bag, and shake till chicken is well coated. Heat oil in a large, heavy skillet over medium heat, add chicken (reserve remaining flour), and brown on all sides. Remove with a slotted spoon, set aside, and loosen any browned bits on bottom of skillet. Using whisk, add 1 cup reserved flour and stir constantly until roux is very dark brown. Remove from heat, add onion, green pepper, and celery, and stir thoroughly and constantly to prevent burning. Transfer to a large saucepan, stir in stock, and bring to a boil over medium-high heat. Reduce heat, add sausage and garlic, and simmer 45 minutes, stirring occasionally. Remove chicken from bones, cut meat into ¼-inch pieces, add to saucepan, and heat through. Season to taste with salt and pepper and serve over steamed rice in individual soup bowls. SERVES 6–8.

CRAB MEAT IMPERIAL

2   Tb. butter
¼   cup minced onion
2   Tb. minced green pepper
2   Tb. minced celery
¼   cup minced tops of scallions
    Salt and freshly ground pepper to taste
1   tsp. powdered garlic
¾   cup fresh mayonnaise
¼   cup Creole mustard (available in speciality food shops)
1   Tb. Tabasco
1   Tb. Worcestershire sauce
1   cup well-drained and minced pimiento
½   lb. fresh lump crab meat, picked
2   Tb. chopped parsley

In a large skillet melt butter, add onions, green pepper, celery, scallions, salt and pepper, and garlic and sauté about 15 minues. Remove from heat, add mayonnaise, mustard, Tabasco, Worcestershire, and pimiento, mix lightly, and let cool. Place crab meat in a large mixing bowl, add sauce, and mix gently to coat crab meat without breaking up lumps. Serve in shells or atop lettuce and sprinkle with chopped parsley. SERVES 2.

RED BEANS AND RICE

4	Tb. oil
1	cup chopped onions
½	cup chopped bell pepper
½	cup chopped celery
2	cloves garlic, minced
½	lb. ham, diced
½	lb. red kidney beans
¼	tsp. thyme
2	bay leaves
¼	tsp. oregano
½	lb. hot pork smoked sausage or kielbasa, sliced
	Salt and cayenne pepper to taste
5–6	cups cooked rice

In a large, heavy skillet sauté onions, bell peppers, celery, garlic, and ham in oil over medium heat till vegetables are soft. Add beans and enough water to cover. Add thyme, bay leaves, and oregano, cover skillet, and cook over low heat till beans begin to break up (about 2 hours). Add sausage, salt, and cayenne to taste, and continue cooking slowly about 1 hour or till beans start to change color and become thick and creamy, stirring occasionally to prevent beans from sticking to bottom of skillet. Serve on top rice. SERVES about 8.

CREOLE SEAFOOD STOCK

2	qts. water
6	celery stalks, cut into 2-inch pieces
2	medium onions, peeled and quartered
2	garlic cloves
½	lemon
	Fresh shrimp heads and/or shells, lobster heads and/or shells, and fish bones (used singly or in combination)

Combine all ingredients in a large saucepan or stockpot, bring to a rapid boil, reduce heat, and simmer slowly 4–8 hours, depending on strength of flavor desired. Strain before using. Yield: 2 quarts.

CREOLE SEAFOOD SEASONING

⅓ cup plus 1 Tb. salt
⅓ cup plus 1 Tb. paprika
⅓ cup cayenne pepper
¼ cup black pepper
¼ cup granulated garlic
3 Tb. granulated onion
2 Tb. thyme

Combine all ingredients in a small bowl and mix thoroughly. Can be stored indefinitely in tightly lidded glass jar. Yield: 2 cups.

ARTICHOKES PRUDHOMME

6 large artichokes
½ fresh lemon
  Butter or olive oil
3 cups Oyster-Artichoke Sauce*
  Freshly grated Parmesan cheese

Cut off artichoke stems and discard. Cut top of leaves (about ¼ inch from top) with scissors. Remove center leaves and thistle in center. Rub cut surfaces with lemon juice to prevent discoloration. In a large kettle of rapidly boiling water to which a small amount of butter or olive oil has been added, poach artichokes till leaves pull easily from center (about 20–30 mintues). Remove with slotted spoon, invert on paper towels, and drain well. Just before serving bring water to boil in a large kettle, cook artichokes till completely heated, remove with slotted spoon, and drain thoroughly. To serve, preheat oven to 400° F. Place artichokes in small individual heatproof serving dishes and fill center of each with ¼ cup Oyster-Artichoke Sauce. Sprinkle generously with Parmesan cheese, transfer dishes to a baking sheet, and bake about 10–15 minutes or till Parmesan is golden.

* OYSTER-ARTICHOKE SAUCE
1½   cups cold water
36   fresh oysters
¼   cup flour
1   stick unsalted butter, melted
1   cup chopped scallion tops
2   Tb. Creole Seafood Seasoning
8   fresh artichoke bottoms, thinly sliced, or 1 8½-oz. can water-packed artichoke hearts, well drained and thinly sliced

Pour water over oysters in large bowl and let stand 15 minutes, stirring occasionally. Remove oysters with slotted spoon and set aside, reserving oyster water. Combine flour and butter in a small bowl and beat constantly with a whisk till smooth paste forms. In a large skillet melt butter over medium-high heat, add scallion tops, and sauté till soft. Add reserved oyster water and seafood seasoning and bring to a boil. Add roux and stir constantly till sauce is consistency of heavy cream. Reduce heat and simmer 10 minutes. Add artichokes and oysters and blend well. Remove from heat and let stand in warm place for up to 1 hour. When ready to serve, stir sauce and adjust consistency with small amount of water if desired.

CRAB AND CORN BISQUE

1   stick butter
1½   cups chopped scallions
2   Tb. flour
1¼   tsp. Creole Seafood Seasoning
1   tsp. granulated garlic
     Pinch thyme
4   cups Crab Stock*
2   12-oz. cans whole kernel corn, drained
1½   cups heavy cream
1   lb. lump crab meat

Melt butter in a 3-quart saucepan over medium heat, add scallions, and sauté till wilted. Stir in flour, seafood seasoning, garlic, and thyme and continue cooking till flour begins to stick to pan. Blend in stock, reduce heat, and simmer 15 minutes or till slightly thick. Add corn, simmer 15 minutes more, slowly stir in cream, and blend well. Gently add crab meat, remove from heat, and let stand 30 minutes. Reheat gently over very low heat, being careful crab meat does not break up into flakes and cream does not curdle. SERVES 8.

* CRAB STOCK

1½	qts. water
6	medium hard-shell crabs
6	celery stalks
2	medium onions, quartered
1½	Tb. liquid crab boil (optional and available in speciality food shops)

Combine all ingredients in a large saucepan, bring to a boil, reduce heat, and simmer 3 hours, adding more water as necessary to make 1 quart stock. Strain before using.

LIGHT SEAFOOD GUMBO

2	qts. seafood stock
16	crab claws
3	cups diced onion
2	cups diced green pepper
1	16-oz. can whole tomatoes, undrained
1	cup tomato puree
3	Tb. gumbo filé (available in speciality food shops)
2	10-oz. packages frozen okra, thawed
¼	cup Creole Seafood Seasoning
1½	Tb. granulated garlic
1½	tsp. thyme
1¼	tsp. saffron
4	bay leaves
½	tsp. salt
60	large raw shrimp, peeled and deveined
24	fresh oysters, shelled
1	lb. lump crab meat

In an 8-quart saucepan or Dutch oven combine stock, crab claws, onion, green pepper, tomatoes, and tomato puree, place over medium heat, and bring to a boil. Reduce heat, simmer 10 minutes, add all remaining ingredients except seafood, and return to simmer for an additional 10 minutes. Add seafood and continue cooking 10 minutes more, adding more seafood seasoning to taste if desired. SERVES 8.

SHRIMP CREOLE

¾	stick butter
2	cups coarsely chopped onion
2	cups coarsely chopped celery
2	cups coarsely chopped green or red bell pepper
1	cup tomato puree
6	fresh tomatoes, peeled
3	bay leaves
¾	tsp. oregano
	Pinch thyme
	Creole Seafood Seasoning
2	cups Seafood Stock
½	stick butter
2	cups coarsely chopped onion
1	Tb. brown sugar
2	cups coarsely chopped celery
2	cups coarsely chopped green or red bell pepper
60	large fresh shrimp, peeled and deveined
	Steamed rice

Melt butter in a 3-quart saucepan over medium heat, add onion, celery, and pepper, and sauté 10 minutes. Add tomato puree, tomatoes, bay leaves, oregano, thyme, and seafood seasoning to taste and cook an additional 10 minutes. Stir in stock, bring to a boil, reduce heat, and simmer about 45 minutes or till sauce begins to thicken. Remove from heat and strain, discarding vegetables. Melt remaining butter in a large skillet over medium heat, add onion, sprinkle with sugar, and sauté till golden brown. Add celery and pepper, sauté an additional 3–4 minutes, reduce heat, stir in reserved sauce, and simmer gently 10 minues. Add shrimp, cook just till heated through, and serve over rice. SERVES 6–8.

Eggs Commander's

2   Holland rusks
½   cup Commander's Sauce*
2   poached eggs
¼   cup Béarnaise Sauce**
2   2-oz. cooked Commander's Sausage patties***
    Minced parsley

Arrange Holland rusks on plate and top each with half of Commander's Sauce. Place poached egg over sauce and top each with half of Béarnaise Sauce. Place 1 sausage patty on either side of eggs. Sprinkle with parsley. Serves 1.

* *COMMANDER'S SAUCE*
½   stick butter
¼   cup flour
2   cups chicken stock
2   Tb. pureed yellow onion
1   Tb. white wine
1   tsp. Worcestershire sauce
½   clove garlic, minced
½   tsp. salt
½   tsp. freshly ground pepper
    Pinch garlic powder
6   oz. smoked ham, finely chopped
3   Tb. minced white onion
1   stick butter
½   cup heavy cream

Make roux by combining butter and flour in a small heavy skillet over medium-low heat and stirring constantly till butter is melted and mixture forms smooth paste. Remove from heat and set aside. In a medium saucepan bring stock to boil over medium heat, reduce heat, and simmer gently till reduced to 1 cup. Add onion, white wine, Worcestershire sauce, garlic, salt, pepper, and garlic powder and blend well. Stir in roux and continue to simmer over low heat till mixture is consistency of slightly whipped cream (about 20 minutes). Meanwhile, sauté ham and minced onion in a small heavy skillet till onion is soft. Remove sauce from heat and add butter in chunks a little at a time, whipping constantly with whisk. Gently stir in cream, add ham and onion mixture, and blend well. Yield: 3 cups.

** *BÉARNAISE SAUCE*
1 Tb. white wine
1 Tb. finely crumbled dried tarragon leaves
4 egg yolks
   Juice of ½ lemon
1 Tb. white wine
1 tsp. vinegar
1 tsp. Worcestershire sauce
   Pinch cayenne pepper
4 sticks unsalted butter, melted
   Salt to taste

In a small skillet heat white wine with tarragon over medium-low heat till wine evaporates. Combine yolks, lemon juice, remaining white wine, vinegar, Worcestershire sauce, and cayenne in top of double boiler over gently simmering water. Whip together with whisk till sauce begins to thicken, add butter in slow steady stream, and whisk constantly till sauce is creamy and thick. Stir tarragon mixture into sauce, blend well, and season with salt if desired. Yield: 1½ cups.

*** *COMMANDER'S SAUSAGE*
½ lb. veal, finely ground
½ lb. pork, finely ground
½ lb. beef, finely ground
½ cup Creole Seafood Seasoning
6 scallions, chopped
½ tsp. fennel
½ tsp. garlic powder
½ tsp. freshly grated nutmeg
   Dash thyme
   Salt and freshly ground pepper to taste

In a large mixing bowl combine all ingredients and blend well. Place mixture on a 12-inch length of aluminum foil and form into cylinder shape about 1½ inches in diameter. Chill in freezer till firm enough to cut without mashing (about 1 hour). Cut into 12–14 patties about ½-inch thick, fry in skillet over medium-high heat till brown, and drain well on paper towels. Yield: 12–14 patties.

STAR-SPANGLED BOURBON

•••••••••••••••••••••••••••••••••••

NOT TOO long ago a certain columnist for the Associated Press, obviously a little put out with a dreary world, closed his eyes for a moment, let his imagination run wild, and came up with the most enviable daydream: "If today weren't an ordinary day and I were allowed to do anything I wanted, I would like to skip rope with Cheryl Tiegs, have dinner with Julia Child, and beat Jimmy Connors at tennis." Before that, when Cecil Day Lewis was named poet laureate of England and informed he would receive the equivalent of $183 a year for the distinguished office, he made but a single comment: "Almost enough to keep me in Bourbon whiskey a day or two." And when one of our oldest citizens, a certain Charlie Smith of Bartow, Florida, celebrated his 130th birthday, he didn't hesitate for a moment to tell a Louisville reporter that he liked a glass of Bourbon every morning just to get started.

Dixie Nectar, Liquor Joy, Milk of Old Age, Old Friend, Good Company, Constant Companion are all well-known synonyms for Bourbon, the great American spirit and the only liquor ever designated by congressional resolution (in 1964) as "a distinctive product of the United States." As any connoisseur of fine wines and spirits knows, all the accolades awarded our best indigenous whiskey are based on the same respected standards as those associated with the tightly controlled production of French Champagne or genuine Cognac. Unfortunately, far too many people, convinced of the absurd and outright embarrassing notion that no liquor is worth touching unless it's imported, not only take Bourbon too much for granted but have absolutely no concept as to why the spirit is so special. And special it is! I know, for I was virtually weaned on the stuff, two-finger measures at a time. Take, for instance, the Bourbon formula, spelled out by law in one long breath: "A spirit, distilled from a fermented mash of grain which is at least 51 percent corn; distilled at not more than 160 proof; withdrawn from the cistern room of the distillery at not more than 125 proof and not less than 80 proof; and aged for not less than two years in new-charred white-oak containers." Government regulations further stipulate that nothing whatsoever may be added to distilled Bourbon except the pure limestone-filtered spring water used to lower its alcoholic proof; that all bonded whiskey (i.e., barreled under federal supervision and identified by a green tax stamp on the bottle caps) sold in the United States must be 100 proof (or 50 percent alcohol); and that, unlike Scotch or Canadian whiskey, any Bourbon less than four years old (practically speaking, very little is marketed younger) must specify its age on the label. The rules are tough, to say the least—so tough, in fact, that even a superlative sour mash whiskey like Jack Daniel's is forbidden to include the word *Bourbon* on the label simply because the distiller includes the additional procedure of seeping the liquor through charcoal (or "leaching") before transferring it from the still to barrels. It may all seem unnecessarily strict but, because of such quality control, anyone buying Bourbon is assured of receiving the genuine product.

It's often said that the year 1789 signifies three important events in the country's history: Washington was elected the first president, the Constitution was adopted, and the first Bourbon was made. According to Gerald Carson's *The Social History of Bourbon,* rye whiskey was being distilled by the Dutch on Staten Island as early as 1640; applejack was produced in Monmouth County, New Jersey by 1698; and the first "western" distillery for the production of whiskey was erected in Pittsburgh in 1770. But it was not till 1789 that, ironically, a pioneer Baptist preacher named Elijah Craig began making a corn whiskey—which was later named in honor of the place he produced it: Bourbon County, Virginia—the area that later became Bourbon County, Kentucky. There, where corn was plentiful and the indigenous limestone water was pristine and iron-free, the early distillers learned that when barley malt was mixed with a cooked mash of corn, rye, and pure water, the enzymes of the malt mysteriously converted the grain starches to fermentable sugar. They also learned that the higher the corn content, the lighter the whiskey, and the higher the rye content, the more amenable the whiskey became to longer aging. Each perfected his own formula for superior Bourbon, the secret was passed on to the next generation, and today family distillers (including those located outside of Kentucky) guard these formulas as closely as their proud ancestors did.

Equally valuable to the great distillers of Kentucky are the carefully cultured yeasts that are so important to start the fermentation process. Although fresh yeasts are used to begin each new batch of mash, these come from prized old cultures (some more than half a century old) that Bourbon families have always taken great precaution to preserve. During Prohibition, one distillery transferred its sacred yeast cultures to the basement of the family home, while another shipped its treasure to Canada for careful supervision. Today distillers keep their cultures in refrigerated safes, and it's been said that you'd probably have better luck trying to rob Fort Knox than break into the yeast vault of a Bourbon distillery.

Most of what you hear about "sour mash" whiskey is nonsense. Ninety-five percent of all straight Bourbon (86 or 90 proof) is sour mash whiskey, which simply means that when a new Bourbon mash is started, part of the spent "distiller's beer" from a previous run is allowed to sour overnight, then is added to the new batch for combined fermentation. As in the production of nonvintage Champagne when wine from a previous year is blended with new wine to assure uniformity year by year, sour mash gives Bourbon a "continuity," and whiskey makers pride themselves on preparing their product so carefully that each bottle of a brand tastes exactly like all the rest.

The practice of aging Bourbon is new-charred white-oak barrels is both intriguing and, to an extent, inexplicable. To this day no one knows exactly how the caramelized wood sugars produced by charring the insides of barrels give Bourbon its characteristic flavor and deep amber color; but, according to law, no barrel may be used twice to age Bourbon. Since one of these new barrels can cost $50 or more, distillers are forced to spend millions each year just on barrels, the only solace being that Scotch and Canadian distillers will gladly pay a fraction of the original cost for a second-hand Bourbon barrel.

A great deal has been written about the various technological procedures, the body of lore, and all the strange legends associated with the production of Bourbon. But the only way to appreciate fully the present-day industry and its unique social culture is to drive through north-central Kentucky, visit the distilleries, chat with members of families whose unassailable Bourbon bloodlines go back generations, and, to top it all off, attend the Derby with a mint julep in hand.

A good amount of superior Bourbon (like Old Grand-Dad) is distilled in Frankfort, along the Kentucky River, but most of the well-known brands are produced either in Louisville or just to the south, deep in Bluegrass country. In town, the distilleries of some of the greatest names in Bourbon sprawl along the Ohio River: Brown-Forman, Glenmore, Old Fitzgerald, Seagram, I. W. Harper, National, Schenley, Old Taylor, and Old Charter. A few miles south of Louisville, the largest producer of all, Beam, is located at Clermont; and right down the road are Barton, Waterfill & Frazier, and Willett. Some distilleries and warehouses resemble austere medieval fortresses with their towers and flapping pennons; others are no more than huge red brick buildings that house thousands of barrels and boast four-story-high continuous stills; but those that dot the countryside are generally low, old-fashioned tin constructions surrounded by precious springs (and fences which, according to an old federal inspection law, can be no higher than the head of a man riding a horse). Large or small, commanding or humble in appearance, they are all part of an industry steeped in hard-core tradition and dedicated to producing the best whiskey in the world.

Descendants of the old distilling families make up a protective aristocracy that is unmatched anywhere in the country. They are proud and closely knit, and some are the wealthiest inhabitants in and around Louisville. Many of the Bourbon barons live in handsome Georgian manor homes; most belong to the exclusive River Valley Club and the Pendennis Club (social bastion of the Bourbon empire); and they all know everything there is to know about Bourbon. Of course, things aren't exactly as they used to be. No, sir. "Pappy" Van Winkle, for example, went to his reward some time ago at the age of ninety-one, leaving Stitzel-Weller Distillery (Old Fitzgerald) to members of the family. Julian Van Winkle, Jr. continued running the company for a few years, but eventually he and his kin decided to turn over holdings to the New York firm of Somerset Importers Ltd. Yale-educated Frank Thompson, Jr., whose grandpappy founded Glenmore Distilleries in 1872, is president of the business but finds more time to devote to his plant nursery. And modern technology has allowed some firms to expand in a diversified way their founders would never have dreamed of. Brown-Forman, for instance, not only owns Jack Daniel Distillery in Tennessee and Jos. Garneau (exclusive importer of Martell Cognacs, Cruse wines, and Veuve Clicquot champagnes) but the company is also the sole distributor of California's Korbel champagne.

At the entrance to the Old Fitzgerald distillery, a sign still stands that reads: "No Chemists Allowed! Nature and the old time 'know-how' of a Master Distiller gets the job done here. Because traditional

Kentucky Whiskey is a natural product, we disdain synthetics, scientists, and their accompanying apparatus. This is a Distillery, not a whiskey factory." A few decades ago no one would have questioned the sign's dictum, but today the big bosses realize the technological advantage of chemical experts, exact measuring devices, controlled distillation levels and warehouse temperatures, and chill-filtering of the aged whiskey.

In a way, it's sad to see this type of homespun enterprise modified by the wonders of science. On the other hand, it's reassuring to know that as long as the industry is tightly regulated by the government (only federal tax agents, for example, own keys to the warehouses), there's hardly any way the increasingly sophisticated methods of automated production can actually alter the quality of Bourbon. L. L. Brown, Jr., the young president of Brown-Forman, admits that "with bigness, it is probably inevitable that you lose some of the personal touch"; but he's quick to add that "those of us in the young and middle group coming on know that we have been and must be a quality company. We are going to be involved in many areas of the business in the years to come, and at many levels, but it always will be at the premium level."

Of course, a few veteran warriors are determined always to make their Bourbon just as it was made a century ago, and none is more proud of his craftsmanship than T. William Samuels, owner of Star Hill Distilling Company and a fourth-generation distiller whose family dates back to 1840 in the Kentucky Bourbon business. Nestled in the rolling hills of Marion County south of Louisville and just a few miles off the Bluegrass Parkway, Star Hill is the producer of Maker's Mark, considered by many experts to be one of the best of the sippin' whiskeys. The story of Samuels's success is a Bourbon story. Following Prohibition, he attempted to expand the old family business, only to lose control and eventually sell the firm. Other business endeavors proved unrewarding and downright boring; after all, Samuels was a distiller with Bourbon in his blood. Convinced that fine whiskey could not be mass produced, he acquired in 1953 near Loretta an old farm distillery dating back to 1878, refused to update most of the early equipment, and has devoted the past thirty years to making Bourbon in the traditional slow manner of his great-grandfather. Kentucky produces thousands of barrels of whiskey every day; Samuels's output is about seventeen barrels. He has no pressurized tanks for fast blending; each grain (including a little wheat) is added separately in composing the brew; the original steam engine is still used in the yeast room; each filled bottle is hand-dipped into hot sealing wax; and every label is hand-cut by a few employees. In many respects, the emblem on the square bottle of Maker's Mark relates the whole story of the master craftsman: a circle containing a star (the location of the distillery), the letter *S* (for Samuels), and the figure *IV* (designating the fourth generation of a great Bourbon family).

Although Kentucky produces about 70 percent of all Bourbon and pays the federal government hundreds of millions of dollars in taxes each year, more than half the counties in the state (including Bourbon County) are dry. Incredible but true. Of course, it's a well-known fact (a fact, I say) that most pinkcheeked Kentuckians—like most good ole God-fearing Southerners—never touch a drop of whiskey; they just make the stuff. Maybe on special occasions, when someone's gracious enough to drop in, they might pull out a rare bottle and take a nip or two in the name of hospitality; but when the polls open, an awful lot of sippers vote "dry." Local gossip also has it that more than one of the famous horse breeders of Kentucky became involved in the sporting world mainly to avoid discussing their activities in the whiskey business and their personal drinking habits. For some, talking Bourbon is one thing; revealing drinking capacities is another.

Well, I'm not about to risk guessing how much Bourbon is consumed in the open on home territory, but you can be sure that members of the Pendennis Club in Louisville drink their fair share, with unconcealed pride and with a gusto unequaled anywhere. The name of the club, which refers to the famous English castle along the coast at Falmouth, is derived from the Welsh words *Pen Dinas,* meaning a "high place." And high the club is—not only in the social hierarchy of distillers and horse lovers but also in the quota of Bourbon served in the elegant wood-paneled rooms. Without doubt, this baronial club stocks more Bourbon than any other watering hole on earth, and it's a rare day that at least eighty or ninety *different* brands are not artfully displayed on the long counter behind the bar. It goes without saying that such international aristocrats as Old Fitzgerald, Maker's Mark, Early Times, Old Crow, I. W. Harper, Glenmore, Old Forester, Wild Turkey, and Old Grand-Dad take up most room among the bottles on the front row. But equally exciting for the connoisseur are lesser-known brands like Rebel Yell, Virginia Gentleman, Kentucky Tavern, and Yellowstone (the largest seller in Kentucky); not to mention Beam's "limited editions" of Santa Fe and The Huntsman, both in ceramic bottles; eleven-year-old Weller Masterpiece; and rare David Nicholson.

It's common knowledge around Louisville that any drinker worth his weight in sour mash sips nothing but the 100-proof variety. But which is the most popular Bourbon with club members and their guests? As one bartender put it, "If a senator steps up and asks me to chose, I look around to see which distiller is nearest the bar, then recommend two or three fingers, on the rocks, of one of his brands."

No one really has a convincing explanation why certain brands of Bourbon are readily available in one section of the country and virtually nonexistent in another, but apparently this curious factor is due in part to regional preferences. Is it true, for instance, that Southerners generally like sweet Bourbon, while sippers in the North and West usually opt for a more full-bodied, longer-aged whiskey? And why—to cite an extreme example—are such limited-production brands as Chapin & Gore, "1492," Schnuck, Old Rivermont, and Rocking Chair shipped almost exclusively to St. Louis?

Whatever the answers, it's for sure that Bourbon aficionados must be the most discriminating drinkers in existence, for it's even got to the point where certain social and professional clubs throughout the nation not only order particular brands but also request that distillers print their respective designated names on the labels. In Washington, D.C., members of the Press Club enjoy their "Gentlemen of the Press" Bourbon. The same is true at the Press Club in San Francisco, the Princeton Club in New York, and the University Club in Chicago. And it's even possible for private consumers demanding the ultimate in chic to make arrangements with certain distillers (e.g., Maker's Mark) for special deliveries of Bourbon with personalized labels.

Some of the finest cocktails on earth owe their celebrity to bourbon. Although those Kentuckians who do "touch the stuff" still consider it barbaric to destroy the mellow flavor of good sippin' whiskey by blending it with anything more alien than water, millions of people, nonetheless, appreciate the spirit most when it's mixed with other ingredients to make sours, mists, fogs, punches, Stingers, toddies, grogs, eggnogs, and who knows how many other potables. Without doubt, the most famous Bourbon cocktails are the Sazerac from New Orleans, the Manhattan (introduced by Lady Randolph Churchill in the 1870s at New York's Manhattan Club), the Old-Fashioned (supposedly invented by a bartender at the Pendennis Club, then later popularized at New York's old Waldorf-Astoria Hotel), and—well, I refuse to become still another culprit in the never-ending heated controversy over the legendary mint julep and its correct preparation. Suffice it to say that experts at the Pendennis *never* crush a mint leaf and that perhaps the most sensible method of concocting the drink is one suggested by a Louisville newspaper editor and great Bourbon admirer:

"Pluck the mint gently from its bed, just as the dew of the evening is about to form upon it. Select the choicer sprigs only, but do not rinse them. Prepare the simple syrup and measure out a half-tumbler of whiskey. Pour the whiskey into a well-frosted silver cup, throw the other ingredients away, and drink the whiskey."

I don't know whether an all-inclusive Bourbon cookbook has ever been published, but if one hasn't, someone somewhere has a fascinating job ahead compiling the incredible number of recipes for all types of food prepared hither and yonder with our great American whiskey. Personally, I would never consider any kitchen well stocked that didn't have at least one bottle of good whiskey on the shelf—but, after all, I was raised on a cuisine that included dozens of dishes flavored with more Bourbon than salt and pepper. To mention only a few of the delectable creations: Bourbon pâté, Bourbon onion soup, Bourbon-and-cheese soup, Boubon-lobster bisque, raw oysters "cringed" in Bourbon, onions braised in Bourbon, lobster, steak, and hamburger flamed in Bourbon, Bourbon pie covered with shavings of bittersweet chocolate, Bourbon cake that is literally aged for days, and, of course, cocoa-and-walnut-filled Bourbon balls.

Bourbon is an important ingredient in some of America's finest sauces. Anyone who has ever tasted the Henry Bain Sauce placed on every table at the Pendennis has never forgotten it, and more than one epicure would like to have the exact recipe for Old Fitzgerald's Bluegrass Steak Sauce, composed partly of chutney, pickled walnuts, and very old Bourbon—unfortunately, not for sale on the commercial market. One of the best Bourbon sauces I know is easy to make and goes particularly well with beef:

For about six moderate portions, combine ¼ cup soy sauce, ½ tsp. ginger, ¼ cup Bourbon, ¼ cup brown sugar, 2 Tb. vinegar, 2 Tb. molasses, ¾ cup orange juice. Mix well and serve with meat or use as a splendid marinade for beef.

Whether it's poured on the rocks, blended into hundreds of cocktails, used to add unique flavor to food, or (prepare yourself) splashed on a miniature palette by a member of Whiskey Painters of America (WPA), star-spangled Bourbon remains one of America's proudest contributions to the gustatory, social, and even artistic world. Born with the Constitution and nursed by the pioneers, this magnificent spirit is part of the heritage that has made America what it is. And no one has summed up its glory more poetically than the old Kentucky judge who advised: "Sip it and say that there is no solace for the soul, no tonic for the body like Old Bourbon Whiskey."

BOURBON SPOON BREAD

2	cups milk
1	cup white cornmeal
2	sticks butter, softened
½	tsp. salt
1	Tb. sugar
5	eggs, separated
1½	Tb. Bourbon

Preheat oven to 350° F. In a saucepan, scald the milk, stir in cornmeal, beat thoroughly, and cook over low heat till thick. Remove from heat, add butter, salt, and sugar, beat well till butter has melted, and set aside to cool. Beat egg yolks and stir into mixture. Beat egg whites till stiff, fold into mixture, and add Bourbon, mixing lightly. Pour mixture into a buttered casserole and bake about 40 minutes or till inserted straw comes out clean. Serve as a breakfast dish. SERVES 4.

BOURBON PORK ROAST

1	3-lb. pork loin roast
	Juice of 1 lemon
1	Tb. brown sugar
1	tsp. flour
1	tsp. paprika
½	tsp. salt
	Freshly ground pepper
¼	cup water
¼	cup Bourbon
2	springs fresh parsley, chopped
1	bay leaf

Preheat oven to 350° F. Rub entire roast with lemon juice. Mix together brown sugar, flour, paprika, and salt, and rub mixture over entire roast. Add freshly ground pepper to roast, place roast fat-side up on a rack in baking pan, cover, and let sit about 1 hour. Combine water and Bourbon and pour mixture into bottom of pan. Sprinkle parsley over top of roast, add bay leaf to liquid, and roast uncovered about 2½ hours, basting frequently the last hour. SERVES 4.

EGGNOG PIE

1   envelope unflavored gelatin
¾   cup cold milk
3   eggs, separated
½   cup sugar
½   cup heavy cream
¼   tsp. nutmeg
⅛   tsp. salt
⅓   cup Bourbon
½   cup seedless raisins
1   9-inch baked crumb pie shell

In a small bowl, soften gelatin in ¼ cup of the milk. Beat egg yolks in top of double boiler, stir in ½ cup milk, ¼ cup of the sugar, cream, nutmeg, and salt and cook over hot water, stirring constantly, till mixture thickens and coats spoon. Remove from heat, add softened gelatin, stir till dissolved, and cool thoroughly. Stir in Bourbon and chill till slightly thickened. Beat egg whites till foamy, add remaining ¼ cup sugar, and beat whites till stiff. Fold egg whites plus raisins into Bourbon mixture. Turn into pie shell, sprinkle with a little extra nutmeg, and chill thoroughly. SERVES 8.

Bourbon Pralines

2	cups granulated sugar
1	tsp. baking soda
1	cup buttermilk
	Pinch salt
2	Tb. butter
2⅓	cups black walnuts or pecans, broken
2½	oz. Bourbon

In a large kettle combine sugar, soda, buttermilk, and salt and place candy thermometer into mixture. Over high heat cook 5 minutes, or to 210° F, stirring constantly and scraping bottom of kettle. Add butter and nuts. Continue cooking, stirring and scraping continuously, till a little of the mixture placed in cold water forms a very soft ball. Remove from heat, add Bourbon, let cool about 1 minute, then beat by hand 5 minutes. When mixture begins to thicken, drop by tablespoons onto a cookie sheet covered with wax paper and allow to harden. Yield: about 2 dozen.

MY PIG BEATS
YOUR COW

••••••••••••••••••••••••••••••

I DON'T claim to be the foremost authority on the centuries-old
Southern tradition of barbecue (the dish, the event, and the cooking
process), but I can assure you that, since I was born and raised in
North Carolina, the undisputed barbecue center of the world to the
more enlightened, I know plenty about the subject. The first fact is
that the only meat in the world that can absorb such flavors as pepper,
sugar, and smoke without losing its identity is pork. The second is that
Texas beef barbecue, good as it is, really can't approach what Tarheels
do with pork. Of course, people all over the South will tell you this and
that about where to find the best pit-cooked barbecue, but over the
years I've eaten every type from Montgomery to Newman, Georgia to
Williamsburg, and I'm here to tell you that when it comes to superlatives, North Carolina barbecue has no serious competition.

In Virginia, where (in case Texans don't know) the first barbecue
took place at Jamestown a couple of years after the first settlers arrived,
they used to turn out some pretty good meat; so good, in fact, that even
George Washington once spent three entire days devouring pig at an
outdoor feast in Alexandria. But then, after the War, they gradually
lost interest or became too fancy in their eating habits, and today Virginia barbecue is scarcely anything to rave about. You'd also think the
tradition would have thrived in the coastal low country of South
Carolina and Georgia and in southern Louisiana, territories where, in
the heyday of river-plantation society, the most lavish barbecues recorded in history were thrown. Well, there's still some decent barbecue
to be found in those areas, but generally, I'm afraid South Carolinians
and Georgians just don't have the knack anymore, and I know that a
lot of what's served at barbecues in Louisiana has been too deeply in-

fluenced by all the beef, chicken, antelope, shrimp, wild turkey, pumpkin, and Lord knows what all else they barbecue in Texas.

So how have North Carolinians managed to stay so enlightened, and
what makes the barbecue fixed all over the state the best anywhere?
Some natives (including all my barbecue-loving kin) say it's mainly
due to family pride since so many of today's commercial barbecue
houses have been passed down from one generation to the next; others,
in the eastern part of the state, swear that without all the barbecues
there's be no place to talk tobacco; still others rap on about the superiority of Carolina hogs and the state's great abundance of hickory wood
used to cook the meat. Without doubt, there's some truth in all these
theories, but to me the most logical explanation is that Tarheels simply
love and understand barbecue (and country ham) more than anyone
else in God's creation. I'm also convinced that if there were such a
thing as a state food (like state birds, flowers, and all that), North
Carolina's without question would be barbecue.

Predictably, nobody laughs louder at Texans and their beef roasts
than all the barbecue connoisseurs of Carolina. (When you're talking
about barbecue, there's only one Carolina.) On the other hand, Tarheels will argue each other up a tree defending their convictions as to
which area of the state produces the greatest barbecue. Personally, I
don't squabble over any I eat, for, frankly, it doesn't vary in quality
that much from one place to the next. And for good reason. All Carolinians follow the time-proven deep-pit method of roasting over hickory coals. Whether the pork is fixed at a restaurant, on church or
school grounds, or in a family's backyard, you can be fairly well assured of finding at least one pit from 3½ to 4 feet deep. Some experts
dig a hole in the ground, then line it with bricks; others construct ce-
ment pits that can be used year after year. Traditionally, one or more
grain-fed pigs are dressed, split in half, bound in chicken-wire racks,
and cooked very slowly for up to sixteen hours over hickory coals. At
regular intervals, the meat is basted with a special homemade "big
yellow-back" sauce (best applied with mops), turned, and the coals are
replenished with more hickory chips. When the pork is flaky and
tender, it's removed from the racks, cooled, boned, defatted, chopped,
mixed with a little more sauce, reheated in a large pot, and dished up.

The resulting barbecue is all that any great barbecue should be:
lean, greaseless, not too moist, and delicious. Serve it with red-pepper
vinegar, peppery coleslaw, fresh hush puppies (crisp, crunchy balls of

corn bread fried in deep fat), a bowl of Brunswick stew (that thick, soupy concoction made with chicken, beef, ham hock, corn, butter beans, okra, and about ten other ingredients), and either beer or iced tea, and you're set for some real good eating.

Although you find Carolina barbecue places (i.e., restaurants) from the Outer Banks to the Great Smokies, perhaps the most legendary are the dozens of spots that dot the back roads of the tobacco belt in the eastern part of the state. Usually they're pretty easy to pick out: small cinder-block buildings with dirt parking lots full of big shiny cars, smoke rising from the pits in the rear, and the single word BARBECUE (and *not* BARBEQUE or Bar-B-Q) either painted somewhere on the front or written on a board suspended from a Coke sign. When you approach Rocky Mount on Interstate 95, you're smack in the middle of the territory. In fact, the last time I turned onto old Route 301, heading toward Melton's (a name known throughout the state), two huge billboards side by side confirmed my whereabouts. The first read YOU ARE IN KLAN COUNTRY; the second identified Rocky Mount as THE BARBECUE CAPITAL OF THE WORLD.

No matter which place you end up in, the scene's always about the same: a counter with short stools, plain wooden tables and chairs, paper napkins, plastic forks and iced-tea glasses, bottles of red-pepper vinegar, maybe a little country music on the spanking-new jukebox and an inexpensive portrait of Jesus, and lots of God-fearing and respectable old boys with thick necks and bulging bellies and strong appetites. The second you take a table, up comes a healthy-looking, well-fed waitress wearing a spick-and-span white uniform.

"What'll it be, honey, sandwich or a tray?" she begins, pulling a pencil from her hair and taking for granted you know the difference between a simple barbecue-filled bun and a divided platter (like those they used to feed children from) with equal portions of chopped barbecue, coleslaw, Brunswick stew, and either hush puppies or fried corn bread on the side.

"I'll take a tray—and a beer, please."

"Now, honey, you know we don't serve alcoholic beverages in this place," she whines, allowing you credit for also having that bit of knowledge. "Just iced tea, coffee, and milk."

Irritated that you've hit upon a dry place (a chance you always take in regions crawling with religious folk) but determined to tolerate anything to have some superb barbecue, you are about to opt for tea when the ordering is interrupted by a friendly fellow at the next table.

"Hey, Edna, how about bringing us a couple more sandwiches and a basket of hush puppies, you sweet little thing."

"Mr. Thomas, I'll be happy to get you some more sandwiches as soon as I've finished taking this gentleman's order, but you know as well as I do, Mr. Thomas, that hush puppies don't come with the sandwiches." She says all this slowly and with great authority.

"Aw, now, honey, don't be like that. You know we'll pay extra for the hush puppies, but, confound it, we're still hungry as dogs and have to be down the road shortly."

I should point out that the Mr. Thomas type contributes as much to the local color of the place as anything else. Physically, he makes an interesting contrast with the hard-core folks he's sitting with and is not exactly the figure you'd expect to find crouched gulping down barbecue over a wooden table. He's well dressed in an expensive dark business suit, his hands and impeccable fingernails betray the fact that he hasn't hit a lick of manual labor in years, and if you stick around long enough for him and his cronies to finish their barbecue, you'll see him get up, speak to every roughneck in the place, pop big Edna on the fanny, then zoom away in his long two-tone-green Lincoln Continental.

What does Mr. Thomas do? Well, first, he happens to own the largest tobacco warehouse in the territory, plus God knows how much land from Rocky Mount all the way to the coast. He's a member of the country club, the Jaycees, and the First Baptist Church, and if, by chance, he belongs to the Klan, you can be sure his gown is cleaned professionally by the finest firm in town. Mr. Thomas is a devoted family man and a leader, and he takes care of folks he likes. He's also a fanatic about the dry, salty barbecue featured in the area, and even though his pretty wife wouldn't be caught dead eating barbecue in a public barbecue place (she sends out for it when she "takes a notion"), Mr. Thomas loves nothing better than joining the working boys every day for lunch and knocking off a couple of trays or two or three sandwiches overflowing with what many will defend as the best chopped barbecue on earth. One day he may go to Melton's in Rocky Mount, the next, to Parker's over in Wilson, and it's not beyond him to drive down to one of the places in Goldsboro or Kinston. Outside his home region, however, he won't touch the stuff, swearing that all that barbecue in the piedmont around Lexington and Concord is too moist and peppery; at Flip's in Wilmington, it's too bland, as is the slaw; in Charlotte they have the gall to serve it sliced as well as chopped—and often without the traditional Brunswick stew; and at one place in Durham the meat is full of cracklin' (crisp skin). In some respects, Mr. Thomas is, uh, decidedly different from most Tarheels, but when it comes to pit-roasted pig, his discriminating expertise is about the same as the next fan's.

Although Carolina barbecue is prepared and sold commercially in huge quantities twelve months of the year (despite Southerners' apprehension about eating pork during the summer), the barbecue season officially begins with the coming of fall weather. Generally, every weekend from September through March, schools, churches, civic and political groups, and families all over the state throw bashes to raise funds, to promote a political candidate, or simply to honor an occasion. Down around Wilmington, the most popular to-do is called a pig-pickin', and they do just that—barbecue a hog and pick the meat off with their fingers while slugging down washtubs of cold beer. Back in the mountains of western Carolina, a few of the small country-ham producers still celebrate the killing of hogs after the first frost by roasting a couple, inviting neighbors from all around, and serving up the barbecue with plenty of corn bread and cider (or corn liquor). And in and around Charlotte, a week hardly passes that at least one church doesn't sponsor an affair intended to attract barbecue lovers by the thousands.

For some strange reason, Carolina barbecue has always been linked with the most God-fearing people—as if the Almighty Himself had sanctioned a bond between man and pig—and nowhere is this more evident than at the famous barbecue thrown every third Wednesday in September at Williams Memorial Presbyterian Church in Charlotte. It all began back in 1945, when the choir wanted to raise money for a new organ, and every year since it has been an event people flock to from miles around. The day before starts early when they start roasting forty whole hogs and twelve hundred pounds of pork shoulder, but when they're planning to feed five and six thousand enthusiasts, a lot has to be done, and almost everybody in the congregation lends a hand. (So important is the occasion to some that they take a day of vacation to work at the barbecue.)

At 8:00 A.M., the hickory coals are started in three rows of concrete pits that line the screened-in barbecue shed outside the church kitchen. At about 11:00, J. B. Blasingame (chief barbecuer for over thirty years) cocks his baseball cap, sticks a fresh cigar in his mouth, pulls on a pair of heavy working-gloves, checks the chicken wire, and directs his helpers in placing the meat-filled racks over the coals. All day and well into the wee hours of the following morning, the pork cooks slowly, releasing a fragrance that entices passersby to stop their cars, stand at the screens, and watch. The Reverend Marcus B. Prince, Jr., now retired as minister but not as captain of the meat-chopping team, shows up sometime after midnight and, with other male members of the congregation, works with the meat and mixes it with some of Mrs. Blasingame's homemade sauce before putting it into large refrigerators to cool. Later, any grease that's accumulated is removed and the barbecue is reheated. In the meantime, Mrs. Nancy Brown has begun frying up hundreds of hush puppies, Mrs. Prince has mixed her special coleslaw, and by noon the white-covered tables in the community building and outside under stately old oak trees are filled with people gorging as if they hadn't eaten in a month. The price? About four dollars for the works, including refills of coffee or iced tea. Cokes cost extra.

Since visitors to North Carolina in search of great barbecue are not likely to experience one of these big group affairs unless they happen to be entertained by local friends who know what's going on in the area, I'll give a quick rundown of what most Tarheels agree are the best commercial places in the major barbecue districts. I've already mentioned Melton's in Rocky Mount, Parker's in Wilson, and Flip's in Wilmington, all three of which are legendary in the eastern part of the state and should not be missed by anyone making a barbecue pilgrimage. In Lexington (where traditionally they don't serve Brunswick stew), there must be fifteen or twenty places within spitting distance of each other, but for the leanest meat with good spicy flavor, your best bets are City Barbecue, Smokey Joe's, Lexington Barbecue No. 1, and Beck's (which I've often been tempted to proclaim the king of barbecue houses). Not too far away, in Concord, it's Troutman's and The Red Pig Drive-In; in Newton, the Little Pigs Barbecue, and in Shelby, Alston Bridges' Barbecue. (For directions in these small mill towns, just stop at any filling station.)

As for Charlotte (where I've been eating barbecue for as long as I can remember but where dumb pollution laws have pushed the houses farther and farther outside the city), there's no doubt that some of the most authentic fare is served at barbecues sponsored fairly regularly by such organizations as the Moose and the Masons, and I'd make a drive any day, out to Matthews to pick up a shoulder custom-prepared at Gus Purcell's. But in town there's nothing wrong with Spoon's on Pineville Road, Roger's on Atando (off Graham Avenue), and the Old

Hickory House on North Tryon (one of the few places that serves beer). If, after sampling your first mound of hickory-smoked pork barbecue in any of these havens, you can honestly say you've ever tasted better meat, then either I'm awaiting some cosmic revelation or your only hope is to become a vegetarian.

GOAT-ROPING GRUB

••

SIX SWAGGERING country-and-western musicians who call themselves "The Promised Band" strike the final chords of "I'm Goin' Home to Armadillo" and begin crooning something about how "the blue skies of Texas turned dark when I lost you." Spread about the walls and beams and ceiling of this popular Houston eating establishment known as the Texas Tinhorn Barbeque and Saloon are Texas cowboy hats, Texas license plates, Texas longhorns, Texas flags, beer signs, and big ox yokes. In the vinyl booth behind mine, two Western-garbed women stare misty-eyed at the bandleader while downing fresh unpeeled Texas fries and mugs of Dr. Pepper. A man and woman in formal dress slide off the saddles that serve as bar stools and join other couples dancing the do-si-do—denim clashing with Ultrasuede, diamonds outglittering brass studs. I unload my overcrowded tray of barbecued brisket, ribs, beef-sausage links, coleslaw, sliced white bread, red beans, jalapeño chili peppers, peach cobbler, and beer.

"Well, you said you wanted authentic Texas food," says my Houstonian companion across the table, popping a jalapeño into her mouth. "Just hope it's what you expected."

Following her example, I take a bite of the innocent-looking chili pepper.

"Better watch that, honey," she warns calmly. "You're not used to those, you know."

Wondering exactly what she's talking about, I continue chewing while taking a handful of paper napkins from the dispenser. Then it happens. Gradually, very gradually, my mouth becomes ablaze, then my throat, then what appears to be every membrane in my head. I take a slug of ice-cold beer, another slug, the whole mug, indiscriminate amounts of brisket, beans, bread, anything to douse the fire.

Nothing works. I dash to the rest room and gargle cold tap water for a good ten minutes. Although relief is only partial, I return to the table where my companion is lovingly consuming still another of those demonic green incendiaries. Her single remark of consolation: "Now you'll begin to notice the wonderful flavor of the chili."

Although I had one of the great meals of my life at the Texas Tinhorn Barbeque and Saloon, no one could have convinced me that evening that by the time I left the Lone Star State I'd not only be accustomed to, but would actually admire, the fiery flavor of jalapeños, serranos, anchos, poblanos, piquins, colorados, and who knows how many other varieties of chili pepper used so profusely in Texas cookery. On the other hand, the very fact that I was in Texas for the sole purpose of eating contradicted my blind but resolute conviction that most food down there was, at best, some form of fodder consumed by asbestos-palated goat-ropers for no other reason than to sustain human life. I, like most other Americans, had come to identify Tex-Mex food with all the garbage served at those infamous taco joints all over the country, or with the grease-drenched combination platters featured in 99 percent of the so-called Texas-American restaurants. Most of the "Texas chili" I'd tried was no more than a bland, mushy stew made from little more than fatty hamburger meat, canned tomatoes, beans, and some traces of onion and seasoning. Milk-battered chicken-fried steak I found disgusting, as well as all those soggy refried beans. And as for Texas barbecue, I, having been weaned on North Carolina pork barbecue, simply refused even to acknowledge the existence of barbecued beef brisket.

Well, to suggest that I now champion the cause of Texas cookery is a triumph of understatement—not to mention an admission of acute guilt and embarrassment. I don't know whether it all started back at the Texas Tinhorn Barbeque and Saloon in Houston, or after I sampled baby cactus blended with dried shrimp into eggs at an elegant border-food festivity in Brownsville, or when I tasted a truly great "bowl of red" (chili con carne) at Tolbert's Native Texas Foods and Museum of the Chili Culture in Dallas. What I do know is that I've been converted and am now as enthusiastic about barbecued goat, S.O.B. stew chock-full of marrow gut, jalapeño buttermilk corn bread, venison sausage, and *enchiladas verdes* with *salsa di chili* as I am about the exquisite sturgeon caviar currently being produced in California and Oregon. To be sure, I'll still argue with any Texas kicker in favor of pork barbecue over beef, but, in general, I need no more convincing that the regional dishes of Texas are not only some of the most inspired in the nation but also some of the most delicious—when, that is, they are consumed in the state of Texas and prepared by serious cooks.

To try to define precisely the Texas table would be futile, for the simple reason that each area of this gigantic state has various cultural and ethnic styles of cooking that can be vastly different from those of other areas. Polish, Swedish, Danish, Alsatian, Creole, Czechoslovakian, Mexican, German, American Indian—such are the diverse origins of large ethnic communities, and all contribute in some way to the state's gastronomic makeup. What has emerged from this vast melting pot, however, are four basic types of food that all Texans love and that constitute the overall identity of this regional cookery: Tex-Mex (or border food), barbecue, chili con carne, and what can only be described as Texas rural. By no stretch of the imagination are any of these what you call refined, and blessedly few Texans would have it any other way. On the other hand, there is a remarkable subtlety about this fare as it's served on home ground, a memorable flavor that can rarely be produced elsewhere so successfully and that Texans estranged from their region never cease to crave. Only real Southerners can equal Texans when it comes to the pride and emotion evoked by their food. The inhabitants of San Antonio and Austin and Houston may occasionally sample French, Italian, Chinese, and other such "sophisticated" cuisines, but for the most part they'd rather have a well-seasoned brisket barbecued over mesquite or oak, an aromatic shrimp stew, sourdough biscuits, roast beef hash with a little jalapeño, roast venison with lots of gravy, enchiladas with a good hot sauce and plenty of grated cheese and chopped onions, a buttery vinegar pie, and, of course, a bowl of peppery chili *without* beans. However much outsiders might criticize even the best prepared Texas food for its lack of delicacy, only the most pretentious would deny its singularity and, indeed, its downright goodness.

TEX-MEX: THE TASTIEST MIX

"Come on out here and meet my tamale man," yells Mary Yturria from the well-tailored front lawn of the large house in Brownsville. "This is Enrique Ybarra, and he's been delivering me his tamales for as long as I can remember. Rumor has it down here in the Lower Rio Grande Valley that I can turn out some pretty good border food, but let me tell you, nobody's tamales can hold a candle to Mr. Ybarra's, and I just don't know what I'd do if he ever quit making them."

Although you can find good restaurant border food (or Tex-Mex, depending on which Texans you happen to be talking with) in Austin, San Antonio, Houston, Laredo, and El Paso, I doubt that any could compare with that served at the lavish dinner parties of Mary, a radiant, energetic, self-confident woman who somehow finds time to prepare her specialities for up to 200 persons (less, of course, if she happens to be throwing a picnic at the Yturria ranch about fifty miles north). She also took time to show me how she shops for ingredients across the Mexican border at Matamoros. And once you've watched her dash from one small market to the next—grabbing bags of jalapeños, garbanzos ("beans"), and Mexican vanilla, inspecting avocados and baby cactus leaves ("only the tender spring nopalitos"), discussing in Spanish the quality of cabrito ("kid") with her butcher—you know this lady takes her food very seriously.

To one not accustomed to genuine border food, attending one of Mary's bashes guarantees sampling flavors which are nothing less than revelation: corn shuck-wrapped tamales that make all previous ones pale by comparison; a wooden bowl of guacamole that bears little resemblance to the runny green paste served at most restaurants; a pleasantly assertive jalapeño pie; soft, delicate enchiladas with a white regional cheese and a suave chilichocolate sauce; rice mixed with diced potatoes and vegetables and enriched with a zesty *salsa picante;* beans cooked with ham hock, coriander, and jalapeño; Mary's beloved Gypsy barbecued brisket which she learned to prepare as a child; roasted cabrito, the luscious taste and texture of which leave me wordless; cactus prepared with bell peppers, dried shrimp, and eggs; a feathery mango mousse; and a milk and sugar dessert called *leche camada* that requires two hours of constant stirring and resembles fudge. It's a far cry from all the tough enchiladas and greasy tacos and tasteless tostados we've come to associate with Tex-Mex food.

So exactly what is it that makes these dishes so special? "Well, first you've simply got to have these fresh local ingredients for authentic border food," Mary insisted, "which I suppose is one reason Tex-Mex dishes are what they are in other parts of the country. Take chili peppers, for example, probably the most important agent in so many of our dishes. I wouldn't think of using anything but fresh chili pulp, but what you find elsewhere is all that commercial chili powder. And believe me, the difference in flavor is vast. The same holds true for the Mexican chocolate in my enchilada sauce, which just can't be substituted if you want the sauce to taste right. Or the *masa harina* ("finely ground cornmeal") which we use to make our breakfast tortillas."

Why, I wondered, didn't restaurants and individuals seek out correct ingredients and try to produce at least a decent facsimile of the real thing?

"Listen," she declared pointedly, "it's the same problem as that involved with so much bad food in this country. Tex-Mex has been streamlined and commercialized to the point of utter crudeness, and today people just don't know the difference. *Frijoles* serve as a good case in point. When we prepare these beans at home, we use fresh garlic and coriander, carrots and onions, ham hock, and jalapeño or chili piquin for a subtle zip, but in restaurants they'll just dump in a lot of chili powder, bacon grease, and—if you can imagine—tomato catsup! It's a disgrace. Or take these tamales, which are pure Texan. Much of their flavor comes from the soaked corn shucks. Well, just like down in Mexico, most people use so much *masa* and chili powder you can't even taste the meat, and would you believe that lots of the tamales you find today are bound with some sort of paper instead of natural shucks? Thirty years ago there was no such thing as a factory-made tortilla. And I'd say that what makes my guacamole different from that same old mixture you're served from coast-to-coast is both the quality of the avocados and the touch of cream cheese and *homemade* mayonnaise I add. I know I complain a lot about all this, but let me tell you, I don't complain half as much as the real Tex-Americans who live here in the valley."

BARBECUE: BRISKET, RIBS, AND LINKS

Mary Yturria may be a bit outspoken on the topic of enchiladas and tamales, but she's no more concerned about her border food than the Texans who specialize in barbecue—and it does seem that any Texan who cooks (and most do) specializes in barbecue. I'm still convinced that pork is the only meat in the world that can absorb such flavors as pepper, sugar, and smoke without losing its identity, but, after

sampling more examples of barbecued beef in Texas than I care to remember, I'm beginning to understand fully why Texans are so passionate about the stuff.

If, by chance, you're under the impression there's some remote connection between the barbecued briskets, ribs, and links prepared on
ranches and in restaurants by serious-minded Texans and the hot dogs,
hamburgers, and chickens that are charred elsewhere by suburbanites
on their little backyard grills, you have a lot to discover about barbecue. And if, by chance, you think Texas barbecue lovers are less emotional about their staple than chiliheads are about their bowl of red,
just bring up the question of why the Texas legislature decided to cer-
tify chili as the official state dish instead of barbecue. "The case for
barbecue is overwhelming," a founding member of the Texas Barbecue
Appreciation Society raved. "Barbecue cookery is truly an art. It requires real skills like fire building, wood choosing, pit knowledge, sauce
manufacture, and carving. The hardest thing about preparing a pot of
chili is finding someone to eat it. Finally, the process of natural selection has proved barbecue's superiority over chili. Most restaurants of
less than the highest pretentions offer something they call chili, but it's
next to impossible to get a true bowl of red in a restaurant these days.
Chili parlors, once the scourge of the land, have all but disappeared. In
the Dallas Yellow Pages, for example, there are 109 listings under barbecue, but only two under chili. The public has spoken. Why wasn't
the Legislature listening?"

Such high-strung convictions in Texas are not unusual, and such
voices are not quickly stilled, the point being that many native sons are
willing to fight an outright gastronomic and political war to prove that
barbecue is a great deal more than broiled or grilled meat. Which, of
course, it is. Whether you're talking about brisket, ribs, steaks, sausages, shoat, venison, or cabrito, genuine Texas barbecue is meat that is
thoroughly dry-seasoned, cooked long and slowly out of doors on a grill
over mesquite or oak coals (or pit-cooked so that it steams in its own
juices), and basted constantly with a special sauce. Although real barbecue is always well-done, professionals of the art know how to turn
out meat that is raven black on the outside yet juicy and succulent on
the interior. It is always served with a spicy barbecue sauce, the components of which vary from individual to individual and usually remain
a closely guarded secret.

At elaborate ranch barbecues like those once staged for hundreds by
the late President Johnson at the LBJ ranch, the meal traditionally in-

cludes such dishes as chuck wagon potatoes (similar to hashed browns), smoked beans, sourdough biscuits, spicy coleslaw, sliced tomatoes and raw onions, fried pies, and plenty of beer and iced tea. The accompaniments in restaurants that specialize in barbecue rarely vary throughout the state: coleslaw, potato salad, jalapeño peppers, some form of relish, plain white bread, and gallons of beer and iced tea. If you've never sampled Texas barbecue, the best idea in restaurants is to order a combination platter of brisket, links, and ribs. Ideally, the meat should be lean, moist, and tender; the sauce spicy, but not so hot as to overpower the flavor of the meat. The finest restaurants also serve barbecue sandwiches, and believe me, you haven't lived till you've tasted one made with only the charred ends of brisket coarsely chopped and cloaked in sauce.

CHILI: A BOWL OF RED

I may have the courage to take sides in the great barbecue war between pork-loving North Carolinians and beef-chomping Texans, but never would I dare have the audacity (or fortitude) to become in any way involved in the many controversies surrounding the official state dish of Texas. The truth is that outsiders no more understand chili con carne than non-Southerners understand fried chicken or country ham. To be sure, we all have the right to taste, compare, and express opinions, but I'm convinced that only Texans weaned on chili (and which ones were not?) have the background and experience to actually discuss it. And what discussions! When one native heretic had the nerve to analyze in painful detail in a local magazine why "I *Still* Hate Chili," another regional expert immediately came to the dish's defense in another article entitled "Gourmet Chili": "Chili is the essence of gourmet cuisine. Some of the finest chefs in this country dine on chili in the kitchen while their patrons are forced to submit to foods like escargots and veal marsala among the hordes in the dining room. The chef knows what's good. A simple, but elegant, bowl of red." And when one longhorn moved to California and started a moneymaking World Championship Chili Cookoff in competition with the legendary one at Terlingua, a culinary range war started in the Sun Belt that is still far from subsiding.

Chili is a big issue in Texas, to say the least—so big, in fact, that a cult of sorts has developed around the dish. When purists founded the Chili Appreciation Society International (CASI) in 1951 to help protect their foodstuff from never-ending adulteration, things were pretty quiet. Then, in 1966, a Midwesterner by the name of H. Allen Smith published an article in *Holiday* entitled "Nobody Knows More About Chili Than I Do," making the outrageous claim that "no living man can put together a pot of chili as ambrosial, as delicately and zestfully flavored as the chili I make. This is a fact so stern, so granitic, that it belongs in the encyclopedias as well as in all the standard histories of civilization." Frank Tolbert, an enraged columnist for the *Dallas News,* tested the recipe and proclaimed Smith's concoction "a chili-flavored low-torque beef and vegetable soup." He encouraged one Wick Fowler—considered the finest chili maker in Texas—to challenge Smith to a cookoff, and chili history was made in 1967 when the first World Championship Chili Cookoff was held in the remote Texas town of Terlingua (the Smith-Fowler contest was eventually declared to be a tie).

Suffice it to say that today members of CASI are more active than ever (the president is called the "Great Pepper"); that Frank Tolbert, after the publication of his book *A Bowl of Red* and the opening of his chili parlors in Dallas, is the King of Chili, Prince of the Pod; that every weekend from April to November there are at least three or four chili cookoffs somewhere in the state; that as many as twenty thousand chiliheads show up for the World Championship at Terlingua each November; and that one mustached aficionado, Hal John Wimberly, even publishes a monthly newspaper, the *Goat Gap Gazette,* devoted exclusively to the chili culture and cookoffs.

Now, in case you wonder just what a chili cookoff is like, I can tell you the rather amazing details, since I went out of my way to attend a bash in Houston. Naturally, there were hundreds of contestants (doctors, lawyers, farmers, oilmen, you name it) cooking chili with every ingredient from beef to snake to chicken to raccoon, all with the intention of earning more winning points that would qualify them for the Terlingua competition. Since points are also made through showmanship, contestants cooking "Roman Red" chili were dressed as gladiators, those preparing "Deadman" chili cooked out of a coffin, and a team from Corpus Christi dramatized their "Crab Claw" chili by tossing live crabs at squeamish spectators. Then, of course, there were wet-T-shirt contests for the women, lemon rolls, egg tosses, shoot-outs, and other "games of high skill," not to mention dancing and marathon beer drinking. Throughout all this excitement and chaos, the chili pots simmered away, and when the judges finally made their choice, everybody but the elated champion threw hats on the ground, swore, and went on about how nobody knew anything anymore about what constitutes great chili.

I wouldn't exactly coax the uninitiated or weak at heart to attend any chili cookoff, but you simply haven't tasted real chili till you've eaten chili made by Texans. Generally, the great examples have much in common: hunks of tender beef that have been marinated in beer and browned first in beef suet; subtle seasonings of garlic, cumin, oregano, coriander, paprika, and chili pepper pulp (*not* chili powder); a light binding of *masa harina;* a deep purplish red color; and no onions, no tomatoes, no bell peppers and, heaven forbid, no beans. "Keep things as simple as possible with chili," advises Frank Tolbert. "The main thing in good chili is for no one ingredient to overpower any other. And, above all, remember that it's not the heat but the taste that counts."

RURAL: GOOD HOME COOKING

Although Tex-Mex fare, barbecue, and chili are no doubt the three most fascinating foods associated with Texas, there are certainly other day-to-day staples in the Longhorn State which illustrate the enviable rich bounty of fresh foods with which Texans are blessed almost year-round. In one home where I've stayed, good food is constantly in evidence, and my host thinks nothing of shopping every day for the ripest homegrown tomatoes and cucumbers, the pinkest Ruby Red grapefruits, the freshest range chickens, the sweetest Hidalgo onions. Breakfast is never a ridiculous piece of bland bread or pastry with coffee, but rather a serious meal involving items like thick-fleshed cantaloupes, stewed fruits, farm-fresh *huevos rancheros* ("ranch-style eggs"), country sausage, roast beef hash with bits of jalapeño, fried ham with raised gravy, and fresh hot biscuits with homemade peach preserves and hot pepper jelly.

Perhaps what impresses me most about the Texas table and the people's eating habits is the total absence of pretension. To be sure, Texans can and will throw a "gourmet" feast grand enough to shake up even the snootiest visitor, but what they love most are friendly, informal meals with an old-fashioned abundance. Attend even a glittering, Bourbon-scented party in San Antonio, and what you find on the buffet is a mountain of fat Gulf shrimp simply boiled, spicy meatballs sparked with poblano chilies, bowls of "Texas caviar" (pickled black-eyed peas), tiny barbecued ribs, fresh tamales, baked ham, plenty of cheese and pecans, and large bowls of *chili con queso* with crisp tostados for dunking. At home no one makes excuses for serving roasted meats with oceans of gravy, platters of jalapeño corn bread, chicken-fried steak, shrimp stew, okra and tomatoes, refried beans, jam cakes rich with fresh ice cream, and gallons of iced tea.

Having sampled hither and yonder on recent trips such other regional specialities as venison sausage, tamale pie, barbecued lima beans, onion steak, prune aspic, pumpkin bread, and vinegar pie, I left this remarkable territory with an entirely different attitude toward its contributions to American gastronomy. Surely the only other cooking style in this country that can testify so fully to the benefits of mingling cultures would be that of New Orleans, and surely no Americans are prouder of their heritage than Texans, whose pioneer ancestors by force of sheer necessity developed culinary ideas that would later result in numerous codified dishes. Today, of course, the flavor of Texas and the taste buds of Texans are being at least partly influenced by the rapid influx of the same "refined" restaurants and trendy cooking schools that have infiltrated the rest of the country, and it is sad but true that the number of chili parlors, old-fashioned barbecue houses, and authentic Tex-Mex restaurants are dwindling more and more in favor of pseudo-French and pseudo-Italian restaurants, exotic Szechuan palaces, and those disgraceful salad-bar emporia. On the other hand, Texans have always had the independence, intelligence, and outright rebellion in the soul at once to absorb and apply sensible new ideas and unhesitatingly reject anything that clashes with natural instinct, a character trait that could help more than anything else to preserve a fascinating cookery that should be allowed to evolve. It's for sure that Texans love to eat well, and unless I'm badly mistaken, the next time I visit that big, sprawling, overgrown empire, there'll still be plenty of tasty vittles—three times a day.

Jalapeño Pie

1   7-oz. can jalapeño peppers, drained, rinsed, and seeded
½ lb. sharp Cheddar cheese, coarsely grated
4   eggs, beaten
    Salt to taste

Cut peppers into thin long slices and line bottom and sides of a 9-inch pie plate. Press grated cheese over peppers. Add salt to eggs, beat slightly more, and pour over cheese. Bake at 350°F for 25–30 minutes. Slice pie into small wedges and serve as finger food with cocktails, or slice into equal wedges to serve as a luncheon dish. SERVES 4–6.

Nopalito (Cactus Casserole)

2   qts. salted water
1   lb. young cactus (packaged), washed and cut into strips
    available in specialty food shops)
2   Tb. shortening
1   onion, chopped
1   green bell pepper, chopped
2   Tb. hot chili sauce
½ cup dried shrimp (packaged), soaked in hot water
3   eggs, beaten
    Salt and freshly ground pepper to taste

In a large kettle bring water to full boil, cook cactus 20 minutes, and drain. In a heavy skillet melt shortening, add onion and bell pepper, and sauté over medium heat till tender. Add hot chili sauce, cactus, shrimp, and stir thoroughly. Add eggs, salt and pepper to taste, and stir slowly till eggs have set. Serve as a side vegetable. SERVES 4–6.

GYPSY BARBECUED BRISKET

BARBECUE SAUCE
1   bottle Worcestershire sauce (10 oz.)
1   bottle hot pepper sauce (2 oz.)
1   stick butter or margarine
1   Tb. black pepper
½   Tb. hot red pepper, finely chopped
1   Tb. salt
    Just less than 1 pt. white vinegar

In a large saucepan combine all ingredients and bring to a boil. Lower heat, stir thoroughly, and simmer about 10 minutes. Cool and refrigerate till ready to use.

"I usually buy the biggest, thickest brisket I can find," says Mary Yturria. "Then I line a large roasting pan with foil, put the meat in it, cover the meat with sauce, and fold the foil over the meat. This is done in the morning. After lunch I put meat in the oven at about 325° F, and after four or five hours, when meat is almost done, I fold the foil around the sides and allow the meat to finish cooking uncovered. The meat should brown thoroughly and soak up all the sauce. The meat is so moist and tender, with such a delicious flavor, that you really do not need to serve sauce on the side. If the spirit moves you, you can cook the meat over charcoal outside, but be sure that it is done in a pan so that the meat can absorb the sauce. This brisket will feed at least a dozen people."

ENCHILADAS

8	Tb. bacon drippings
5	Tb. flour
1	clove garlic, finely chopped
6	Tb. pulp from boiled colorado or ancho chilies (available in specialty food shops)
1	qt. hot water
	Salt to taste
4	squares Mexican chocolate, mashed (available in specialty food shops)
2	large onions, chopped
1	lb. sharp cheddar cheese, grated
1	lb. Monterey Jack white cheese
1½	cups vegetable oil
10–12	tortillas

In a heavy skillet heat bacon drippings, add flour, garlic, and chili pulp, and stir over low heat about 5 minutes. Add hot water, stirring, then add chocolate and salt to taste, stirring constantly. Continue cooking till medium thick, then set aside. In a bowl combine onions and cheese and mix thoroughly. Heat oil in another large skillet and add a tortilla just long enough to soften. Remove from oil, dip in sauce, fill with a little onion and cheese mixture, roll up neatly, and arrange in a large baking dish. Continue rolling tortillas till dish is full (one layer only). Sprinkle remainder of onion and cheese mixture on top, pour on enough sauce to fill half the dish, and bake at 350° F. About 20 minutes or till bubbling hot. SERVES 4–6.

Brownsville Shrimp

4½   lbs. fresh shrimp, shelled and deveined
½   tsp. cayenne pepper
3   cloves garlic, crushed
    Paprika to dust
    Filé powder to dust (available in speciality food shops)
2   lemons, thinly sliced
1   lb. butter
½   cup lemon juice
¼   cup chopped chives
1   tsp. salt
2   oz. Tabasco

In a large oblong baking dish arrange layer of shrimp, sprinkle cayenne evenly over surface, add half the garlic, dust with paprika and filé powder, and arrange half the lemon slices over surface. Add another layer of shrimp and repeat procedure with cayenne, garlic, paprika, filé powder, and lemon slices. Combine remaining ingredients in a saucepan and simmer slowly till butter is melted. Pour butter sauce over shrimp and bake at 350° F for 20 minutes. Serve with plenty of hot Mexican or French bread to dip into sauce. Serves 6.

Congealed Mango Mousse

2   cups boiling water
8   oz. lemon Jello
    15-oz. can mangos (including juice)
4   oz. cream cheese, softened
    Sour cream

Dissolve Jello in boiling water. In a blender place mangos, juice, and cream cheese, and blend till smooth. Whisk mango mixture into dissolved Jello and mix well. Pour into a 1½-qt. mold, chill thoroughly, and unmold on lettuce leaf. Garnish with sour cream. Serves 4.

Frank Tolbert's Quintessential Chili

Mastermind behind the World Championship Chili Cook-off at Terlingua, author of the definitive *A Bowl of Red,* and owner of two famous chili parlors in Dallas, Frank Xavier Tolbert knows more about chili con carne than anybody else on earth. Although the much-sought-after recipe he gave me might sound a bit complex and involved, I've decided to reproduce it with minimum editing and tampering. Read the recipe carefully at least three times to absorb the facts and get in the chili-making mood; then get to work and learn what truly great Texas chili is all about.

"The main vehicle in the formula is three pounds of mature beef or venison, and we usually call for lean beef when we can get it. I successfully made the chili on the North Cape in Norwegian Lapland, hundreds of miles above the Arctic Circle, with reindeer meat, and my brother in Alaska uses caribou (same as reindeer) and moose.

"At the start, we marinate the beef in beer and keep this liquid in the cooking process. Cut the meat into thumb-sized pieces or put it through a grinder at the coarsest setting. We sear the beef until it is gray in rendered beef kidney suet, which adds a sweet flavor, but you will probably do the searing in vegetable oil. Vegetable oil is okay. The searing will seal in meat flavors and solidify the beef for the cooking process, same as you would sear a steak. I use about an eighth of a pound of rendered kidney suet, and a like amount of vegetable oil should do. Many old time chili cooks sprinkle some chopped-up onions on the meat while it is being seared. Go ahead if you think it'll suit your taste.

"Chili peppers, such as sun-dried anchos or jalapeños, can be obtained in most Mexican food stores. For mild chili use two average-sized chili pepper pods for each pound of beef. For 'elevated' chili use four pods. Put chili peppers in a blender along with enough water to make a puree, transfer to a large pot along with the beer marinade and meat, and cook the seared meat, first bringing it to a boil and then simmering for about 30 minutes. Take the pot off the stove for a while.

"Add fresh garlic to taste, two level tabelspoons of crushed cumin seed or powdered comino, one level tablespoon of salt, one level tablespoon of cayenne pepper, and a few pinches of oregano. We go very slow with the oregano. Too much oregano can give a spaghetti sauce flavor. If you use yellowish, greenish, or purplish chili peppers, you can sprinkle in some paprika to add a reddish hue to the chili. It won't affect the taste. Wick

Fowler, one of the greatest of chili cooks, put 15 ounces of tomato sauce in a recipe calling for three pounds of meat. He said it adds color and thickening and most of the tomato flavor surrenders to the more power- ful spices. Wick also "tightened" the chili with *masa harina* (corn flour), but I think it gives too much of a tamale taste.

"With the spices in there, put the pot back on the stove, bring to a boil, and then simmer about 45 minutes, stirring some but keeping the lid on as much as possible. This last time for simmering isn't arbitrary. Cook the meat till it's tender and has the taste you're looking for. Keep the chili in the refrigerator overnight to seal in the spices. This also makes it easy to spoon off any grease at the top which you don't want in your chili. Actually, though, a little grease helps the flavor.

"If you want pinto or red beans with your chili, for God's sake cook the beans separately, and there's no need to make the beans highly fla- vored. I'm constantly running into people who cook beans in with the meat in making chili con carne. These people flunked chemistry."

CONFRONTING AMERICAN GOURMANIA

AMERICA'S PASSION, AMERICA'S GUILT

OF COURSE you love them! French fries are your secret yen, the source of your most deep-seated guilt. Admit it. Oh, I know how you try to hide it. The writer says, "Baked or French?" You hesitate, you cringe, you wonder why in hell he couldn't simply serve the steak with a baked potato and not mention French fries. But now you're forced to choose, and you know there is no choice; by God, you want the fries, diet or no diet, pimples or no pimples, and damn the cholesterol. You say, "I think maybe I just might have the French fries tonight," forgetting that you ate half a pound three evenings ago. When they arrive you pick around at the mound one fry at a time. You think you'll eat just a few. Halfway through the steak, you're downing them by the handfuls, and by the end of the meal you've devoured the batch, long thin ones, short fat ones, charred ends, every remaining greasy or dry, oversalted or undersalted, catsupy or non-catsupy morsel.

Of course you're now ridden with guilt, you're miserable, demoralized because you have given in. The pleasure of French fries is fleeting. But if you take my advice, it needn't be.

Americans love French fries violently—all of us, not just the grease-smacking kids and their asbestos-palated guardians. Even the country's most respected epicures admit directly or indirectly to being fanatics. When Julia Child was asked what she thought about McDonald's fries, she described them as "surprisingly good," while Craig Claiborne pronounced them "first-rate." Gael Greene swoons over the French fries at Carrols, Roy Andries de Groot still dreams of those he tasted at Arthur Bryant's in Kansas City, and James Beard becomes passionate while discussing the *pommes frites* at La Grille in Paris. As for myself, I have about as much moral fiber when I see, sniff, or hear about great fries as when I contemplate the idea of a second Bourbon Manhattan.

No one has feared developing leprosy from eating French fries, or any form of potato, ever since the brave Frenchman Parmentier disproved that possibility a few centuries back, but we all do know that fries make us fat (or fatter), cause blemishes, induce indigestion, nourish ulcers, and make havoc of cholesterol counts. Yet everybody keeps on stuffing them down, at steak and fish houses, at thousands of fast-food joints, on street corners, in the air, at ball parks—and in the finest restaurants, too. So much I understand. But the odd thing is that for most people the greasier and more awful the French fry, the better. Here my own taste and the national yen part company. I think that what passes for French fried potatoes at most places today is both a crime against nature and an insult to our addiction. Give one second of serious thought to what one usually finds: fries that have been precooked, frozen, freeze-dried, reconstituted, or "re-created" from powdered potatoes in an ingenious new machine that spits them out like artillery cartridges; fat, greasy fries that are undercooked in filthy oil reeking of fish, chicken, and heaven knows what other alien flavors; charred fries that taste like pure carbon; lukewarm fries served in sacks that bear close resemblance to barf bags on airplanes; and so forth and so forth.

I refuse to put up with these, and you don't have to either. I mean, if you really crave French fries, learn to recognize what great ones are. If you're going to give in, do so to quality, not junk. And know, too, that there's lots of truth in the old-fashioned idea that a portion of properly cooked French fries can have a lower calorie count and cause fewer other problems than a baked potato dripping with butter or full of all that other stuff people plop on baked potatoes.

So exactly what is a flawless French fried potato? A perfect French fry is, above all, fresh, meaning the oblong has been cut from an absolutely fresh potato no more than an hour before being deep-fried in clean fat. A perfect French fry is thin, smooth and not crinkled, consistently golden brown in color, firm, crackly crisp on the outside with a slightly soft interior, and dry enough for most salt to fall off. Anyone who's ever tasted delicious *pommes frites* in France or Belgium knows what I'm talking about and will agree that the fries in those countries are generally just the opposite of the soggy matchsticks or fat greasy tubers we have thrown at us in fast-food places and undistinguished restaurants. I'm not stating that the French and Belgians are the only ones aware of the difference between a good and bad potato, but they at least accord the same care and respect for the humble *frites* as for most other comestibles that grace their universally admired tables.

This may all sound like too much of a production over something as common as French fried potatoes, but again, if you're really after perfect fries, you'll learn that making them correctly yourself involves a lot more than cutting up potatoes and throwing the pieces in hot oil. Although the procedure for preparing great fries is virtually the same in your own kitchen as in a restaurant, I must give fair warning that deep-fat frying at home is not only a mess but (recalling a few terrifying experiences) potentially dangerous. (On TV, Julia Child introduced a fire extinguisher as the first ingredient.) When grease reaches a certain temperature it can catch fire, and unless you're accustomed to regulating the heat with a deep-fat thermometer, you could easily burn yourself up and your house down. Restaurants usually install huge automatic Ansul fire extinguishers close to fryers and exhaust vents, but for home frying the best idea is always to keep both a portable extinguisher and a big box of baking soda within arm's length, and remember never to allow so much as a drop of water to come near hot fat.

Contrary to what many people think, perfect fries must be made from mature, mealy potatoes containing minimum moisture. The finest examples grow during the summer months in California and Missouri, but since it's unlikely that many people outside those regions will ever have the opportunity to use the exquisite potatoes, it's sensible to say that the one and only variety to buy is the long Idaho. Some cookbooks (and some chefs) say you can fix French fries with Maine potatoes, Long Island potatoes, new potatoes, etc. Don't! They contain too much water and will not give you ideal results.

Now for the actual preparation and frying of the potatoes. Forget everything you ever learned about cooking French fries, for I guarantee if you follow this fail-proof procedure step by step with no shortcuts, you'll not only produce the celestial fries you've always dreamed about but you'll also be able to speak with authority when inquiring about the potatoes served in public. The method may sound a bit unorthodox, but it represents the collective results of everything I've learned from experts both here and abroad. It works.

1. Peel the raw Idahoes by hand. Cut oblongs exactly 3¾ inches in length and ⅜ inch in width, soak in cold water at least two hours to wash out starch, then soak in *ice* water thirty minutes to help the potato regain its firmness.

2. Dry each potato individually by hand with paper or cloth towels, wrap loosely in another towel, and set aside. Absolutely no cheating. To brown properly, the potatoes must be *completely* dry.

3. Although the ideal cooking equipment consists of two deep-fat fryers with built-in thermostats, there's nothing wrong with two more practical and economical large, deep, iron pots into which you can lower fry baskets and a deep-fat thermometer. Fill the first pot ½-to-¾-full of fresh rendered beef suet (the preferred cooking fat), hydrogenated shortening, or peanut oil, and heat to 360 ° F. Prepare the second vessel in like manner and heat to 390 °. Always keep a close check on the thermometers, and make sure the fat never smokes. The fat must be fresh and there must be enough of it to assure that there will be no significant change in temperature when the cold potatoes are added.

4. Never cook more than two handfuls of potatoes at a time, and do not blanch them before frying. Lower the first batch into the 360 ° fat and fry till light golden in color but with no brown spots. This will take six minutes. Transfer the container *immediately* to the 390 ° fat and finish the fries to a golden brown—about 2 or 2½ minutes. Watch them constantly in both cookings. (You can begin a second batch in the first vessel while the other batch cooks.)

5. Dump the fries *inside* a brown paper sack, shake quickly to absorb all grease, salt to taste, then devour. (The fat can be used again—only for French fries!—if filtered through muslin, covered, and kept refrigerated.) To avoid nauseating carbon buildup, the cooking equipment should be soaked in hot water and baking soda after every session.

There you have it, and once you've become accustomed to your own perfect fries, you should accept nothing less than this same quality in restaurants. (It goes without saying that since you can now cook all the fries you want, you have no reason to wander out to fast-food joints and the like.) When a surly captain or waiter mumbles "baked or French fried," you ask right off if the potatoes are fresh, thin, crisp, and whether or not they're fried in the same fat as other edibles. If, after they're served, you find he has lied, raise hell. Pinch a fat, soggy tuber to expose the grease, tell him you smell and taste the shrimp flavor, send back the whole rotten mess, demand a doggy bag for your steak, go home, fry up a batch of beauties, and suffer in ecstasy.

BURGER TRUTH

●●●●●●●●●●●●●●●●●●●●●●●●●●●●●●●●●●

I DON'T hesitate for a second to state that I'm as mad about all-American hamburgers as anybody else and am proud that this is still by far the most beloved of our yummy staples. Not hot dogs, or apple pie, or fried chicken, or even steak. But hamburgers. On buns. I know I'm not really supposed to love hamburgers, but I do. Good ones.

I'm also prepared to state that if the country's destiny were dependent solely on the quality of most burgers being hustled off today, we'd go to pot quicker than you could say jackrabbit. It's depressing enough facing up to the fact that chain restaurants and fast-food operations now account for almost one-third of the sales of the gigantic food service industry, and that before we know it, old-fashioned, custom-produced, family-style meals will most likely be something of the past. But what has already happened to the good old American burger is an absolute disgrace, a sin, an insult to our culinary heritage. In all likelihood you've actually *forgotten* what an honest-to-goodness hamburger is like, and your children may never have even tasted one. Well, it's high time you reacquaint yourself with an aspect of our background that's as important as liberty itself.

Now there's no sense trying to analyze exactly how everything went wrong with hamburgers, but it's for sure that those outrageous computerized sandwiches you find from sea to shining sea are a far cry from the luscious original introduced by German immigrants at the 1904 Louisiana Purchase Exposition in St. Louis. Just consider for a moment the standard type of cheap burger that has overwhelmed the masses during the past two decades. Stuck between two fat hunks of bread is a pitiful three ounces of meat charred to the consistency of a tennis ball. (Yes, I know, you were promised a quarter-pounder, but don't forget the meat shrinks about 25 percent in cooking.) Once you study the minuscule patty (which you usually locate only on the second bite), you may see a dollop of mustard, catsup, or some gluey mayonnaise dressing, perhaps a faint suggestion of minced onion, and, if you're lucky, two razor-thin pickles. That's it. If you eat cheese, the price begins to soar, and if you want the plasticized tomato and lettuce usually included on the super-duper sandwiches (super-duper, indeed!), you really shell out—and *still* for nothing. Add to this an order of string-like, tasteless fries and a soft drink overwhelmed by ice, and . . . admit it, somebody's making a sucker out of you.

You'd think things would be better over the grill at home, but since almost everybody's forgotten what a real hamburger is like, few people ever serve up a really smashing example. Of course, today's fanatical obsession with weight and cholesterol and fats and all that nonsense hasn't exactly enhanced the image of the ideal burger *I'm* forever seeking out, but even more menacing to the authentic sandwich's future is the increasing willingness of consumers either to settle for cheap, flavorless ground meat that's reduced to nothing when cooked or, even worse, to buy those new scientific marvels known as texturized beef and soybean extenders with the intention of stretching the yield and the dollar. Heaven knows I have to watch the buck as closely as the next guy, but when it comes to fixing a great hamburger, I'm unalterably convinced there simply can be no shortcuts. After all, the problem in most restaurants is disastrous enough without our denigrating in our own homes the one staple capable of bringing us the maximum in gustatory bliss.

So exactly what is a great hamburger, how did it used to be fixed, where can you still find one, and how do you prepare a truly classic example? Well, I'll tell you, detail by luscious detail. The old-timey real McCoy was, above all, thick, and when I say thick I'm talking about 1½ inches of meat. It wasn't only thick as sin but wide. So wide it stuck out on every side of the bun. I can still see in my mind's eye one old expert now frying up my order in a small joint I patronized for years. He reaches in the refrigerator, pulls out a fistful of fresh red meat, shapes it into a fat patty, and throws it on a flat grill (and I'm not referring to a charcoal grate). After a few minutes he flips it over, and, since I want a cheeseburger with all the trimmings, lays a slice of American cheddar (nothing more fancy, mind you) on top to melt all down the sides. In the meantime, he takes a hot, soft sesame-seed bun out of a bread warmer, smears both sides with gobs of mayonnaise plus a little catsup, and neatly arranges, on the bottom half, one fat cut of

Bermuda onion, two slices of *real* tomato, and two or three leaves of crisp iceberg lettuce. On top of all this he spatulas the burger, adds the top half of the bun, and then, with the palm of his hand, pushes slightly down on his creation so that the meat juices begin saturating the other ingredients. Finally, he tongs a mess of piping hot French fries on the plate, an unspecified number of sliced sour pickles, and casually plops the miracle on the counter. No one ever argues with his technique, and no one gives a hoot about his hands coming in contact with the food. He's a genius.

Eating this sort of burger with your hands has never been an easy feat, but nobody in his right mind would ever consider the absurd possibility of using a knife and fork. Of course, there was, and still is, a set approach to the ceremony of downing a great hamburger. First you salt and pepper the meat, next you salt and catsup the fries and gobble down a few to get things rolling; then, naturally, you guzzle a big slug of Coke. (Some people order milk shakes, root beer, or some other unorthodox soft drink, and I personally wonder why they don't choke.) Now comes the inimitable moment to take the first compelling, mouth-watering, sensuous bite of the burger. You grasp the corpulent creature with both hands, squeeze hard, and begin gradually, ever so carefully, trying to edge it into your salivating mouth. You close your eyes, chomp down, and—mummm . . . mummm—you're on your way. The meat, cheese, onion, tomato, lettuce, mayonnaise, catsup: each makes its own special contribution to the whole, yet the flavors and textures harmonize almost synesthetically. Wow! you say. Now *that's* damn good eatin'!

When your teeth finally meet, all hell breaks loose as the juices start to explode and bits and pieces of garnishment try to go their own way. It's dripping . . . all down your chin and through your fingers and across your wrists and onto the plate; red, green, white particles bombarding the countertop and the single, innocent, worthless paper napkin resting in your lap. Trying not to lose grip on the bun, you slowly, respectfully return matter to rest on the plate, rearrange the components, grab frantically for a *handful* of napkins, tidy up fingers, chin, lips, clothing, counter, and prepare for the next assault. It's rough going for a while, but you know the reward is great. So you stay in control and eventually win out over every burger-bite, French fry, pickle, and ounce of Coke.

Now let me assure you that such perfect hamburgers are indeed still around, and if you're a true burger hound you'll sniff them out anywhere and everywhere you go, refusing to ever accept second best. Sometimes I spend hours in unfamiliar towns walking around in search of my ideal burger, just as on the highway I'll drive twenty miles out of the way if I have reason to believe a place exists where my craving will be satisfied. The first notion to keep in mind is that great hamburgers are rarely found today in hotels, motels, and fine restaurants. (Temples of gastronomy might be able to turn out delectable steak tartares and spectacular *tournedos Rossini,* but they know zero about the fine art of fixing superlative American burgers.) Although some of the most memorable patties I've consumed have been in ordinary coffee shops, without doubt the best old-fashioned hamburgers are to be found at truck stops, side-street saloons, hidden away holes-in-the-wall, and plain old greasy spoons. Yes, I realize none of this sounds too chic and elegant—just good. In fact, nothing pertaining to real hamburger-eating is chic and elegant. Never has been, never will be.

Again, it all depends on what you want and to what extent you're willing to sacrifice hoop-de-la for burger perfection. If, like most of this sad world, you prefer the convenience of a fashionable cafe serving spiffed-up phony burger plates at outrageous prices, you won't have to look too far. Or if you enjoy forcing down a quick plastic sandwich in a plastic container at an antiseptic plastic table, you'll have no problem spotting a fast-food place. If, on the other hand, you demand the type of hamburger God intended us to eat, you'll seek and search and yearn and think nothing of nesting in ordinary wooden booths or perching on twirl-around barstools at unpretentious but clean short-order counters. It's all a question of gastronomic value—of how much you really love your stomach.

As for making hamburgers at home, there's simply no excuse in anybody's not attaining absolute perfection. The first rule is never to buy chopped meat that's prepackaged and full of bone and gristle and heaven knows what else. Generally the best idea is to pick out a nice piece of chuck, top or bottom round, or rump (always with enough fat to insure good flavor and juiciness) and either have the butcher grind it twice or grind it yourself. If you're willing to go to a little extra trouble, as I do, you'll first grind up some lean round or sirloin, then an equal amount of lean chuck, then enough fat to make up about 20 percent of the whole, and finally mix everything together lightly. Exactly why grinding the ingredients separately produces such outstanding hamburgers I don't really know. But it does, and I see no need to question it further.

To cook the ideal burger, measure about seven or eight ounces of chopped meat (eventually you'll be able to simply grab a handful and instinctively feel the correct weight), roll it into a ball, flatten it out evenly with the palm of your hand till it's about 1½ inches thick, place it in a cold cast-iron skillet with a little butter (or, if you insist, on a charcoal grill), and cook over moderate heat about six minutes per side or till the meat has a good crust with a pink interior. (Note: If you plan to char this sublime meat to the point of petrifaction, you might as well go to a fast-food outlet.) Turn the patty only once, place a slab of natural American cheddar on top if desired, and never—but *never*—press down on the meat with a spatula to speed up cooking or extract precious juices. (Second note: If you're fanatical about consuming fats, just forget altogether about trying to make a great hamburger and settle instead for a boringly healthy boiled-chicken sandwich.)

The bun is as important as the burger, so shortly before you begin frying, heat the oven slightly, wrap a good-quality sesame bun tightly in foil, and allow it to warm till it's soft but not delicate. Put plenty of mayonnaise on both halves of the bun (true hamburger lovers *hate* mustard on their patties) and a shake of catsup, stack on the bottom half a slice of raw onion, ripe tomato, crisp lettuce, plus any other garnish you happen to fancy, transfer the burger from the pan to the sandwich *without* draining, salt and pepper everything in sight, position the top half of the bread, and press down just hard enough so the juices begin to drip down through the ingredients.

Now you're almost ready. Once the burger is fixed, place it smack in the middle of a large plate, surround it with mounds of potato chips (or fresh homemade French fries) and half a dozen sour or bread-and-butter pickles, open a cold bottle of Coke or Pepsi (to be drunk from the bottle, naturally), spread a large dish towel across your lap, and prepare to devour a juicy hunk of Americana even more exciting than *The Adventures of Huckleberry Finn.*

CLAWED KING
OF THE DEEP

●●●●●●●●●●●●●●●●●●●●●●●●●●●●●●●

OF ALL the sensuous experiences associated with the art of eating in America, few can equal the summer ritual of devouring a fresh lobster on the New England coast. The fact that one can enjoy live-cooked Northeastern lobsters in restaurants all over the country does little to explain the almost mystical appeal of this delicacy on its home ground. Perhaps it's strictly psychological—like eating *boeuf bourguignon* at a rustic country inn in Burgundy or crawfish in New Orleans. But you simply have never tasted truly great lobster until you've pulled up to a seaside cottage or restaurant in Maine or on Cape Cod, breathed deeply the fresh ocean air, strapped on a big, clumsy bib, and indulged in all the primitive cracking, twisting, digging, and sucking involved in an old-fashioned lobster feast.

The grandest of lobster dinners are inevitably the simplest, and memories of them get tangled with the smell of spruce and wharves permeated with salt, or the sound of small boats knocking companion-ably at a dock. If you're staying with family or friends, half the ritual is sheer expectation: the trip, perhaps by boat, to the local lobsterman to pick out some hefty fighters fresh from the trap; the ceremonious small talk as he boxes them in layers of cool seaweed; the injunction to chil-dren to please stop poking the lobsters. Lobsters probably taste best cooked outside on the beach or the ledges (in days gone by, they were steamed in seaweed over hot rocks, an almost lost art), but if the fog is rolling in or appetites grow impatient, they're almost as good indoors.

Just before dinner, out comes the huge lobster pot (still smelling faintly of other summers), and someone runs to the tideline for seawa-ter—just a few inches for the bottom of the pot. Lobsters in and steam-ing, butter melting, rolls heating, salad tossed, beer or wine chilled, ev-eryone mills about, helpless with expectation. Suddenly there are more experts on the matter of timing a lobster than anyone needs in one house. The hostess's pride—the beauty of a long table with a steaming red lobster at every place—lasts but a second. With a concentrated hush, the joyous twisting, cracking attack begins: butter drips; fingers tear and pluck; the tiniest, most secret shreds of sweetness are extracted from the depths of the shell. The sighs, crunches, and groans would be familiar to cavemen. For hours after, the subtle essence of lobster still clings to even the best-scrubbed hands.

If it's true that such a down-home lobster orgy is a gastronomic tradition that can only be classified as pure American, it's equally true that the day could be approaching, even in New England, when such a feast will be something most people can do it any more than read about. The great American lobster, or *homarus Americanus,* has become so scarce and expensive that it can almost be placed in the same luxury class as beluga caviar, fresh *foie gras,* and even truffles. No doubt, at the height of the summer lobstering season, visitors to remote coastal villages in Maine can occasionally still buy quarters (1¼-pound lobsters) for around three dollars a pound. But elsewhere the story's the same: the demand for clawed Northeastern lobster is so great and the supply so low that even during July and August (when prices everywhere go down slightly), only the affluent and overindulgent can afford the delicacy on any sort of regular basis.

In the not-so-distant past, Americans frequently enjoyed preparing fresh steamed lobster at home or choosing a bunch of mean, green two-pounders from a cold restaurant tank and ordering them up steamed or boiled. Ever since refrigerated jet transport made live Maine and Canadian lobsters available coast-to-coast—and even abroad—we've taken a ready supply for granted. The way things look now, however, these treasures of the deep, dwindling in number each year, will soon be so special that most of us will savor them on red-letter holidays only. "Those who wish to believe that the American lobster resource is in good condition must deliberately ignore the facts," states Robert Dow, research director of the Maine Fisheries Department. "With nearly twenty years of declining landings throughout its range, the lobster supply is obviously in trouble both biologically and economically."

What has happened to bring about the demise of this delicious arthropod so cherished throughout the country—and much of the civilized world? Ironically, today's predicament contrasts dismally with the prodigal past when lobster was as ordinary as corn and molasses.

The early New England colonists, in fact, were so indifferent to these crawly green monsters washed ashore by storms that they used them primarily as fertilizer for crops and bait for codfish, rarely deigning to actually eat the things. When a shipload of starving colonists landed at Plymouth Rock three years after the original settlement, Governor Bradford apologized that "the only dish they could presente their friends with was a lobster, without bread or anything else but a cupp of fair water." And later Captain Frederick Marryat of the Royal Navy noted in awe that the thirty-pound crustaceans off the Boston coast were so prodigious that "one could stow a dozen common English lobsters under their coats of mail."

For two centuries after, the lobster remained undisturbed in the cold Atlantic, its gustatory glory unrecognized until the newly rich of the mid-nineteenth century ushered in the custom of lavish dining. Once the delicacy caught on, there was no limit to its appeal. And with no statutory laws to control the size of the catch, there was no limit to what lobstermen could and did haul in, day after day. Records show that by the last years of the century, the annual harvest from Labrador to North Carolina hovered around 130 million pounds, enough to satisfy the demands of what Lucius Beebe once called "lobster-palace society"—but also enough to assure thereafter a steady decline in supply from overfishing. At such celebrated New York haunts as Rector's, Café Martin, the Knickerbocker Grill, and Bustanoby's, the likes of Diamond Jim, "Bet-a-Million" Gates, Lillian Russell, and Lillie Langtry tucked away eight-course lobster dinners for no more than $1.25. Even until World War II it was still possible (and indeed fashionable) to order a good-size Maine lobster at Lüchow's for about $2.00. Conservation laws were passed, to be sure, but extravagance had already sunk an incurable wound into the industry, and by the late sixties the total American catch had been reduced to an annual 70 million pounds (only 18.5 million of which were landed in Maine waters).

Today, a thicket of measures has been enacted or introduced in various state legislatures to protect the troubled industry: more in-depth studies of water temperatures; restrictions on the number of fishermen allowed to land (only Maine residents, for instance, can qualify to trap Maine lobsters); changes in regulations governing the legal minimum and maximum sizes; increasing the Maine license fee to eliminate the small or part-time lobsterman; improving lobster traps to reduce mortality rates; tighter laws governing pollution; improved methods of shipment; and, finally, an unpromising attempt to breed lobsters artificially in controlled pounds (lobsters cannibalize each other).

Furthermore, Canada (which produces up to 65 percent of the average annual volume) is shipping more and more of its catch to Europe, thus reducing the supply available to this country and driving up prices. In Maine, 8,000 lobstermen use the most sophisticated modern equipment and venture out as far as 200 miles to sow their pots, yet their yield is still nor more than that produced by 2,600 salts in 1892. "Just forty-five years ago we were dealing annually with half a million pounds of lobster at 25¢ a pound," says a wholesale dealer in Stonington. "Today we pay $3.40 per pound and get half that amount." And out at Montauk on the tip of Long Island (where absence of size regulations allows lobstermen occasionally to bring in gigantic twenty- and thirty-pound behemoths), a long-time dealer is hardly more optimistic: "At the rate things are going, the industry will be down to 2 million pounds a year in twenty years. We've seen the results of overfishing both in New England and off Long Island, and it all boils down to the fact that when you see the size of lobsters decreasing as steadily as today, it simply indicates that the overall stock is definitely being depleted."

The truth remains that of all the varieties of so-called lobster found around the world (and most are disappearing even faster than the American lobster), none can compare in size, flavor, and texture with the beauties we know so well. The closest thing to a Maine and Canadian lobster is the small-clawed *homarus vulgaris* trapped in the waters around Scotland, England, and Norway, a colorful crustacean that yields reasonably sweet but relatively little meat. Even smaller is the clawless species in various European waters known as Danish Dainties, *demoiselles de Cherbourg*, Dublin Bay prawns, or even scampi. And when it comes to all the varieties of clawless, spiny lobsters caught off Florida, Califonia, France (*langoustes*), South Africa, Australia, and New Zealand, you're talking about the bland, woody "lobster tails" similar to those found in the frozen food departments of every supermarket. No doubt all these varieties have their valued place in the annals of world gastronomy, but for one accustomed to the solidly packed, tender, salty-sweet meat that characterizes the *homarus americanus,* there is simply no equal.

For those stubborn epicures who, price be damned, still insist on the king of crustaceans, the best advice is to go on and splurge during July and August when lobster is most plentiful and least expensive. Half the fun, of course, of eating lobster is in those age-old debates about how to do it. No two lobstermen's wives or New York chefs agree about the ideal size or cooking method, or about what does or doesn't go best with lobster. Most enthusiasts will tell you, for example, that the ideal weight for a lobster is from 1½ to 2 pounds, young enough for tenderness yet mature enough to yield full flavor. But personally, I love nothing more than a terrifying 4- or 5-pounder. What you hear about giant lobsters being tough is sheer nonsense. Anyone going through all the effort and mess of eating a lobster should eat it like a warrior. "Size really has nothing to do with texture," I was once told by a lobsterman up in Nova Scotia. "Two things toughen any lobster: holding it on ice too long and overcooking. Plain and simple."

While nothing can be more tasty (and economical) from time to time than a lobster prepared Newburg style or à l'américaine, the delicacy is never quite so luscious as when simply steamed or boiled, then dipped in hot melted butter spiked with lemon juice or served cold with fresh mayonnaise. Of these two cooking options, I find steaming preferable to boiling for the simple reason that any food submerged in boiling water seems to lose a certain amount of flavor. (And a boiled lobster gets too much water in the shell.) Debate rages eternal over the correct amount of time to boil lobster, if boil you must, but the most sensible rule of thumb to avoid overcooking is roughly five minutes for the first pound and three minutes for each additional. Broiled lobster I consider nothing less than a sacrilege, not only because this method of cooking tends to dry out and toughen the flesh, but because, more often than not, delectable parts, like the small legs and the tomalley, end up a charred disgrace. Unfortunately, since few restaurants care to deal with tremendous cauldrons of boiling water and heavy-duty steamers, most people have to settle for broiled lobster when they dine out. At home, however, there's little excuse for broiling when so many other possibilities exist.

If you're a native of the coast of Maine, what you mostly do with lobsters is steam them. That's what one lady I know on Penobscot Bay does, and believe it or not, a mess of lobsters is just about as special a feast down there as it is anywhere. "Lobsters," she has told me, "are not just something you heave in a pot and cook. I take my great big ten-quart canning pot and put in no more than four inches of water. Of course, sea water's the nicest because that's what they live in. But if you're not right down at the harbor, a heaping tablespoon of salt in tap water is good enough. After the water comes to the boil, stick them in as much headfirst as you can, and steam them, covered, of course, fifteen minutes *after* the water boils again. It's the steam that cooks them. I suppose I could cook up to eight in a pot, but for eight people I usually do two pots, four in each. Put plenty of paper napkins on the table, and a couple of big bowls for the empty shells. And, of course, your little dishes of melted butter to dunk your lobster in. What's lovely with lobster is a big tossed salad, with everything fresh from your garden in it, or corn on the cob in August or peas in July. The menfolk like plenty of hot yeast-muffins, too. If they've got any room left, there's homemade blueberry pie with ice cream for dessert."

Over in Cape Porpoise, Maine, another veteran lobsterwoman agrees about the steaming and differs on everything else. "The secret to cooking lobsters is not to murder them. Give them a nice, slow, respectable way out. I put in two inches of water, whether I'm cooking two lobsters or fourteen. I take a salt container and with the spout I pour it three times around the pot (about three teaspoons). When the water is boiling, put in the lobsters, put the lid on, and steam them for twenty minutes. Not a minute less or a minute more. That's how my grandfather showed me, and I've done it his way ever since. When they're done, draw up your butter and serve the lobster with a dish of vinegar, potato chips, hard rolls, and butter, as well as plenty of beer or soft drinks."

Naturally, tastes differ with all lobster lovers. Some like their two-pounders with salad, hot biscuits, and white wine; others prefer salad, Italian bread, and beer; and still others insist upon cottage fries, fried onion rings, and iced tea. Purists, on the other hand, eat lobster and nothing but lobster, as I learned from none other than my worldly barber who makes regular pilgrimages to a place in Louisbourg, Nova Scotia called The Lobster Kettle.

"What does the place look like?" I asked.

"Oh, I don't know," he mumbled disinterestedly. "I think it looks like a boathouse and has lots of wooden tables and nets. And there's a sink, with lots of soap and towels, right near the front door, where you can wash up after you're done. Now let me tell you: this guy goes out every day, traps his own lobsters, pulls the boat right up to the side of the restaurant, and unloads the greatest looking lobsters you ever saw. Big black things, much darker than the ones you see all over the U.S."

"What size do you eat?" I continued.

"Well, the last time, I had a seven-and-a-half-pounder, mainly because the guy was trying to convince me the big ones are as good as the little. And it was terrific, best damn lobster I ever put in my mouth. Steamed. And I ate every bite of that jumbo by myself."

"What do they serve with it up there?"

He looked totally puzzled. "You know, I don't think they serve anything. Wait a minute, I think they do have some fish chowder to start with. But when I eat lobster, I just don't fool with all that other stuff and I don't think anybody else does either. Sure wish you could have tasted that lobster."

Suddenly I had the definite impression not only that I was missing out on something very important but that all the lobsters I'd consumed over the decades in the States were mere shadows of what they have in Nova Scotia. I vowed then and there to one day visit The Lobster Kettle. In the meantime, however, I have full intention of devouring any and every sweet red *homarus americanus* placed before me—steamed, boiled, stewed, and, yes, even broiled—and to hell with the price.

HOW TO STEAM LOBSTERS

Place a rack in a very large pot or canning kettle, add 2–3 inches sea water, or tap water with 1 Tb. salt per quart, and bring to a rapid boil. Place lobsters headfirst on rack, cover, and when boil returns, begin timing according to the following: 1–1¼ lb. lobsters, 10–12 minutes; 1½–2-lb. lobsters, 15–18 minutes; 2½–5 lb. lobsters, 20–25 minutes. To serve, turn the lobster bottom-side up, and with a heavy chef's knife, slit down the middle of body and tail. Place whole lobsters on individual platters and provide either individual bowls or one large communal bowl for shell scraps, bowls of hot drawn butter, nutcrackers, oyster forks, and plenty of napkins.

HOW TO EAT LOBSTER

While the lobster cools, you can twist off the small legs and squeeze out the meat with your teeth—or save them until later. Most people go for the large, sweet claws first. Twist them off the body, crack with nutcrackers, and break away the small end to draw out the slim fin of cartilage, and remove the meat. Separate the tail from the upper body by grasping the lobster firmly and twisting until it cracks. To get at the tail meat, hold the split tail soft-side up and bend both sides back until it cracks. Be sure to remove the dark intestinal vein running down the tail. There is lots of goodness in the upper body too. Pull the head from the chest shell and crack open the chest as you did the tail. Discard the stomach sac in the head part, and scoop out the soft green tomalley and red coral (if any) to eat. There are sweet chunks of meat between the cartilage where the legs join the body, and many people find the soft white matter inside the chest delicious. No true warrior is finished until he has cracked even the hinged tail flippers.

STEWS, RAGOÛTS, BURGOOS

●●

No MATTER where I travel, my nose is twitching and my tentacles are out for anything stewing in a pot: beefy *casoeula* with *polenta* in northern Italy, fishy cioppino and *chaudrée* in California and France, chicken *pipían* in Mexico, catfish stew and burgoo in the American South, rabbit-enriched *stiphádo* in the Greece of my ancestors, and muttony hot pot in England. Yes, there are a few foods—comfort foods, if you will—of which I never seem to tire, and topping this short list is certainly any form of stew. Even in the fanciest of restaurants, while my companions debate the merits of eel in aspic and marvel over the elegant presentation of raw duck breast with rose petals, I—who find most of *la nouvelle cuisine* an utter bore—search the menu for an authentic *boeuf bourguignon* or lamb stew or gumbo.

I'm fully convinced that no matter how sophisticated America's taste becomes, there are very few people who can resist, deep down, the earthy, sensual aroma and flavor of meat, poultry, or fish gently boiled with or without vegetables and flavored with herbs and spices. Who can fail to recall the experience of entering a home or small restaurant where an honest, soul-warming stew has been simmering for hours? Just the thought stimulates the appetite, and if the scene happens to take place on a frigid winter day, the memory is even more vivid. A lusty stew brings out the primitive in all of us, suggesting, as it does, the prehistoric need to appease hunger in the simplest and most savory way possible. There's no culture on earth that cannot pride itself on at least one stew recipe, and it's safe to say that throughout history the very survival of developing countries (America, above all) depended, in part, on man's ability to combine basic nourishing ingredients in a pot and prepare them in a palatable fashion.

Throughout the centuries, these varied concoctions have been given enough names to fill a special dictionary: *solianka* in Russia, *baeckaoffa* (or *baeckenoffe*) in Germany and Alsace, *carbonnade* in Belgium, *gúlyas* in Middle European countries, ragoût, fricassee, *navarin*, and *daube* in France, *cocido* in Spain, *bigos* in Poland, and hot pot and stew in Britain and America. The name derivations are often as mysterious as the origins of the dishes themselves, and even the English word *stew* comes from an archaic French term (*estui,* a medieval food vessel) that today has no gastronomic significance whatsoever.

Matters become even more complicated when you try to pinpoint the differences between a ragoût, *blanquette,* and *navarin;* or between a fricassee and sauté; or between a Brunswick stew and Kentucky burgoo. It's easy enough to say, for example, that a ragoût is small pieces of meat, poultry, or fish that are turned in fat before being simmered in stock or water, but then you realize that a dish such as *moules à la marinière* is technically a ragoût of mussels in white wine. A fricassee supposedly should apply only to braised poultry and a *blanquette* to simmered veal with a *velouté* sauce, but restaurants abound that now serve a fricassee of sweetbreads or snails and *blanquettes* of everything from vegetables to lobster with any sauce imaginable. The people of Louisville, Kentucky will list beef, chicken, squirrel, corn, tomatoes, potatoes, okra, lima beans, green peppers, and onions as the essential ingredients in an authentic burgoo; my prized recipe for what I consider a genuine Georgia Brunswick stew includes the exact same items.

Since *stew* implies ingredients simmered in liquid for a reasonably long period of time, some might question applying the term to such fish dishes as cioppino, *bouillabaisse,* Portuguese *caldeirada,* or the Swedish cod stew known as *torsksoppa,* none of which should be boiled very long. Well, as far as I'm concerned, these are indeed stews, if for no other reason than because there is simply no better terminology to describe the cooking process. Much more important is that these dishes, like all stews, should be prepared with a great deal of care and imagination. "As much as Americans love a great stew, most are actually afraid to order one in a restaurant," I was told by one pro. "I guess they've had just too many of these cheap, fatty, steam-table disasters made with anything and everything that can be tossed into a pot. But stew can be a wonderfully artistic dish, with the right interplay of flavors, enticing aromas, and a pronounced taste of impeccably fresh ingredients. All you have to do is treat stew with the same respect as anything else you cook."

What determines the difference between a good and bad stew is based more on the quality and advance preparation of ingredients than on the cooking itself. The fact that stew, like hash, can be a very economical dish to serve does not automatically mean it has to be cheap in character. Nothing illustrates this point better than good old American beef stew. To make a lousy beef stew (and that's the only adjective to describe the recipes given in far too many cookbooks), all you have to do is throw chunks of leftover beef, old potatoes, sprouted onions, and shriveled carrots into a pot of water, add salt and pepper, simmer a few hours, and thicken with plenty of flour and water. It's a disgrace. To make great beef stew, you buy a small chuck roast, cut it up yourself according to the natural seams of the meat, trim carefully, and dry each piece with paper towels. Then you sear the meat in butter or bacon fat, pour off the excess fat, deglaze the pan with a little red wine, then combine all the freshest vegetables and herbs available and the best stock or bouillon added to water. While the stew simmers, you periodically taste for seasoning and check to make sure the meat and vegetables are not falling apart, and when time comes to deal with the liquid, you skim any fat and thicken with kneaded flour and butter or arrowroot. It requires a little extra time and attention, no doubt, but the stew you end up with makes a mockery of those bland, overcooked, watery atrocities, that, unfortunately, most people identify as American beef stew.

As a result of our myriad background, no country in the world now has the incredible variety of stews found throughout the regions of America. The boiled dinners and Irish stews of New England, the *pots-au-feu* and gumbos of the South, Philadelphia's famous veal-and-tripe pepper pot and Texas's infamous "son-of-a-bitch" stew, the goulashes and German veal stews of the Midwest, the fish kettles and game stews of the West Coast and Rockies—all are unpretentious one-dish meals that can't help but inspire warmth and hunger on any occasion.

Southern Brunswick Stew

6   slices bacon, chopped
2   squirrels, disjointed, or 1 3-lb. chicken, quartered
1   lb. boneless chuck, trimmed and cut into chunks
1   cup chopped celery (with leaves)
1   cup chopped onions
1   green pepper, chopped
1   medium ham hock, trimmed
3   tomatoes, chopped
2   sprigs parsley, chopped
1   small hot red pepper, seeded and minced
1   tsp. salt
½   tsp. each, basil and thyme
2½   qts. water
1½   cups each, corn kernels, sliced okra, and lima beans
1½   cups mashed potatoes

In a large, heavy skillet fry bacon till crisp, drain on paper towels, and crumble. Brown squirrel or chicken in fat, transfer to a dish; brown boneless chuck, and transfer to same dish. Pour remaining fat into a large casserole, add celery, onions, and green pepper and sauté till vegetables are soft. Add squirrel or chicken, chuck, ham hock, tomatoes, parsley, seasonings, and water, bring to a boil, reduce heat, and simmer covered for 45 minutes, skimming from time to time. Remove squirrel or chicken with a slotted spoon and continue to simmer mixture 1½ hours. When squirrel or chicken has cooled, skin, bone, shred the meat, and set aside. Bring mixture to a boil, add corn, okra, and lima beans and cook over moderate heat 30 minutes. Remove ham hock with slotted spoon, bone and shred meat, and return to casserole along with reserved shredded squirrel or chicken and reserved crumbled bacon. Add mashed potatoes, stir well, and continue cooking 15 minutes. SERVES 4–6.

California Cioppino

1   medium lobster, hacked into serving pieces
1   lb. fresh shrimp, shelled and deveined
1   doz. mussels, scrubbed thoroughly
1   doz. clams, scrubbed thoroughly
3   lbs. firm white fish, cut into serving pieces
½   cup olive oil
1   cup finely chopped onions
1   cup finely chopped green pepper
3   cloves garlic, chopped
6   ripe tomatoes, peeled, cored, and coarsely chopped
2   Tb. tomato paste
2   cups dry red or white wine
½   cup chopped parsley
    Herb bouquet (bay leaf, basil, oregano)
    Salt and freshly ground pepper to taste

In a large kettle place lobster, shrimp, mussels, and clams in 1 inch of boiling water, cover, and steam about 10 minutes or till shells of mussels and clams open (discard any that remain closed). Remove shellfish, strain broth, and reserve. In a large casserole sauté onions, green pepper, and garlic in oil till tender, add tomatoes, tomato paste, wine, parsley, herb bouquet, salt, pepper, and reserved broth and simmer about 15 minutes. Add white fish, cook 10 minutes; add shellfish, cover, and simmer about 15 minutes more. Taste for seasoning. SERVES 4–6.

PHILADELPHIA PEPPER POT

1	qt. water
1	qt. chicken broth
1	lb. honeycomb tripe, cut into bite-size pieces
1	veal shank, sawed into 2 pieces
1	clove garlic, crushed
4	black peppercorns
1	dried hot red pepper
½	tsp. thyme
½	tsp. marjoram
1	tsp. salt
½	stick sweet butter
1	cup finely chopped onions
½	cup finely chopped celery
½	cup finely chopped carrots
3	Tb. flour
1½	cups peeled potatoes cut into ½-inch cubes

Pour water and chicken broth into a large, heavy casserole and add tripe and veal shank. If necessary, add more water to cover by 2 inches, bring to a boil, and remove scum. Reduce heat, add garlic, peppercorns, hot red pepper, thyme, marjoram, and salt; cover, and simmer 2 hours or till tripe is tender. Transfer tripe and veal shank to a cutting board, remove meat from shank, and cut into bite-size pieces. Strain liquid into a bowl and reserve. Melt butter in casserole over moderate heat, add vegetables, and sauté till soft. Add flour, stir well, add reserved liquid, and cook over high heat till mixture thickens slightly. Add meats and potatoes, reduce heat to low, cover, and simmer 1 hour. SERVES about 4.

Tex-Mex Chicken Stew

1	4-lb. chicken, cut into serving pieces
2	onions, quartered
½	bell pepper, cut into strips
2	carrots, cleaned and halved
1	tsp. coriander
2½	cups chicken stock or broth
6	ancho chili peppers, seeds removed and rinsed
½	cup shelled roasted peanuts
2	Tb. vegetable oil
⅛	tsp. ground cloves
¼	tsp. ground cinnamon
¼	tsp. thyme

Place chicken in a large casserole with onions, bell peppers, carrots, and coriander. Add chicken stock plus, if necessary, water to cover. Bring to a boil, reduce heat, and simmer 30 minutes. Remove chicken and vegetables with a slotted spoon, strain and reserve stock, rinse out casserole, and return chicken and vegetables to casserole. Tear chili peppers into pieces, soak for 1 hour in ½ cup hot water, place in a blender, reduce to a paste, and transfer to a bowl. Place peanuts in blender, pulverize, and mix into chili paste. Sauté paste in the oil about 4 minutes, add 2 cups stock, and stir in cloves, cinnamon, and thyme. Pour over chicken, cover, and simmer 30 minutes or till chicken is tender. SERVES 4-6.

Rabbit Stew

8   slices bacon, finely chopped
1   5-lb. rabbit, cut into serving pieces
    Salt and freshly ground pepper to taste
½   cup flour
2   onions, finely chopped
1   clove garlic, finely chopped
1   cup dry red wine
1   cup chicken stock or broth
2   Tb. brandy
1   tsp. currant jelly
1   bay leaf
¼   tsp. rosemary
¼   tsp. thyme

In a large, heavy casserole fry bacon till crisp, drain, crumble, and set casserole aside. Wash rabbit, pat dry, salt and pepper to taste, and lightly dust with flour. Over high heat brown rabbit in casserole, transfer pieces to a plate, pour off all but 2 Tb. fat, then sauté onions and garlic 4 minutes or till soft. Add wine and stock, stir in brandy, jelly, and herbs, and return rabbit to casserole. Add crumbled bacon, cover casserole, and simmer over low heat 1½ hours. SERVES 4–6.

Old-Fashioned Pork Stew

1   large onion, chopped
2   Tb. butter
2½   lbs. boned pork shoulder, cut into serving pieces
1   large apple, sliced
     Salt and freshly ground pepper to taste
¼   cup flour
     Small bunch seedless grapes
3   dates
⅛   tsp. sage
1   sprig parsley, chopped
2   stalks celery, chopped
½   orange
1   cup red wine
     Brown stock or bouillon

In a large, heavy skillet sauté onions in butter for 2 minutes and transfer to a casserole. Add pork to skillet, brown evenly over high heat, and transfer to a plate. Cover onions with apple slices and season with salt and pepper. Dust the pork with flour, season with salt and pepper, and place on top of apples. Add grapes, dates, sage, parsley, and celery. Peel orange, cut peel into narrow strips, and add to casserole. Remove pith and seeds from orange, cut into quarters, and place around the meat. Add wine and stock or bouillon to cover meat, cover casserole, and simmer 2½ hours or till meat is tender. SERVES 4–6.

COUNTRY VEAL STEW

1 small onion, chopped
3 Tb. butter
2 Tb. vegetable oil
2 lbs. boneless veal shanks or shoulder, cut into chunks
2 tsp. salt
   Freshly ground pepper to taste
½ tsp. sage
1 sprig parsley, finely chopped
2 ripe tomatoes, coarsely chopped
½ cup dry white wine
1 10-oz. package frozen peas, thawed

In a large, heavy skillet sauté onions in butter and transfer to a heavy casserole. Add vegetable oil to skillet, brown veal well, and transfer to casserole. Add salt, and pepper to taste, sage, parsley, chopped tomatoes, and wine. Bring liquid to a boil, lower heat, and simmer about 1½ hours or till veal is tender. Add peas to stew, raise heat slightly, and continue cooking about 10 minutes. SERVES 4–6.

Papa's Greek Lamb Stew

2   onions, chopped
2   cloves garlic, minced
4   Tb. butter
1   Tb. olive oil
2   lbs. lean boneless lamb, cubed
    Salt and freshly ground pepper to taste
2   bay leaves
1   stick cinnamon, cut in half
3   cloves
½   tsp. rosemary
1   8-oz. can tomato sauce
1   16-oz. can whole tomatoes
1   cup white wine
1   lb. macaroni
    Feta cheese
½   stick sweet butter

In a large, heavy skillet sauté onions and garlic in 2 Tb. of the butter till soft. Add remaining butter plus olive oil to skillet, season lamb with salt and pepper and add to skillet, and continue sautéing over medium heat about 2 minutes. Add bay leaves, cinnamon stick, cloves, tomato sauce, tomatoes, and white wine. Stir well, cover, reduce heat, and simmer about 1 hour or till lamb is tender, adding water to cover when necessary. Cook macaroni according to package directions, drain, and arrange half on a heated platter. Crumble a little feta on top, add remaining macaroni, and top with more cheese. Melt butter and pour over macaroni, then arrange lamb with its juices on top, adding a little more feta. SERVES 4–6.

REINVENTING THE
SANDWICH

●●●

THE NOTION that England's greatest contribution to world gastronomy is the sandwich not only discredits that country's distinctive style of cooking but also totally misrepresents an edible that is now essentially as American as, well, apple pie. Forget that the sandwich was named for John Montagu, the eighteenth-century British fourth Earl of Sandwich who once ordered his meat between two pieces of bread to avoid having to leave the gambling table. Forget these thin, skimpy concoctions with cheese, sliced hard-boiled egg, and slivers of tongue you see bibbers nibbling with their pints of bitter in London pubs. And forget even the pristine cucumber and watercress morsels served during afternoon tea in the English countryside. There is a time and place, I suppose, for what the British and Scandinavians call a sandwich, but when it comes to the real McCoy, in no country has the art of the sandwich been more developed and appreciated than in the United States. Sandwiches have always been to most Americans what pasta is to Italians or rice to Chinese.

Granted, in certain circles sandwiches have fallen out of favor. The upwardly mobile business executive, with his fancy expense account French lunch, began to associate subconsciously the sandwich with eat-and-run, middle-class fast food. And, of course, the plague of finicky eating that has swept the country over the past few years has brought in a whole slew of alternatives, such as the fads for quiche, tofu, yogurt, and *pasta primavera*. Slim-hipped calorie counters automatically—albeit erroneously—assumed that because of the bread, sandwiches were excessively fattening. Now, however, with carbohydrates back in vogue—their nutrient value reestablished—the country is finally aiming for a well-balanced diet, and food fanciers are becoming aware of the infinite creativity and imagination with which a sandwich can be assembled.

I, for one, really love a good sandwich, and I would opt any day for a juicy hot pastrami on rye with ice-cold beer rather than something so innocuous as veal paillard, mixed salad, and mineral water. Don't get me wrong. Not for me a soggy bologna on white in a coffee shop. Ah, but lead me to a delicatessen where the corned beef is sliced by hand and stacked high and evenly on a Kaiser roll; or show me a well-trimmed Club sandwich on which the chicken is tender, the tomatoes, lettuce, and mayonnaise impeccably fresh, and the bacon plentiful and crisp.

The fact is that there are very few foods that can't be incorporated into a superb sandwich so long as the ingredients are first-rate and the preparation skillful. The first thing I seek out when visiting my native North Carolina is a chopped pit-cooked pork barbecue sandwich or plate of small country-ham biscuits moistened with red-eye gravy. In New Orleans, I know right where to go (Mother's Restaurant on Poydras Street) for the best Po' Boy in town, and I couldn't imagine leaving Dallas or Houston without devouring at least one bun bursting with the spicy charred ends of barbecued beef brisket. If two pieces of sourdough bread filled with Dungeness crab and avocado represents for me a high point on any trip to San Francisco, just the thought of sinking my teeth into a turkey with Russian dressing on white, a hot pastrami or sardine on rye, a Reuben, or a lox and cream cheese on a split bagel at one of many New York delis is mouth-watering.

Although my all-American passion for great sandwiches (as for substantial breakfasts) remains virtually incomprehensible (and often reprehensible) to most foreigners, this does not deter me in the least from trying to satisfy this particular craving from time to time when I travel outside the United States. And, ironically, in most countries there are usually a couple of preparations that at least approximate our concept of the sandwich: Danish open-face *smorrebrod,* Mexican *tortillas,* Chinese *dim sum,* Cuban *medianoches,* Russian *blinis,* and a number of assemblages made with *phyllo* dough in certain Mediterranean and Middle Eastern countries. In Italy, the small squares of fried *polenta* topped with everything from ricotta cheese to sausage to wild mushrooms known as *crostini* can make for a delightful lunch, and one of the greatest Italian classics of all time, *mozzarella in carrozza,* is basically a fried egg-coated cheese sandwich served with a garlicky anchovy sauce. The

Greeks make a delicious *keftedes* sandwich of lamb meatballs on either hard rolls or pita bread; the Portuguese love to snack on *linguiça* rolls stuffed with smoked garlic sausage and chopped onions; and for centuries pasties filled with meat, seafood, and vegetables have been a staple in the diet of the English in Cornwall.

For an American addicted to sandwiches, it's no easy feat finding a good version in France, but when you do, the moment can be memorable. A *croque monsieur*, properly made with egg-drenched *pain de mie*, lean ham, and grated Gruyère is perhaps the ultimate ham and cheese sandwich, while a genuine *pan bania* (French bread stuffed with a variety of *salade niçoise*) represents the very soul of Provence. During my student days in Paris, I would watch with amazement in cafés and brasseries as waiters prepared my *saucisse chaude* by ramming a baguette down a hot steel spike, spreading the interior of the bread with eye-watering Dijon mustard, and dropping a long sausage down the hole. Today the spike contraption has disappeared, the baguette is now split with a knife, Gruyère is added to the frank, and the menu reads "le hot dog," but in Paris there's still quite nothing that sends the spirit soaring like sitting at a sidewalk café, ordering this succulent sandwich and a *demi* beer, and allowing the crusty bread and mustard to "break in" the roof of the mouth.

Fascinating as these foreign creations might be, they can hardly be said to fill the same important role in the various countries' gastronomic makeup as the sandwich does in the United States. Over the decades there has developed in this country a veritable repertory of sandwiches that can now only be termed classic American: Who can say in all honesty, for instance, that childhood would have had its same wonderment without those addictive peanut butter and jelly sandwiches, crisp grilled cheese, creamy egg or tuna or chicken salad, hot dogs, and thick homemade hamburgers—sandwiches which, for better or worse, few of us ever outgrow completely? From the various regions there emerged sandwiches that today have overall national appeal: pimiento cheese, oyster loaves, fried fish, and pork barbecue from the South; fried egg, hot dogs (German *wursts*), and hamburgers (German Hamburg chopped steak, introduced, as was the hot dog, at the St. Louis World's Fair) from the Midwest; Sloppy Joes, beef barbecue, and tacos from Texas and the Southwest; cheesesteaks from Philadelphia; Silver Dollars, Denvers, Heros, crab, and Monte Cristos from the West; lobster rolls, brisket, and baked beans and bacon from New England; and from New York City and vicinity, hot pastrami and corned beef, chopped chicken liver and onions, Reubens, sardine, lox and cream cheese, and Coney Island dogs.

Some of our favorite sandwiches evolved naturally (BLT, hot roast beef, meat loaf, turkey, sliced steak), while others will most likely always be shrouded in a bit of mystery. Exactly how did the names "hot dog," "Monte Carlo," "Po' Boy," "Hero" (or "Hoagie," "Submarine," and "Grinder"), and "Sloppy Joe" come about? Sandwich aficionados know that the toasted corned-beef-sauerkraut-Swiss-cheese-on-rye beauty known as the Reuben was conceived decades ago in New York at Reuben's delicatessen on Madison Avenue and Fifty-ninth Street, but is it true (as James Beard seems to recall) that the original was corned beef, turkey breast, Swiss cheese, coleslaw, and Russian dressing on pumpernickel and was *not* toasted? The origins of our most celebrated triple-decker, the Club, have been identified with any number of bars, restaurants, and country clubs, and was easily the favorite sandwich in the plush club cars of such legendary trains as the Twentieth Century Limited?

A great sandwich demands the same imagination, care, patience, and top-quality ingredients as a fine stew, and those interested in perfecting the art might keep the following basics in mind.

• • • Most sandwiches should be assembled just before serving to guarantee freshness and avoid sogginess. If advance preparation of cold sandwiches is absolutely necessary, use only dry fillings, make sure all interior bread surfaces are well coated with spread, and wrap tightly in plastic before refrigerating. Never prepare hot sandwiches in advance.

• • • Be generous with mayonnaise and butter, and be sure to extend both spread and filling to edges of the bread.

• • • Crusts help keep sandwiches fresh, but when trimmed toast is preferred, trim crusts before toasting and dress bread with spread the second it is done. Never begin a sandwich with cold dry toast, and never use burned or scraped toast. Never stack toast—it becomes soggy.

• • • Never make a sandwich with unsoftened butter, wet or wilted greens, hard tomatoes, tough or fatty meats, stringy bacon, canned vegetables and seafood, or undrained tuna and sauerkraut.

• • • To assure a good texture and proportion, use several thin slices of meat, cheese, and vegetables instead of a single thick one—including such ingredients as meat loaf, steak, raw onion, and pickle.

• • • The only thing worse than an overly bready sandwich with a skimpy filling is one so packed with food it virtually falls apart. All hot and many open-face sandwiches should be served with a knife and fork, but any sandwich to be eaten by hand must be manageable—especially double-deckers. Square and rectangular cold sandwiches are best cut in half.

• • • Keep all salad-type fillings well chilled before making sandwiches, and make sure such fillings are creamy, not soupy.

• • • Whether used for cold or hot sandwiches, hard and semihard cheeses are often better (culinarily and visually) grated than sliced.

• • • Never overwhelm the one or two main ingredients of a sandwich with other assertive fillings and spreads, and always think twice about whether certain combinations are compatible.

• • • Although garnishes add eye appeal and help round out the meal, all should be as simple as possible and none should detract from the sandwich itself.

With these basics in mind, the imaginative chef is free to create literally hundreds of sandwiches of varying styles, combinations, and textures. The recipes that follow represent only a few tasty possibilities, each illustrating how, with slight modification, classic sandwich concepts can be transformed into new dimensions by the use of different breads, fillings, spreads, and assemblage techniques. At first glance, some combinations might appear strange, but behind each there's logic: sweet kiwi instead of traditional fruit jelly or preserves with peanut butter; the supple texture of sardines and capers contrasting with the toothy quality of a Kaiser roll; the use of guacamole instead of avocado chunks or slices to emphasize the delicacy of crab meat; the quiet zing of Roquefort butter to add character to bland fresh vegetables; the crunch of almonds against Brie running sensually over tender chicken breast. Consumed with a fine ale or lager or a simple wine, these sandwiches are not only delicious but prove indeed that this aspect of American cookery can be just as stylish as any other.

Pseudosophisticates who enjoy sneering at the great American sandwich might do well to thumb through the pages of none other than Escoffier, the distinguished French master who didn't think much about preparing dainty tea sandwiches but was fascinated enough by something called a Bookmaker to reproduce its lengthy recipe. Essentially this is an entire loaf of bread sliced in half, buttered and filled with a thick grilled steak seasoned with horseradish and mustard, wrapped in sheets of blotting paper, and squeezed tightly in a press for ½ hour. Now *that* is a sandwich!

Fresh Vegetables in Pita Bread

¼ cup raw spinach
¼ cup cauliflower or broccoli florets, blanched
¼ cup zucchini strips, blanched
    A few fresh alfalfa sprouts
3 Tb. grated raw carrot
2 Tb. raisins
2 Tb. chopped pecans
4 Tb. yogurt
2 Tb. lemon juice
    Freshly ground pepper to taste
1 pita bread
    Roquefort Butter*

In a mixing bowl toss together vegetables, raisins, and nuts, then add yogurt, lemon juice, and pepper and mix lightly. Slit open the side of the pita, spread the interior with Roquefort butter, and fill bread with vegetable mixture, allowing part of the vegetables to show.

ROQUEFORT BUTTER:
  1 Tb. mashed Roquefort cheese worked into ¼ cup soft butter.

Serve with a rice and shrimp salad in scooped-out half tomato.

Pastrami Reuben on Onion Bread

2 slices onion rye bread
¼ cup Russian dressing
2 oz. lean pastrami, sliced very thin
1 oz. uncooked sauerkraut, drained
2 slices Gruyère cheese
1 Tb. butter

Spread Russian dressing over one side of each bread slice. Arrange pastrami on one dressed slice, add sauerkraut, arrange cheese on top of sauerkraut, and cover with remaining bread slice, dressing-side down. Melt butter in a skillet and brown sandwich till golden and cheese begins to melt. Serve with dill pickles, coleslaw, and fresh potato chips.

CREOLE CROQUE MONSIEUR

2   slices slightly dry French or Italian bread
    Creole mustard (available at speciality food shops)
3   oz. Gruyère cheese, grated
1   slice lean ham or Canadian bacon
    Nutmeg and freshly ground pepper to taste
1   egg beaten with 1 Tb. water
1   Tb. butter

Spread Creole mustard evenly over one side of each bread slice and sprinkle half the grated cheese evenly over one slice. Add ham, sprinkle remaining cheese on top of ham, season with nutmeg and pepper, and top with other bread slice. Pour egg mixture into a shallow dish and into it carefully dip both sides of sandwich. Add butter to a skillet and brown both sides of sandwich about 5 minutes or till golden and cheese begins to melt. Serve with marinated dill mushrooms with crushed red pepper on a bed of fresh fennel.

SARDINE CLUB

1   Kaiser roll, sliced into two equal halves
      Anchovy Butter*
3-4   small skinless, boneless sardines, divided in half
      Capers to taste
2-3   raw onion rings
      Sprigs watercress

Spread anchovy butter evenly over interior of roll. Cover bottom layer with sardines interspersed with capers to taste. Place onion rings on center layer, add watercress, and top with remaining layer of roll.

* *ANCHOVY BUTTER:*
½ tsp. anchovy paste, ½ tsp. minced parsley, and a few drops lemon juice worked into ¼ cup soft butter

Serve with cucumber rounds and black olives stuffed with cream cheese.

CRAB AND GUACAMOLE BURGER

1	ripe avocado
½	small ripe tomato, peeled, seeded, chopped, and patted dry
1	tsp. finely chopped scallions or onions
¼	tsp. chili powder
¼	tsp. coriander
	Salt and freshly ground pepper to taste
½	tsp. olive oil
1½	tsp. lime juice
1	large sesame bun, split and toasted
4	oz. king crab leg, cut into chunks

Peel avocado, remove pit, place in a mixing bowl, and mash with fork. Add tomato pulp, scallions, chili powder, coriander, salt and pepper, olive oil, and lime juice and mix thoroughly with the mashed avocado. Spread guacamole generously over interiors of bun, add crab meat evenly to bun bottom, and cover with bun top. Serve with corn and pimiento salad on romaine lettuce.

STEAK TARTARE AND CAVIAR

1	lb. sirloin or top round, cut into chunks
1	small onion, finely chopped
1	tsp. finely chopped parsley
½	tsp. Dijon mustard
½	tsp. salt
½	tsp. freshly ground pepper
1	egg yolk
1	Tb. Cognac
1	thin slice pumpernickel
	Chive Butter*
1	Tb. chopped hard-boiled egg whites
1	Tb. fresh sturgeon caviar

Grind beef by hand or chop to a smooth consistency in a food processor and transfer to a mixing bowl. Add onions, parsley, mustard, salt, pepper, egg yolk, and Cognac, mix thoroughly, and refrigerate steak tartare till ready to use. Spread Chive Butter evenly over one side of bread, spread on even layer of steak tartare, sprinkle chopped egg whites around edges of sandwich, and spoon tablespoon of caviar in center.

* *CHIVE BUTTER:*
1 tsp. minced chives worked into 2 Tb. sweet butter.

Serve with watercress and endive salad.

TOASTED BRIE WITH ALMONDS ON CHICKEN

1	slice black bread
	Tarragon Mayonnaise*
2–3	shredded chicken breasts
3	oz.-wedge Brie cheese
	Sliced almonds
2	Tb. melted butter

Spread mayonnaise evenly over one side of bread and arrange chicken on bread. Carefully slice Brie in half lengthwise and place the two slices on chicken. Cover top of cheese with a layer of almonds and dot with droplets of melted butter. Place sandwich on a cookie tin, place tin on middle rack of oven, and broil sandwich slowly till almonds brown slightly and cheese just begins to run.

* *TARRAGON MAYONNAISE:*
1 leaf minced fresh tarragon, or 2 tsp. dried, mixed into ¼ cup fresh mayonnaise.

Serve with fresh peach chutney on bed of chopped roasted red bell pepper.

Britannia

2	slices Irish soda bread
	Horseradish Mayonnaise*
2–3	slices fresh turkey breast
1	hard-cooked egg, sliced
2	oz. Cheddar cheese, grated
	Chutney to taste

Spread mayonnaise evenly and generously over one side of each bread slice. Place turkey slices on one half and arrange slices of egg on top. Sprinkle on Cheddar cheese, add chutney, and cover with other bread slice.

* HORSERADISH MAYONNAISE:
  1 Tb. prepared horseradish mixed into ¼ cup fresh mayonnaise

Serve with pickled onions and a half pear stuffed with quince jelly.

SOUR MILK WITH A COLLEGE EDUCATION

I'M TRYING, God knows I'm trying, with dogged determination to learn to love the slimy stuff. It all began back in the fifties when, as a student in France, I almost gagged to death when coaxed to taste my first spoonful of yogurt. Since then I've made good progress, but today it's still a struggle. Plain, from those waxy cartons, mixed with every ingredient from black cherry to crushed almond to peppermint stick, homemade in a special machine, spooned atop fresh fruit, salads, and baked potatoes, incorporated into pies and cakes, crammed into pancakes, licked off a stick—you name a way to eat yogurt and I've tried it. Repeatedly. Once I used it in preparing a beef Stroganoff. Another time I even tried it as a substitute for mayonnaise on a fat hamburger. And most recently I desecrated a precious forty-four-buck serving of fresh beluga caviar by crowning the eggs with a plop of alien culture.

Although generally I suppose I've come to like yogurt, it's for damn sure I still don't *love* it. Over the years I've developed a passion for tripe soup, stuffed goose neck, and those tiny birds known as ortolans which you eat bones, eyeballs, and all in a single bite. But not yogurt. So why all the great effort to savor something that basically bores me? Well, let's simply say that, like millions of other Americans, I can't help wanting to partake in what has become a veritable yogurt revolution. I mean, I feel I *should* be eating yogurt, just as I should be devouring vitamins C and E, slurping down niagaras of mineral water, and jogging two ridiculous miles a day.

And after all, the claims made for this fermented goo may be, in part, highly suspect, but they're nonetheless overwhelmingly engaging: yogurt is rich in protein, vitamin A, thiamine, riboflavin, and niacin; it promotes longevity (look at those TV ads with those healthy 120-year-old yogurt-eating Russians and Greeks); it benefits digestion and re-establishes intestinal *flora* for those receiving antibiotic therapy; it reduces cholesterol as well as the blood level; it helps to control obesity; and it's a possible cure for cancer, gallstones, hepatitis, migraines, arthritis, and wrinkled skin. In short, according to what you hear and read from coast to coast in this country, yogurt is the gastronomic *summum bonum*.

So just what is this thing called yogurt? Where did it come from, and how is it helping to revolutionize our eating habits? Since, frankly, I have no intention or desire to understand fully all the weird technology involved in producing the stuff, all I can tell you is that yogurt is essentially low-fat milk (containing something like 1.6 percent butterfat) that is injected with lactic cultures, placed into scientific incubators, and left at warm temperatures to be transformed into the custardlike substance we eat.

Apparently the whole business began back in 1910 at the Pasteur Institute in Paris when a Russian scientist named Metchnikoff became obsessed with the thought of dying and discovered that century-old Bulgarians enjoyed a steady diet of sour buttermilk. Eventually he isolated the agent in Bulgarian yogurt that "would chase poisonous bacilli from the intestines by making acid in the milk." Hoping to live to be at least one hundred, Metchnikoff devoured yogurt for twenty years. He died at the age of seventy-one.

After World War I, one of the largest companies then marketing yogurt in Europe was headed by Isaac Carasso, who, having first manufactured the product in Spain, expanded his interest into France, put his son Daniel in charge, and appropriately named the yogurt Dannon. After later emigrating to the United States, Daniel was joined in the Bronx by Joe Metzger and his son Juan, old family friends from Spain, and today Juan Metzger, chairman of Dannon (the largest-selling yogurt in the country) is known as the "King of Yogurt."

Although there are more than one hundred different brands of yogurt, there is still no national yogurt association and therefore no official standard of identity. As a result, the sky's the limit when it comes to marketing the product, and to say that yogurt is big business is something of a gross understatement. What has made the marketing success is the incredible variety of flavors and seasonings used to cut the tart (once referred to as "sour") taste of plain yogurt. It was the Metzgers who initially added a layer of strawberry preserves to their

Dannon product, an experiment that was to revolutionize the industry by making way for the seemingly endless (and exotic) varieties of yogurt available today: Mandarin Orange, Purple Plum, Dutch Apple, Coffee, Boysenberry, Peppermint Stick, Crushed Almond, Mild Lime, not to mention all the more standard fruit flavors. For those who must have even more camouflage, Dannon issues a booklet packed full of suggestions of what might be added to plain yogurt to enhance the enjoyment: instant cocoa, presweetened tea, maple syrup, carob syrup, marmalade, *crème de menthe*, coconut flakes. And in case all these possibilities fail to capture consumer enthusiasm, Dannon markets yogurt swirled on a cone, soft-frozen, on a stick and coated, and in individual half-pint cups; Knudsen has a frozen "push-up" stick eaten directly from the paper covering; and companies like Hood ("Frogurt"), Johanna Farms ("Lacto"), and Colombo are making every effort to all but exterminate old-fashioned ice cream in their campaigns for frozen yogurt (less calories, more nutritional, easily digestible, and so forth).

If yogurt is considered a chic food, it's because it's consumed in large quantities not only by those who are well-heeled and well-traveled but, especially, by affluent types who are forever concerned with their waistlines. What about all those claims made for yogurt as the perfect dietetic food, the promoter of longevity, and the cure-all for diseases? For years I've gone on yogurt binges when I had reason to knock off a few pounds, and I can say it works as well as anything else and no more. There is nothing magical about yogurt, and I've lost just as much weight by eating nothing but fresh fruit and vegetables or remaining on an overall tasty high-protein diet. Unfortunately, most people forget that while a carton of plain, unsweetened yogurt (which is almost fat-free) contains only 130 to 150 calories, all those better-tasting, fruit-flavored varieties are almost double in caloric value due to the added carbohydrates. Furthermore, don't forget that since yogurt is quickly and easily digested, it doesn't do much for assuaging those hellish and seemingly endless hunger pangs unless you go through three cartons a day, meaning something like 780 calories for fruit-flavored—or the equivalent of two slices of apple pie or a juicy steak. Consumed intelligently (e.g., a single container for lunch with nothing else, or as a substitute for fattening desserts—neither possibility of which I could personally imagine), yogurt can serve as a successful, healthy, and (for some) enjoyable dietetic food.

As to whether yogurt will add years to your life, absolutely no definite proof exists thus far to substantiate the contention. No doubt some of those yogurt-gulping inhabitants in the Caucasus do live well past one hundred, but it's equally true they smoke and they drink vodka. Numerous efforts have been made to explain the possible connection between yogurt and longevity, but at least for the time being, I'll settle for the sensible reasoning somebody made a few yers ago: "If yogurt indeed keeps the bowels working and sets things right in the large intestine, it *might* make a person live longer by making his input-output system function efficiently."

Little medical research has gone into yogurt's therapeutic effects, and whatever conclusions have been made remain mostly controversial. Nobody denies that yogurt is a valuable source of protein, calcium, and vitamins, and most experts agree that such troubles as both diarrhea and irregularity can often be partially controlled by yogurt. No doubt yogurt does help people with intestinal problems, although there is still no actual proof that the substance has any beneficial effect on the *flora* or the normal gastrointestinal tract. As for the effect of yogurt on growth (government scientists have discovered that rats on a yogurt diet grow remarkably big and strong), cholesterol buildup, cancer, arthritis, and any number of other maladies, again far too little research has been conducted to separate myth from fact. I can report from long personal experience, however, that slurping regular milk is more benefieical than yogurt any day when it comes to soothing the agony of my hiatal hernia.

How, you might ask, can you learn to eat yogurt if you're basically repulsed by it but still feel you should be ingesting fermented milk? The first rule is don't, for God's sake, begin with plain, unsweetened yogurt; in all likelihood it will make you gag and turn you off for life. Some people, determined to save money and hold down calories, have had some luck in taking plain yogurt and stirring in everything from onion-soup mix to catsup to tuna fish. Others have crossed the hurdle by starting with a cone of soft-frozen yogurt (so reminiscent of eating ice cream) or a box of yogurt pops coated with chocolate. My own advice would be to take the leap with a container of Black Cherry. Unlike most other flavors, which are little more than sweet flavorings, Black Cherry contains big hunks of the fruit, meaning you have something pleasant to chew on while trying to masticate what feels essentially like a cold cotton ball. And don't chicken out on a first spoonful. Keep going, steadily, not thinking about what you're eating, till you've finished the entire blessed eight ounces. After four or five containers, you'll probably be well on the road to liking yogurt, or at least in the position to test other flavors. Soon you may even learn to love it, in which case you'll be one up on me.

If, of course, you become a true fanatic about yogurt, you'll forget all about the different supermarket brands and simply learn to make your own, either in the home-style method or with one of those fancy yo-gurt-making machines. Frankly, I've never had any desire whatsoever to produce my own yogurt, but for those who like to do things right, here's the basic technique reported to me by a lovely, energetic, dis-gustingly healthy woman of a certain advanced age who eats the yuk as if it were *foie gras:*

> In a large bowl blend ¼ cup commercial yogurt (as a starter) into 1 quart whole or skim milk and heat in oven to 120° F, using a kitchen thermometer to keep careful check on the temperature. Reduce heat gradually to 105°, cover bowl, and let cool to 90°. Maintain 90°–105° for 2 hours by either reheating oven periodically or removing bowl, wrap-ping in heavy towels or a blanket, and letting stand in a warm area till milk has the consistency of junket. (To thicken more, add ½ cup dry milk.) Pour yogurt into glass jars, chill thoroughly, and be sure to retain ¼ cup as starter for the next batch.

Where will it all end? Skeptics would have us believe that yogurt is no more than another fad that will eventually go the way of granola, wheat germ, Metrecal, and copper bracelets, and even the most ardent enthusiasts have to admit it's still basically a fun food eaten primarily as a snack. Whether yogurt eventually becomes as much a permanent part of American life as hot dogs and peanuts remains to be seen. Per-sonally, I couldn't care less what happens, for, come to think of it, I'm much more interested in learning to eat beefalo.

UPGRADING HASH

•••

OF ALL the great American dishes to suffer under the present-day tyranny of gastronomic pretension and snobbism, perhaps none has undergone a more lamentable demise in popularity than that wonderful creation known as hash. Once a delectable staple on the menus of the country's finest restaurants, hotels, and railway dining cars, hash today is considered a plebeian conceit in the minds of many, an unfashionable concoction worthy of no better environment than a coffee shop and no more serious ingredients than whatever leftovers happen to be in the bottom of the refrigerator. To suggest I find all this deplorable is a minor understatement, for by automatically relegating hash to the same truck-stop realm as many would place even the most savory chili, barbecue, and stew, we negate not only an important potential in our culinary evolution but also the possibility of some downright delicious food.

Although technically no food concept is more universal than hash (even the French prepare a *hachis* of everything from beef to lobster to partridge), we in the United States, with our widely diversified ethnic background, have probably done more than anyone over the years to elaborate the dish. Mixing chopped meat or fish, potatoes, and onions with seasoning may seem a typically crude American idea to some, but, actually, this same basic principle, under other guises and names, was drawn upon from numerous foreign culinary traditions and gradually modified to fit our own style of cooking. Think, for a moment, of the *frittatas* in Italy; the *picadillos* of Spain and Mexico; the *labskaus* (corned beef and salt herring hash) of Germany; the croquettes, *mirotons*, and *émincés* of France; the pasties, shepherd's pies, and kedgerees of England; the game *tourtières* of Quebec; and the stir-fry meat and vegetable preparations of China. To be sure, each of these concepts has an identity all its own, yet each, like standard American hash, involves little more than two or more hashed ingredients that are blended, seasoned, and cooked rather quickly. Easterners fry pork scraps with meal and rave over their breakfast scrapple. New Englanders mix flaked codfish with potatoes and call it a cake. Midwesterners of Scandinavian descent add cubed potatoes to chopped ham and beef to make pytt i panna. Gourmands on the West Coast refer to their creation of diced abalone, celery, and potatoes as croquettes. And throughout the country the same initial theory behind something like hot chicken salad can be applied to such other favorites as chicken à la king, crab Imperial, and even chopped chicken livers and onions. Call these dishes what you may, but, in the final analysis, they all add up to be some form of hash.

"Beef, that's nothing. Onion, nothing. Seasoning, nothing," quipped one elderly housewife, "but when I throw myself into my hash, now that's something!" How good the old gal's hash actually tasted I don't know, but she, unlike so many others, did manage to capture the right spirit of the dish. I'm the first to state that nothing is quite so wretched as a hash sloppily made with stale, uninteresting leftovers, but I'm also the first to insist that, especially when the temperature hovers around freezing, an imaginative hash properly prepared with impeccable ingredients makes a glorious addition to any breakfast, weekend brunch buffet, early evening supper, or après-ski occasion.

Although any number of serious gastronomes have extolled the virtues of the dish, surely none has spoken with greater fervor than the distinguished champion of American cookery, James Beard. "The other night," he once related, "I purposely bought more chicken than I wanted to sauté because I wanted to make chicken hash later. I served half the chicken and let the rest cool in the pan, then removed it, added one-half cup white wine to the pan juices, heated them, scraping up the brown bits, and poured this over the cold chicken. Next day I made hash with chunks of chicken, cut-up chicken gizzards, diced potatoes, chopped onion, rosemary, fresh parsley, heavy cream, and a little chicken gravy, and it was so tasty that the next morning I reheated what was left, popped a poached egg on top, and had myself one of the best breakfasts I've ever eaten." James Beard understands hash.

The fact that American hash has suffered undue abuse since the time when well-tailored regulars at the old Ritz Carlton in New York feasted on Chef Diat's chicken hash washed down with champagne does not imply that there are no fine examples around today for those caring enough to search them out. I'd be hard put, for instance, if forced to choose between the succulent varieties of corned beef hash served at Don Hernando's in the Beverly Wilshire in Los Angeles, the Caucus Club in Detroit, and the Regency Hotel in New York. There's probably not a social luminary in this country who hasn't sampled the legendary chicken hash Mornay at New York's "21", a creation whose only local competition is the glazed mound served farther uptown at Mortimer's. At a small inn called David's in Bennington, New Hampshire, it was a crusty lobster hash; at Crawdaddy's in Tampa, a mixed seafood and potato hash; and behind private doors in New Orleans, any number of aromatic crawfish hashes. Probably the most authentic red-flannel hash in New England is served at the Café Plaza in the Copley Plaza Hotel of Boston, and except for the chunky roast beef hash with jalapeño peppers I found throughout the state of Texas, I doubt there's a beef hash anywhere that can touch the version that is baked, then broiled at Locke-Ober in Boston.

No doubt one of the main advantages to hash is that it can be made not only from the more familiar leftover beef, chicken, turkey, and ham but also from pork, venison, veal, lamb, pheasant, sweetbreads, vegetables, and almost any form of seafood. At least part of the difference, however, between a truly great hash and the vast majority of disasters with which we're too frequently confronted lies in the application of the term *leftover*. Like any dish, hash is no better than the quality of ingredients that go into it, and I can no more imagine making hash from dry, fatty, week-old corned beef or rump roast than preparing a stew with old carrots, sprouted potatoes, and cheap wine. If you want good turkey or chicken hash, the initial secret is to use the leftovers no more than a day or so after cooking the birds, and if you're striving for sensational chicken or beef hash, you'll follow my habit of actually purchasing a savory fowl or small chuck roast for the express purpose of turning them into hash immediately.

Equally important, of course, is the preparation and cooking of hash, which, believe me, involves a good deal more than hacking away at meat, potatoes, and onions and throwing the mixture in a frying pan. Generally, all the ingredients for standard meat and poultry hashes should be chopped by hand, and the main ingredient should never be chopped so small as to be indistinguishable. It's tempting, I know, to utilize a blender or food processor, but I've yet to compose an extraordinary hash with the aid of a machine except when trying to add dimension by creating a texture that is altogether different from that of the classic dish. There are no set rules about proportions in hash so long as the major ingredient predominates. In most people's minds, hash automatically implies the inclusion of chopped potatoes and onions, and no doubt these two items contribute much to its basic character. On the other hand, I've had delicious hashes in which the main ingredient was enhanced by everything from rice to diced sausage to chopped hard-boiled egg, and some of the most memorable examples I've sampled were made with no more than a well-seasoned chunky main ingredient bound with a luscious sauce.

Although cooking techniques for hash can be as flexible as the choice of ingredients, there are certain culinary considerations that could have a recognizable effect on the finished dish. Some hashes baked in the oven, then quickly browned under the broiler, are, for instance, just as tasty (and often lighter and more digestible) as those fried or sautéed in a skillet. For best results, roasted or pot-roasted leftovers should only be warmed up whereas boiled or braised meats can usually be simmered without losing their essential texture and taste. To accentuate the various flavors in a complex hash, it's often a good idea to sauté the major ingredients before combining them, and to add a distinctly American savor, a small amount of bacon fat is far better for frying and sautéing than butter or vegetable oil. Whether or not they are served crusty, most all hashes need to be bound with gravy, heavy cream, egg yolk, or a thick cream sauce. Although a fine gravy can add a good deal to either a meat or poultry hash, I normally prefer a more refined simple cream binding, especially when a nice exterior crust is attempted in a skillet.

For those who might still believe that a great hash does not require the same attention to ingredients and cooking precision as the more sophisticated preparations of the repertory, let me relate, as illustration, the difficulties entailed in perfecting the modified verison of "21's" chicken hash. Having obtained the original recipe, yet curious as to how red bell pepper might enhance the dish, two professional cooks and I began testing independently what appeared to be a very simple formula. For two days we had nothing but problems: an initial béchamel sauce like soup; chicken cubes that proved too wet and too large for the sauce; inadequate seasonings; egg yolks that wouldn't thicken the sauce after the cubed chicken was added; cheese that wouldn't incorporate properly into the cream sauce. I knew from long experience what the "21" hash was supposed to taste like, and what we had was off track. Eventually, of course, we relearned that preparing any restaurant dish at home is never like preparing it in large quantities; that baking the béchamel an extra fifteen minutes made all the difference in the sauce's texture; that a young, moist broiler chicken cut into large cubes had a more negative effect on the consistency of the sauce than an older roaster poached a long time and cut into smaller cubes; that the "dashes" of Tabasco and Worcestershire sauce meant ½ teaspoon and 1 teaspoon, respectively; and that, contrary to the master recipe, the sauce simply had to contain heavy instead of light cream and had to be simmered before and after adding the chicken and red pepper in order to absorb the egg yolks properly. All chemistry, to be sure, but it does serve to demonstrate that even a dish supposedly so elementary as hash can be elevated from the prosaic to the sublime when culinary discipline is applied.

No matter what pseudosophisticates care to think, a platter of well-made hash is as satisfying to the appetite and gratifying to the soul as a steaming pot of savory stew, a bowl of genuine chili or chowder, and a juicy hamburger. It may not be a dish for every occasion, but when it comes to those American foods that somehow always evoke casual warmth, wholesome relaxation, and goodwill, a toothsome hash served with green salad, fresh bread, and premium beer is still pretty hard to beat.

"21" CHICKEN HASH WITH RED BELL PEPPER

2   Tb. butter
2   Tb. flour
2   cups milk, scalded
¼   tsp. white pepper
1   tsp. salt
½   tsp. Tabasco
1   tsp. Worcestershire sauce
½   cup grated Parmesan cheese
½   cup heavy cream
¼   cup sherry
3   cups poached white meat of roaster chicken, cut into ½-inch cubes
2   red bell peppers, cut in half, cored, and seeded
2   egg yolks
2   cups cooked and pureed peas

Preheat oven to 300° F. In a heavy saucepan with a metal handle melt butter, add flour, and stir with a whisk 2 minutes. Blend in milk gradually and continue to whisk till mixture is thickened. Season with pepper, salt, Tabasco, and Worcestershire sauce, add cheese, and mix well. Place saucepan, covered, in preheated oven and let bake 1½ hours. Strain sauce into another saucepan, add cream, whip with whisk till somewhat fluffy, and mix in sherry. Place saucepan over low heat and bring sauce to a mild simmer. Stir in chicken plus 1 bell pepper cut into ¼"-dice, bring again to the simmer, and remove from heat. In a medium bowl beat egg yolks, add ½ cup of the hot sauce, stir well, and add to chicken mixture. Stir mixture well with a fork, let rest momentarily, then spoon hash around remaining red pepper cut into quarters and arranged attractively on an oval copper serving dish. Garnish with a border of pureed peas and serve hash over toast or wild rice. Serves 4–6.

Red-Flannel Roast Beef Hash

3	slices bacon
1½	cups diced beets
2½	cups diced boiled potatoes
1	medium onion, finely chopped
2	cups diced roast beef
3	sprigs fresh parsley, finely chopped
¼	tsp. thyme
	Salt and freshly ground pepper to taste
1	egg
¼	cup heavy cream
1	Tb. butter

In a large, heavy skillet fry bacon till crisp, drain on paper towels, crumble, and pour off all but 2 Tb. fat from skillet. In a large bowl combine crumbled bacon, beets, potatoes, onion, roast beef, half the parsley, thyme, and salt and pepper. In a small bowl blend egg with cream and combine with beet mixture, mixing well. Divide hash into 4–6 rounds. Heat skillet over moderately high heat 5 minutes, reduce heat, add butter to bacon fat, add hash rounds, and cook 15 minutes on each side or till crusty brown. Transfer hash to a heated platter and sprinkle with remaining parsley. SERVES 4–6.

HAM AND SWEET POTATO HASH WITH PICKLED PEACHES

¾   lb. baked ham, cut into small cubes
1½   cups diced sweet potatoes, cooked but slightly firm
1   medium onion, minced
½   green bell pepper, cored, seeded, and chopped
½   tsp. basil
    Salt and freshly ground pepper to taste
½   cup heavy cream
½   stick butter
4–6   eggs, poached
    Minced fresh parsley
4–6   pickled peaches

In a bowl combine ham, potatoes, onion, green pepper, seasonings, and cream and mix lightly. In a large, heavy skillet melt half the butter over moderately high heat, add ham mixture, and press down evenly with a spatula. Reduce heat to moderate and cook hash 5 minutes or till underside is browned and crusty. Loosen hash with the spatula and invert onto a plate. Melt remaining butter in skillet and slide hash into it to brown other side. Transfer hash to a heated platter, top it with poached eggs, sprinkle with minced parsley, and garnish edges with pickled peaches. SERVES 4–6.

Curried Turkey Hash Cakes

2   medium potatoes, peeled, boiled, and roughly chopped
1   stick butter
3   cups chopped turkey
½   cup chopped onions
¼   cup chopped celery
½   cup chopped green bell pepper
3   eggs, 2 beaten
½   cup heavy cream
1½   tsp. salt
     Freshly ground pepper to taste
1   tsp. curry powder
¾   cup flour
2   cups pulverized bread crumbs
4–5 Tb. vegetable oil

Mash hot potatoes to a puree, add half the butter in pieces, and beat till butter is completely absorbed. In a food processor or blender, grind turkey, onions, celery, and bell pepper to a medium texture and transfer to a bowl. Add whole egg to mixture and stir well till blended. Add mashed potatoes, cream, salt, pepper, and curry powder and beat well till mixture is smooth. Cover bowl and chill about 30 minutes to firm up texture and allow flavors to blend. Shape hash into oval cakes, dust each evenly in the flour, dip in beaten eggs, roll in bread crumbs, and chill 30 minutes. Melt remaining butter with the oil in a large, heavy skillet and sauté cakes on both sides over moderate heat till golden brown. Serves 4–6.

PORK HASH WITH SAUTÉED APPLES

3	slices bacon
1	onion, minced
1	clove garlic, crushed
2	tomatoes, peeled, seeded, and chopped
1	fresh hot red pepper, chopped
1½	lbs. lean pork, chopped
½	lb. smoked pork sausage, skinned and chopped
3	Tb. lemon juice
	Pinch ground cloves
1	hard-boiled egg, whites chopped, yolks sieved
2	apples, cored
2	Tb. butter
	Shaved roasted almonds

In a large, heavy skillet fry bacon till crisp, drain on paper towels, crumble, and pour off all but 2 Tb. fat from skillet. Add onions and garlic to skillet and sauté till soft. Add tomatoes and red pepper and simmer till mixture is thick. Add pork, sausage, crumbled bacon, lemon juice, and cloves and continue cooking about 30 minutes, stirring. Brown hash under broiler till slightly crusty on top, transfer to a large serving dish, sprinkle with chopped egg whites and sieved yolks, and keep warm. Slice apples into rings, sauté in butter till slightly golden, and arrange around edges of hash. Sprinkle dish with shaved almonds. SERVES 4–6.

YANKEE CLAM HASH

6	slices bacon
½	stick butter
1	small onion, finely chopped
2	cups diced boiled potatoes
2½	cups minced clams, freshly shucked or canned and drained
½	tsp. salt
	Freshly ground pepper to taste
4	egg yolks
¾	cup heavy cream
1	Tb. softened butter

In a large, heavy skillet with a metal handle fry bacon till crisp, drain on paper towels, crumble, and pour off fat from skillet. Melt butter in same skillet and sauté onions till soft. Add potatoes and cook mixture over moderate heat till underside is golden. Add clams plus salt and pepper, sauté mixture 2 minutes, then press down with a spatula. Beat cream with egg yolks, pour over clam mixture, cover skillet, and cook 2–3 minutes or till eggs are just set. Dot surface with softened butter, brown top of hash under broiler, loosen around edges with spatula, and slide onto a heated platter. Sprinkle crumbled bacon over hash. SERVES 4–6.

MIDWESTERN PYTT I PANNA LAMB HASH

4   cups potatoes, peeled, cut into ¼″-cubes, and blanched
½   stick butter
2   Tb. vegetable oil
1   white of leek, finely chopped
1   large onion, finely chopped
2   cups roasted lean lamb cut into ¼″ dice
1   cup smoked ham, cut into ¼″ dice
    Freshly ground pepper to taste
4–6 raw egg yolks
2   sprigs watercress, chopped

Drain potatoes and pat completely dry with paper towels. In a large, heavy skillet heat half the butter and oil over moderately high heat, add potatoes, sauté till golden and crisp, and transfer to a plate. Reduce heat, add remaining butter and oil to skillet, and sauté leeks and onions till soft. Add diced meats and cook mixture, stirring, 5–10 minutes. Increase heat, add potatoes and freshly ground pepper, and sauté mixture, stirring, till it sizzles. Arrange mounds of hash on individual heated plates, make a depression in the center of each mound with the back of a large spoon, and drop egg yolks in the depressions. Sprinkle each serving with chopped watercress. SERVES 4–6.

GLAZED VEGETABLE HASH

3   slices bacon
⅓   cup diced onions
1   clove garlic, minced
⅓   cup sliced red bell peppers
2   Tb. butter
⅓   cup sliced zucchini
⅓   cup fresh sliced mushrooms
⅓   cup broccoli florets
½   cup diced boiled potatoes
1   cup cubed cooked beef, chicken, or turkey
1   cup beef, chicken, or turkey gravy
⅓   cup tomato puree
    Pinch each, thyme and basil
    Dry bread crumbs
    Butter
    Grated Parmesan cheese

In a large, heavy skillet fry bacon till crisp, drain on paper towels, crumble, and pour off all but 2 Tb. fat from skillet. Add onions, garlic, and red peppers to skillet and sauté till soft. Add butter and remaining vegetables, cover skillet, and cook about 5 minutes. Mix in cubed meat and crumbled bacon, add gravy, tomato puree, and herbs and heat thoroughly. Pour hash into 4–6 individual baking dishes and sprinkle top of each with bread crumbs. Dot tops with butter, add generous sprinklings of Parmesan cheese, and brown under broiler to a golden crust. SERVES 4–6.

RUM'S BACK!

●●●●●●●●●●●●●●●●●●●●●●●●●●●

UNLIKE THOSE captives of the present generation in America whose dietary habits never allow for anything more than a glass of white wine at lunchtime or an innocent aperitif before dinner, I demonstrate the same passion for and am as fastidious about the sinful cocktails and highballs I sip as the various foods I consume. What flows over the bridgework generally depends, of course, on place, mood, and season, which, I suppose, accounts for the fact that on a scorching day in summer or in a Caribbean bungalow in winter my bibulous instincts turn automatically to rum.

No doubt the individuals responsible for the high-powered promotion and ever-increasing popularity of this spirit in the United States would prefer that we all down their product at any given occasion twelve months of the year. And from what the figures indicate, more and more tipplers are doing just that by drinking everything from rum Martinis to rum Bloody Marys to rum digestives. But for me, rum is likely to maintain its distinction primarily as the sacred ingredient of those tall, frosty hot-weather potables capable of transforming a sweltering day into a balmy paradise. On the other hand, nothing is more appropriate when the temperature remains below zero than a Hot Buttered Rum, and, to be sure, natives of Alaska have good reason for swilling large quantities of a steaming rum concoction called Moose Milk. But I can't help but believe that when the Almighty inspired man to create rum, His ultimate goals were the Daiquiri, Piña Colada, Mai-Tai, and Zombie. Until I'm proved wrong, I doubt there'll be any more change in my attitude toward this noble booze than in my conviction that Bourbon whiskey's ideal place is in a thin-stemmed Manhattan glass.

For a drink that has always conjured up the colorful and romantic images of swashbucklers, marauding pirates, Spanish explorers, Prohibition smugglers, and deserted tropical islands, it's interesting that rum is only now regaining the popularity it enjoyed throughout the eighteenth century. And well it should, considering its important role in American history. Where facts about rum end and myths begin will always, of course, be left open to conjecture, but I can still spend hour after hour reading about this beverage's past: how Columbus brought the first sugarcane from the Canary Islands to the island of St. Croix on his second voyage; how something known as "kill-devil" was first distilled on Barbados in the early 1600s; how the term derived from either the Latin for sugar (*saccharum*) or the old English term for great tumult ("rumbustion") or the eighteenth-century British officer (Admiral Edward Vernon) who became known as Old Rummy when he introduced a ration of this spirit into the Royal Navy to curb scurvy; how Paul Revere didn't do much shouting till he had stopped by Isaac Hall's tavern for a few draughts of Medford rum; how George Washington won his first seat in the Virginia House of Burgesses by distributing seventy-five gallons of rum to voters; how Fish House Punch was created in Philadelphia at the oldest men's club in the English-speaking world; and how the celebrated Daiquiri became Cuba's national drink after 1898 when two American mining engineers stationed at a copper mine at Daiquiri concocted the drink as a prophylactic against yellow fever.

With the 1807 passage of the Embargo Act and the abolition of the infamous "triangle trade" (whereby West Indian molasses was shipped to make New England rum, which in turn was used to buy African slaves to produce molasses), the golden age of rum gradually dissolved in favor of gin and whiskey. Then, in the mid-1960s, the industry began pumping millions into advertising, the result being that for the past decade the sales growth of rum has surpassed that of all other spirits. Obviously, the steady increase of tourist trade in the Caribbean has had tremendous impact on rum's recent appeal with the American public, but in addition to that, a new generation of "light and white" drinkers throughout the country has adopted rum as the ideal beverage for sipping on the rocks with a squeeze of lime or blending with almost any mix.

Technically, rum is a distillate of the molasses, cane juice, or other residues derived from sugarcane, and unlike most other spirits, it retains most of the natural taste factors inherent in the product of origin. Moreover, rum does not have to be distilled at a very high proof, as do spirits such as gin or vodka, and it can be fermented rapidly or slowly (from twelve hours to twelve days). Since it does not need tannin to enrich its flavor, it can be aged in used casks. Rum receives minimal chemical treatment, and the only coloring used in production is sugar caramel, an agent that has no effect on flavor.

Although rum is made almost everywhere sugarcane is grown (including South Africa, Australia, the Philippines, even India), there are basically three types. First (and by far the most popular in the United States) is the very dry, light-bodied spirit produced primarily in Spanish-speaking Caribbean islands and countries (roughly 85 percent of the rum we consume comes from Puerto Rico and the Virgin Islands). Second is the richer, darker, pungent rum distilled principally on the islands of Jamaica, Haiti, Trinidad, Barbados, and Martinique, as well as in British Guyana (Demerara) and the state of Massachusetts. And third is a light-bodied, aromatic Indonesian Arak made on the island of Java and rarely found in this country. This should not imply that Puerto Rico, for instance, produces only light rums and Jamaica only dark, for although distinct rum types are definitely identified with certain areas, each location can and usually does turn out different kinds. Whatever the variety, all rums, with the exception of New England's, are blends of younger and older rums.

As for which rums go into what drinks, traditionally the lightest type (or White and Silver Labels) is used to make Daiquiris, Screwdrivers, Martinis, Bloody Marys, Collinses, and the like, while the amber-colored Gold Labels make up a good percentage of punches, Piña Coladas, Mai-Tais, sours, coolers, and eggnogs. The heaviest rums, fermented longer and distilled at lower proof to attain richer flavor, are the key ingredients in a Hot Buttered Rum, Planter's Punch, Zombie, Rum Mist, Navy Grog, Ocho Rios, and most of those overly sweet Polynesian-style libations adorned with fruit and flowers.

Curiously enough, once you master the simple basic recipes for a Daiquiri (1 part fresh lime juice, 1 part superfine sugar, and 3 parts light rum) and a Planter's Punch (1½ parts each light and dark rum, 2 parts each pineapple juice, orange juice, and lime juice, plus a dash of grenadine), the variations on these two themes are practically limitless and beautifully illustrate rum's immense taste range. More than once, for example, I've altered the Daiquiri by reducing the sugar, substituting a Bacardi Gold for White and adding a tablespoon of both dark Myers and Triple Sec. Perhaps the best Daiquiri I ever tasted was prepared on the island of St. Lucia by a slighty mad barman who used only Haitian three-star Barbancourt. I can hardly imagine a winter passing without dropping by to visit a notorious professional in San Juan who enjoys inspiring the demon by preparing my Zombies with 1 part each light, smoky-flavored Mount Gay from Barbados, Demerara, dark Jamaican Lemon Hart, plus a lethal float of Bacardi 150 white overproof (which bears a fire warning on the label). And if I ever get to the island of Martinique, I look forward to having placed in front of me a wedge of fresh lime, a bottle of sugar syrup, a bottle of heavy local rum, cold water, and an earthenware jug wherewith to mix my own Rum Punch according to the traditional formula of "one of sour, two of sweet, three of strong, and whatever of weak."

Veteran rum drinkers, of course, usually eschew all the exotic combinations in favor of simple, aristocratic rums sipped neat and on the rocks, and I must admit that even with my enduring passion for all those crispy tall creations that taste so good when the sun is hot, after one or two Piña Coladas or Planter's Punches (both of which tend to be slightly sweet and filling), nothing makes for a better change than a tart Rum Sour made with Demerara, or a light six-star Old St. Croix mixed with no more than soda water and lemon, or a suave Siegert's from Trinidad poured in a short glass over shaved ice. Equally satisfying from time to time is distinguished, well-aged rum taken as a digestive, a custom I was introduced to in England (where, by the way, the finest Jamaican rums are sent for long aging) and one which appears to be catching on more and more in the United States. It may seem a bit unorthodox, but the next time the prospect of having still another Cognac or pear brandy after dinner doesn't quite stimulate the adrenaline, try a snifter of Bacardi Añejo straight up, a fifteen-year-old Rón Del Barrilito, also from Puerto Rico, or, if at all possible, a rare Martinican Rhum Clément. I assure you the experience will be a revelation.

Hot Buttered Rum

½   stick butter, softened
¼   cup brown sugar
¼   tsp. ground cinnamon
¼   tsp. nutmeg
    Pinch ground cloves
    Pinch ground allspice
    Pint warmed dark rum
    Boiling water

In a bowl combine butter and brown sugar, add spices, and mix thoroughly. Place 1 tsp. of butter mixture into each of 8 mugs, add 2 oz. rum each, and fill mugs with boiling water. Makes 8 drinks.

Classic Daiquiri

3   oz. light rum
1   oz. fresh lime juice
1   tsp. superfine sugar

Combine ingredients in a mixing glass, add 3 or 4 ice cubes, and shake vigorously about 15 seconds. Strain into a cocktail glass or serve on the rocks. (For a frozen Daiquiri, combine ingredients in an electric blender with ⅓ cup crushed ice, blend about 20 seconds, and pour into a wine glass.)

Perfect Planter's Punch

1   oz. white rum
1   oz. gold rum
1   oz. Myers rum
2   oz. pineapple juice
2   oz. orange juice
2   oz. lime juice
1   Tb. grenadine

Combine ingredients in a mixing glass and stir thoroughly. Fill a Tom Collins glass ¾ way with shaved ice, pour punch over ice, stir briskly, and garnish top with a slice of lime and a cherry. Serve with a straw.

MAI-TAI

1   oz. light rum
2   oz. dark Jamaican rum
1   oz. fresh lime juice
½ oz. grapefruit juice
½ oz. honey
½ oz. curaçao

Combine ingredients in a mixing glass, stir thoroughly, and pour into glass half filled with finely crushed ice. Stir gently, garnish with a short stick of fresh pineapple, and serve with a short straw.

RUM MARTINI

3   oz. light rum
½ to 1   oz. dry vermouth

In a mixing glass combine rum and vermouth with crushed ice, stir very quickly to chill, and either strain into a pre-chilled cocktail glass or pour onto rocks. Garnish with olive or lemon twist.

RUM BLOODY MARY

2 oz. light rum
5 oz. tomato or vegetable juice
   Squeeze of fresh lemon
   Dash of Worcestershire sauce
   Dash of Tabasco
   Pinch of salt

In a mixing glass combine ingredients with ⅓ cup crushed ice, stir thoroughly, and pour into tall stemmed glass. Garnish with short celery stalk.

ZOMBIE

1 oz. 86-proof light rum
1½ oz. 86-proof gold rum
1 oz. 90-proof dark Jamaican or Trinidad rum
1 oz. pineapple juice
1 oz. papaya juice (available in cans)
   Juice of 1 lime
1 tsp. superfine sugar
   151-proof Demerara or Bacardi rum

Combine all ingredients but the last in a mixing glass with shaved ice and shake vigorously about 20 seconds. Pour into tall frosted glass, float a tablespoon of Demerara or Bacardi on top, garnish with fresh mint and a cherry, and serve with a straw.

TEATOTALER

½ qt. water
4 oz. (½ cup) instant iced tea
8 oz. gold rum
   Sugar to taste

Pour water into quart pitcher, dissolve tea in water, add rum and sugar to taste, and stir with ice till well chilled. Serve over ice in tall 8-ounce glasses and garnish with lemon slices and fresh mint.

PIÑA COLADA

2 oz. white or gold rum
1 oz. cream of coconut (available in cans)
3 oz. unsweetened pineapple juice
½ oz. Triple Sec (optional)

Combine ingredients in an electric blender with 1 cup crushed ice, blend about 20 seconds, and pour into a tall glass. Garnish with a short stick of fresh pineapple and serve with a straw.

El Presidente

3   oz. light rum
½   oz. sweet vermouth
    Dash Angostura bitters

Combine ingredients in a mixing glass with ice cubes, stir thoroughly, and strain into a prechilled Manhattan glass. Twist an orange peel over the drink to release the oil, swish it around the edge of the glass, and discard.

Rum Sour

2   oz. gold or Demerara rum
    Juice of ½ lemon
½   tsp. superfine sugar

Combine ingredients in a mixing glass with ice cubes and shake vigorously about 20 seconds. Strain into a prechilled cocktail glass or pour on the rocks. Serve with an orange slice and a cherry.

Rum Unisphere

2   oz. gold rum
½   oz. lime juice
½   tsp. Benedictine
½   tsp. Pernod
½   tsp. grenadine

Combine ingredients in a mixing glass, add about ⅓ cup crushed ice, and shake vigorously about 20 seconds. Strain into prechilled cocktail glass and garnish with a twist of lime.

CANTALOUPE COOLER

2   oz. light rum
½   oz. lime juice
½   oz. orange juice
½   oz. superfine sugar
¼   cup chopped cantaloupe

Combine ingredients in a blender with about ⅓ cup crushed ice and blend about 20 seconds. Pour into prechilled Old Fashioned glass, add more ice to fill glass to rim, and garnish with cantaloupe cube on a spear.

RUM CREOLE

2   oz. gold rum
1   tsp. lemon juice
    Dash Tabasco
    Iced beef bouillon
    Salt and pepper to taste

In a prechilled Old Fashioned glass place 2 or 3 ice cubes, add rum, lemon juice, and Tabasco, stir well, and fill glass with beef bouillon. Sprinkle with salt and pepper to taste.

HAITIAN RUM OLD FASHIONED

½   tsp. superfine sugar
     Dash Angostura bitters
     Soda water
2½   oz. rum

Place sugar in an Old Fashioned glass, add bitters plus splash of soda water, and stir till well mulled. Add 3 or 4 ice cubes, pour rum over ice plus another splash of soda, and stir thoroughly. Garnish with lime and orange wedges.

III

SHARPENING
THE
BLADE

BEYOND
MEAT LOAF

●●●●●●●●●●●●●●●●●●●●●●●●

"My idea of heaven," said the Reverend Sidney Smith, "is eating *pâté de foie gras* to the sound of trumpets." No doubt the good reverend's hedonistic sentiment has served as inspiration to more than one epicure a bit apprehensive about the hereafter, and, no doubt, were we guaranteed the likelihood of this celestial possibility, we might become a little more adept at tempering our earthly gourmadise. Personally, I could do without the musical fanfare, and, with no disrespect intended towards the reverend's culinary tastes, I'd at least make an effort to obtain a small loaf of crusty bread and a good bottle of wine to complement the occasion. Nor, come to think of it, would I necessarily have to have goose liver pâté to feast on for eternity. A truffled pheasant pâté in puff pastry would do very nicely, or a terrine of woodcock with truffles and Cognac, a sparkling galantine of duck flecked with ham and pistachios, or even a simple country pâté studded with a few unpretentious chicken livers.

Like many others devoted to the art of gastronomy, there is virtually nothing I enjoy so much as pâtés, terrines, galantines, or any other "loaves" made from meats, fowl, seafood, or vegetables that are ground and properly seasoned with fresh herbs, spices and spirits, encased in fat, butter, aspic, or pastry, baked to perfection, and served with nothing more than a few gherkins, a crisp vegetable or mixed green salad, fresh bread, perhaps a little hot mustard, and a refreshing bottle of wine. Anyone who's ever traveled extensively in France is bound to have sampled at least a dozen of these delectable creations, but I doubt there are many outsiders who, over the years, have developed my particular passion for them or savored such a vast array. And the varieties produced throughout France are staggering: the duck, woodcock, and thrush pâtés of Flanders, Languedoc, and the Dauphiné; the wild rabbit terrines of the Ile de France and Roussillon; the delicate pâtés of lark and pigeon of Chartres and the Franche-Comté; the eel pâtés of Charente and terrines of lobster and crayfish all along the Atlantic coast; the galantines of fowl in and around Bresse; and, of course, the sumptuous goose liver pâtés of Alsace and the Southwest. Then if you include in the same family such specialties as the inimitable *rillettes* (shredded pork that is potted) of Tours and Le Mans, the *oyonnades* (jugged goose) of Bourbonnais and *civets de lièvre* (jugged hare) of Savoie and Gascony, plus the meat and seafood mousses made all over France, you're immediately made aware of one of the most important (and often underestimated) glories of French cuisine.

Technically speaking, the term *pâté* in French means "enclosed in pastry," or, more exactly, a pastry enclosing meat, fish, or vegetables. A terrine, on the other hand, is literally no more than a style of cooking vessel, the type generally used to cook a pâté. Over the years the confusion of the terminology (and the dishes) has become so total that it's hardly worthwhile trying to point out the subtle distinctions between pâtés and terrines. Professional chefs know that a genuine classic pâté (like the celebrated *L'Oreiller de la Belle Aurore,* or Fair Aurora's Pillow) must be covered with two separate sheets of puff pastry, while most other compositions without pastry should correctly be called terrines. Therefore, all those wonderful *pâtés de campagne* you've been enjoying in your favorite neighborhood bistros should properly be called terrines. In even the finest restaurants, however, the terms are almost always intermingled, so much so that one can hardly be severely criticized for referring to pâtés as terrines and vice versa (or, for that matter, for calling a galantine—technically composed of only fowl—a pâté). As for those who would extend the terminology to anything from liver paste to meat loaf to tinned ham spread—well, I have no comment.

No doubt the Greeks composed crude forms of pâté, but, at least according to one source, it was Apicius, the well-known Roman epicure, who set down the first recipe. He called the dish *salsum sine salso,* or fish without fish, thereby suggesting the same idea of thrift that millions of cooks would later always associate with their concoctions. According to his directions, you should take the livers of chickens, hares, or lambs; cook them; grind them well; add salt, pepper, and oil; mold the mixture into a fish-shaped mound; and sprinkle with virgin oil. I'm not quite sure how big a hit all that fishy ground liver might be today at a dinner party, but there can be no question the dish was economical and hardly time-consuming.

Although pâtés as we know them today (and the term is now well fixed in the English vernacular) have a French ancestry, it's not wholly unlikely that a few medieval Norman chefs may have picked up an idea or two in the baronial kitchens of England, all of which included a large mortal and pestle, a good chopping board, and a hefty servant whose sole duty was to chop, hash, and mince. In a fascinating tome entitled *English Medieval Feasts,* for example, there are a couple of fragmentary recipes which can't help but arouse our curiosity. "Take veal, hew it, seeth it, grind it small, and cast it thereto"; or "Take eels and flay them, and chop them in fair slices." And as one contemporary enthusiast has pointed out, "it must have been a busy day when the 'grete pye' was in preparation. This epicurean effort consisted of a mixture of beef or 'motton,' 'suet of a fatte beste,' pepper, salt, capons, hens, mallards, coneys, woodcocks, teals, 'grete birds,' marrow, hard yolks of eggs, dates, currants, whole cloves, whole mace, cinnamon, saffron, and other things up to the number of twenty-one, besides the 'coffin' which was the picturesque medieval term for the pastry crust that held the pie filling."

During the French Renaissance, pâtés were already being made with such delicacies as lark, badger, porcupine, and dormouse, and by the seventeenth century, it was not uncommon in noble homes to be served truffled partridge pâté, Amiens duck pâté, or veal pâté from Rouen. To be sure, the great majority of pâtés of those early eras were, like today, thriftily fashioned of leftover ingredients unsuitable for more refined dishes, but it's also true that by the reign of Louis XVI a chef by the name of Jean-Pierre Clause, attendant to the Alsatian Maréchal de Contades, had created one of the glories of classic French cuisine by mixing delicate goose liver with, among other things, veal forcemeat and serving it in a pastry crust. For many of us today, it would be nearly impossible to imagine a world without *pâté de foie gras en croûte.*

While pâtés, terrines, and galantines have remained staples in the French (and European) diet for centuries, it's curious that only in the past two decades have these creations begun to attract the American palate. Exactly why I don't know, but I'd suspect it's more than likely owing to the fact that until recent years, Americans in general not only have never been overly fond of liver and fat in any form but have also tended to shy away from any edible whose components are not clearly identifiable. Whatever the reason, it's for sure that today these delicious "loaves" are catching on more and more over the country—and not only in French bistros. No doubt what you usually find in most restaurants of any merit is a simple, honest pâté composed mainly of ground pork, calf or beef liver, fresh pork fat, a little chicken, onions, and any number of spices and heady herbs. (And I've always insisted that the best initial test of any supposedly fine restaurant is the house pâté, for you can be sure that in most cases, if the pâté is poor, the rest of the meal will be worse.) On the other hand, in many of the nation's better restaurants it's becoming increasingly common to find these preparations made of veal, duck, goose, and game, stunning creations bejeweled with black truffles and green pistachios, gilded in aspic, cloaked in delicate pastry, and redolent of garlic, nutmeg, thyme, Cognac, and who knows what other flavorings. Furthermore, in most major cities there's usually at least one speciality food shop that makes pâtés on a regular basis, enabling those who haven't learned to make their own (or don't care to bother) to buy either whole loaves or simply random slices to serve at home.

Pâté making is not necessarily an easy project, so before embarking it's a good idea to shop carefully for the equipment you might need and also give plenty of thought to a few concepts and techniques that have proved basic to the art. I don't deny for one minute that some of the best pâtés I've turned out were baked in ordinary meat-loaf dishes and bread pans. Contrary to what some so-called experts might say, there's absolutely nothing wrong with these vessels insofar as the actual cooking process is concerned (with few exceptions, pâtés are always baked in a water bath, which means the vessel with the mixture is immersed halfway in another receptacle containing water to cook gently). Unfortunately, these dishes and pans are hardly ideal for presentation at the table, so from the start you'd be wise to look around in quality cookware shops and invest in a couple of attractive porcelain or earthenware terrines of different sizes and shapes. (I don't care for those collapsible metal types, none of which are pleasant to work with or look at.) One word of caution, however: Rarely (and I have no idea why) do you find a good terrine with a reversible lid, meaning that since most pâtés must be weighted after cooking, you'll have to improvise on both lids and weights.

Unless you're willing to chop your ingredients by hand, you'll also need a sturdy meat grinder. Personally, I have little use for even the best food processors when it comes to grinding meats since they tend to reduce a part of the ingredient to puree before the whole is sufficiently ground. Nor, under any circumstances, would I ever have ingredients ground by a butcher for the simple reason that I'm always suspicious of what might have been through the grinder before. If you're truly concerned about producing a forcemeat of ideal texture (i.e., one that is firm, juicy, and not pasty), you'll learn to chop by hand. To do this you cut the meat into small cubes with a razor-sharp chef's knife, then, keeping the point of the knife in fulcrum contact with the cutting board, chop slowly and carefully. When the meat becomes cohesive, begin to chop more rapidly, preferably with two equally balanced knives held above the board and brought down on the meat in a rhythmic motion. Depending on whether you prefer a coarse or fine forcemeat, continue chopping till desired texture is accomplished.

One important word about fat. Most meat pâtés call not only for a substantial amount of fat to be mixed into the forcemeat (as well as added in cubes for decoration) but also for sheets of fresh pork fat with which to envelop the entire contents of the terrine. Much of this fat cooks away, but if you nevertheless tend to shy away from fat, you'd best forget about making meat pâtés altogether, for to bring off successfully even the humblest country pâté you need plenty of fat for flavor and moisture as well as to facilitate serving.

More than once I tried to cut back on the fat content and more than once have I ended up with mediocre pâté. As for the type of fat to use for lining the terrine and covering the mixture, there's simply no substitute for fresh pork fat. People advise that you can use bacon, blanched salt pork, or ham fat. Don't, for these not only disintegrate faster but also tend to give the pâté an undesirable flavor. People also advise that it's practically impossible to obtain sheets of fresh pork fat. Nonsense. I've yet to meet a good butcher (even in supermarkets) who wasn't willing to trim enough fat from a loin to meet my needs. Also, when I buy any type of pork roast, I always make it a point to trim off and freeze as much of the fat as possible.

After baking, most pâtés should be weighted down in the terrine (with a heavy pot, brick, books, anything), cooled to room temperature, and left in the refrigerator at least twenty-four hours before serving to allow the flavors to develop fully and to ensure a compact body. I never keep a pâté more than ten days, and after five or six I usually remove a meat pâté from the terrine, wipe off the meat jelly, and either wrap it tightly in plastic wrap and foil or return it to the terrine to be covered with melted pork fat. You can freeze most pâtés, but I've found the texture is by no means ever the same.

How to serve a cold pâté for lunch? I enjoy slicing directly from the terrine, in which case it's always a good idea before making the presentation to first loosen the pâté with a knife around the edges (taking care not to cut into the fat casing), then to cut a large slice from one end to facilitate cutting center slices at table. If you prefer to unmold the pâté and serve it with aspic, first rest the terrine momentarily on a steaming hot towel to loosen the bottom, cut carefully around the edges, unmold on a chilled platter lined with chopped aspic, and decorate with watercress and tomato flowers. For lunch allow two ½-inch-slices of pâté per person.

Whoever the fool was that said there's nothing of true interest left to be discovered in this overly technological universe apparently never gave much thought to Bach cantatas, romance, stars, or, indeed, pâtés. The following recipes, each illustrating a distinctive type of preparation, should prove my point.

COUNTRY PÂTÉ WITH BOURBON

1½	lbs. lean pork, ground
1½	lbs. calf's liver, ground
1	lb. fresh pork fat, ground
¼	lb. veal, ground
¼	lb. chicken, ground
4	Tb. butter
½	tsp. finely chopped garlic
½	cup finely chopped scallions
½	lb. chicken livers
¼	cup Bourbon
4	Tb. heavy cream
2	tsp. lemon juice
2	Tb. flour
1	egg, beaten
¾	tsp. allspice
2	tsp. salt
	Freshly ground pepper to taste
¾	lb. fresh pork fat, sliced into strips
1	bay leaf

Combine ground meats in a large mixing bowl. In a skillet sauté scallions and garlic in half the butter till soft, and add to meat mixture. Lightly sauté chicken livers in remaining butter and set aside. Deglaze skillet with the Bourbon till reduced to 3 Tb. and add to mixture, along with cream, lemon juice, flour, egg, allspice, salt, and pepper. Thoroughly mix all ingredients. To check seasoning, sauté a spoonful of the mixture in skillet and taste, remembering that once pâté is chilled later on, it will tend to taste underseasoned. Preheat oven to 350° F. Line bottom and sides of a 2-quart terrine with slightly overlapping strips of pork fat, allowing enough to hang over sides to later lap over filling. Spoon half the meat mixture into terrine, press and smooth carefully, arrange chicken livers in a row down center, add remaining meat mixture, smooth top, and bring strips of fat up over meat to bind filling completely. (Use extra strips to cover any exposed gaps.) Lay bay leaf on top, cover tightly with foil, and place terrine in a large baking vessel such as a roasting pan. Pour in enough boiling water to reach halfway up the sides of terrine, place vessel on middle shelf of oven, and bake approximately 2 hours or till juices run clear. Cut either a board or heavy piece of cardboard to fit inside dimensions of terrine and wrap it in foil. Remove terrine from oven, remove foil from top, insert foil-wrapped board or cardboard, and weight the pâté with a pot or casserole weighing several pounds. When cooled to room temperature, place in refrigerator (with weight still in place) for at least 24 hours.

CHICKEN LIVER AND PECAN PÂTÉ

½ lb. chicken livers
2 Tb. melted butter
1 medium onion, chopped
   Salt, freshly ground pepper, and paprika to taste
2 oz. dry sherry
2 oz. Madeira
6 oz. (about 1½ cups) pecans, chopped
1 stick sweet butter, room temperature
¼ tsp. mace
½ tsp. thyme
   Pinch of cayenne

Cut membrane and green spots from livers, dice, and place on a broiler pan. Add melted butter and onion, season lightly with salt and pepper, and dust with paprika. Toss to coat livers with butter and spread livers over pan bottom, leaving a little space between pieces. Broil close to high heat till golden, turn with a spatula, then broil other sides. Mix the wines and pour half of mixture into a blender. Turn on blender, add pecans a few at a time, and blend till smooth. Add remaining wine plus the livers and blend till all ingredients are incorporated, using a rubber spatula to scrape down the sides. Add butter, blend well, then add mace, thyme, and cayenne, blending thoroughly. Serve on a crisp leaf of lettuce. SERVES 6.

FLOUNDER AND SPINACH PÂTÉ WITH PRUNES

1	lb. fresh flounder fillets
1¼	cups butter, softened
1	cup bread crumbs
¼	cup heavy cream
2	egg yolks, beaten
¼	cup spinach, cooked, drained, and minced
¼	cup shallots, chopped
¼	cup fresh dill, chopped
1	tsp. salt
	Cayenne pepper to taste
¼	cup scallions, minced
1	lb. fresh salmon, skinless, boneless, and cut into strips
¼	cup dry white wine
10	prunes, pitted and halved
1	tsp. mace

In a blender puree flounder in batches and transfer to a large mixing bowl. Add 1 cup of the softened butter and mix thoroughly. In another bowl moisten crumbs with cream and fold in egg yolks, minced spinach, shallots, dill, salt, and cayenne. Combine fish and bread-crumb mixtures and beat the forcemeat with a fork till fluffy. In a skillet sauté scallions in 2 Tb. of remaining butter till soft, add salmon strips, dry white wine, and a pinch of salt and cook fish (tossing from time to time) for 2–3 minutes or till flaky. Transfer fish to a bowl or platter, reduce liquid in skillet to 3 Tb., and pour over fish. Preheat oven to 300° F. Line bottom of a terrine with ½-inch layer of forcemeat, arrange a layer of salmon strips, season salmon with a pinch of mace, and continue to fill terrine with alternate layers of forcemeat and salmon, remembering to approximate the center of the pâté and arrange a row of prunes down the middle. Dot the top with remaining butter, seal terrine tightly with foil, set in a larger vessel, pour in enough boiling water to reach halfway up the sides, and bake 55–60 minutes or till surface of pâté is firm and springy to the touch. Remove the terrine from the water, set a light weight on top of foil, allow to cool to room temperature, and chill well in refrigerator. Unmold pâté on bed of lettuce or watercress and serve with homemade green mayonnaise.

RICHARD OLNEY'S VEGETABLE TERRINE

1	cup duxelles:
1	large onion, finely chopped
2	Tb. butter
8	oz. finely chopped mushrooms
	Salt, pepper, and lemon juice to taste
	Handful chopped parsley
10	oz. fresh young sorrel, shredded
2	Tb. butter
2	oz. stale bread, crusts removed, soaked in hot water, and squeezed dry
3	cloves garlic, peeled and pureed
1	lb. spinach, parboiled for 2 min., rinsed, squeezed dry, and chopped
8	oz. green beans, cut into ½-inch lengths and parboiled 8 min.
6	oz. carrots, split, diced, and parboiled 10 min.
1	lb. white beans, well cooked, drained, and pureed
3	oz. elbow macaroni, cooked slightly and well drained
1	tsp. finely crumbled dried herbs
	Salt, freshly ground pepper, and cayenne to taste
½	cup butter, softened

The duxelles: In a skillet sauté the chopped onion in the butter over low heat without allowing it to color for 20 minutes. Add mushrooms, turning the heat high and tossing and stirring till mushrooms' moisture has evaporated. Season, add parsley, and continue cooking over low heat 2 minutes. Stir in an extra drop of lemon juice. In another skillet stew the shredded sorrel in butter, stirring occasionally for 10 minutes or till all the excess moisture has been evaporated and the sorrel is reduced to a puree. Mix the squeezed bread-crumb paste thoroughly with the garlic. Combine all the above with the remaining ingredients in a large mixing bowl and mix thoroughly with your hands. Turn out into a 2-quart buttered terrine, tapping the bottom to settle contents. Preheat oven to 350° F. Set terrine in a larger vessel, pour in enough boiling water to reach halfway up the sides, and let sit about 10 minutes. Place in oven, bake about 1½ hours, remove terrine, set a light, covered weight on top, cool to room temperature, and refrigerate (with weights still in place) for 24 hours.

GALATINE OF DUCK IN ASPIC

Marinade

3	Tb. Cognac
1	tsp. allspice
½	tsp. thyme
½	tsp. salt
	Freshly ground pepper

1	4-lb. duck, skinned and boned, with skin kept in one piece and bones and giblets reserved
1	lb. veal, ground
1	lb. pork, ground
½	cup shallots, minced
1½	Tb. butter
2½	tsp. salt
1	tsp. thyme
¾	tsp. allspice
	Freshly ground pepper to taste
	Small tin of black truffles
2	eggs, lightly beaten (retain 1 egg shell, crushed), plus 1 egg white
¼	cup pistachios, blanched and dried
¼	cup cooked ham, diced
	Bouquet garni (6 sprigs parsley, 1 bay leaf, pinch of thyme)
3	cups chicken stock or broth
1	Tb. gelatin
3	Tb. port

Combine ingredients for marinade in a bowl, cut breast meat of duck into strips, and marinate overnight. Put through the fine blade of a meat grinder the remaining duck meat and add to the ground veal and pork in a large bowl. In a skillet sauté shallots in butter till soft. Combine spices in a small bowl. Drain truffles, reserving liquor, dice, and set aside. Add spices to forcemeat and mix thoroughly. Add eggs, shallots, pistachios, ham, and liquor from the truffles and mix thoroughly. Preheat oven to 325° F. On a large piece of damp cheesecloth spread out the duck skin and arrange in center ¼ of the forcemeat. Arrange ⅓ of marinated strips lengthwise on forcemeat, sprinkle a few truffles in between, and continue filling skin in like manner, ending up with a layer of forcemeat. Bring up sides and ends of skin, sew into a rectangle, tie with string at 2-inch intervals, then wrap and tie in cheesecloth. Line a large terrine with reserved chopped duck bones and giblets and add bouquet garni. Lower galantine into terrine, add chicken stock, place in oven, and bake for 2½ hours, basting frequently. Transfer galantine to a platter, remove cheesecloth, strain stock into a bowl, and chill thoroughly. Return galantine to the terrine, place a heavy weight on top, and chill in refrigerator overnight. When stock is well chilled, skim off all fat, pour stock into a saucepan, add crushed egg shell and egg white, and beat well. Slowly bring stock to a boil, stirring constantly, then simmer without stirring for 15 minutes. In a bowl mix gelatin with port and let sit 15 minutes. Strain stock through cheesecloth into bowl and stir thoroughly. Chill aspic till syrupy, remove string from galantine, and spoon on layers of aspic, chilling each layer till set before adding the next. Chill the galantine a few more hours before serving.

TAKE A LEAF OF
LETTUCE AND . . .

●●

In this weight- and nutrition-conscious age, surely no food in this land has risen to such heights of popularity as the composed salad. Originally served either as a simple course in the venue of a complex meal or as a complementary dish to be nibbled at on the side, salads started to come into their own in the 1920s, particularly in southern California. Heading the list were the chiffonade salad, the Caesar, the Waldorf (created by the famous Oscar of the old Waldorf Hotel in New York in 1893), asparagus and egg, grapefruit and avocado, cucumber and carrot, dandelion and tuna, orange and pineapple, and heaven knows what other simple but tasty combinations. Eventually, after the trend spread throughout the nation and the salads took on greater importance, things became more elaborate. By the fifties there weren't many people who hadn't tasted whole tomatoes (on lettuce) stuffed with chicken salad or tuna; shrimp salad with onions, celery, and capers; avocados or artichokes stuffed with shrimp and black olives and topped with Thousand Island or Louis dressing; lobster, crab meat, or beef salad; and any number of congealed fruit salads. In the sixties nothing would do but to start a meal by dividing a gigantic *salade niçoise* or spinach and bacon salad or even a chef's salad full of tomatoes, raw onions, radishes, pimiento, and julienne strips of cheese, turkey, and ham. And by 1970 there could be no doubt that the composed salads served in restaurants and homes were considered main-course items around which the rest of the meal revolved.

Now the trend continues at an ever greater tempo. Just a few decades back a stylish lunch automatically implied two or three Martinis followed by a heavy three-course meal, but today it's never uncommon, even in the finest restaurants, to see people ordering at midday no more than a combined salad of one sort or another accompanied by a glass of white wine and a little bread. Nor is it unusual for a host or hostess to construct an evening meal at home around salad, beginning with perhaps a homemade pâté, continuing with a classic Caesar salad or an imaginative chef's salad full of nutritional ingredients, and finishing up with something like a light cassis sherbet. Obviously, no one (including myself, to be sure) cares to make a meal of composed salad every day of the year, despite the claims of those silly dieters who insist they have nothing but salad day and night. But considering the variety of delicious ingredients that can be used to transform a plate of simple leafy greens into a delectable main course, it does make lots of sense to familiarize yourself with all the possibilities and develop the habit of turning out a great salad maybe once a week.

Of course, the first ingredients to consider when planning any composed salad are the greens. Unfortunately, no item in American supermarkets is subjected to more abuse than greens—as anyone knows who's ever watched a produce worker sling a delicate head of Boston lettuce into a bin, or caught a check-out clerk tossing the romaine in the bottom of a grocery bag. Equally guilty are customers themselves who refuse to take time to clean, dry, store, and prepare greens properly. Some people seem to forget that no matter how fine and fresh the principal components of a salad, if the greens used as either filler or embellishment are not of the best quality and in perfect condition, the dish is a virtual flop. And the same goes for salads involving mixed greens that are thrown together without any consideration for blending individual tastes and textures. Succicntly stated, there's no excuse whatsoever in anyone not handling greens with respect, and just in case you think true salad fanciers don't pay any attention to wilted leaf lettuce or brown-spotted escarole, you could be in for an embarrassing surprise.

Escarole, romaine, Bibb lettuce, chicory (often referred to as curly endive), Boston lettuce, iceberg lettuce, and leaf lettuce are the mainstays of most salads. Other greens and leafy herbs that are gaining more and more popularity are Belgian endive, spinach, watercress, arugula, Chinese cabbage, fresh basil leaves, dill, and tarragon leaves. No matter which ones you decide to experiment with, the basic rules for buying and handling apply to every one. When shopping for greens, never settle for any that are wilted, discolored, and not 100 percent fresh. If the Bibb is not crisp, take a look at the leaf lettuce; if the Boston is droopy, don't buy it with the hope of later restoring its texture with cold water; and if the arugula or basil doesn't give off a tangy aroma when slightly pinched and squeezed, forget them.

Wash and chill greens thoroughly the second you get home, and always allow them to crisp in the refrigerator for twenty-four hours before serving. In the case of iceberg letuce (which, contrary to current snobbism, does indeed have its important place in American gastronomy), cut out the core, place the head core-end up in the sink, let cold water run over it, drain, wrap with either paper towels or clean dish toweling, place in a plastic bag, and refrigerate. Romaine, escarole, and chicory need not be cored but after washing should be placed on a slightly tilted drainboard with heads pointed down. To clean delicate Bibb, Boston, and leaf lettuce, hold in the hand, head up, under running water, taking care not to bruise the leaves. Also treat gently the spicy leaves of watercress, arugula, and herb greens, washing them quickly before wrapping in towels and refrigerating. As for Belgian endive, the best idea is to remove all leaves, rinse separately (some experts believe in soaking the leaves in water with a pinch of sugar for two hours), and wrap tightly in a damp towel. The main point to remember is that greens must be fresh, clean, crisp, cool, and sporting no trace of water when added to a salad bowl or used as a base for composed salads of meat, seafood, fruit, and vegetables. Accumulated moisture on greens not only dilutes a salad dressing but can turn an otherwise splendid arrangement into a soggy mess.

Some of the most exciting main-course salads are without doubt those involving primarily a deft combination of different greens tossed with secondary ingredients and a good dressing. A common fault of many salads, however, is that the mixed greens are not selected to complement each other. Escarole and chicory, for instance, should never be combined with Boston or Bibb lettuce for the simple reason that the heavier, tougher leaves overpower the more delicate ones. Nor does it make sense to blend something like arugula with watercress, two spicy greens that are delectable by themselves but not when mixed together. Equally important when working with tossed greens is cutting the leaves properly and coating them with the right style dressing. Large leaves should be either broken into bite-size pieces or left whole to be cut at table, and the salad should never be tossed till just before serving. The dressing should be neither too oily, too acidulous, nor in the least bit sweet (this is one reason I personally object to the current overuse of such fashionable sweet oils as hazelnut and walnut). Generally, the most acceptable dressing for any mixed green salad is a good vinaigrette made with top-grade olive or peanut oil, wine vinegar or fresh lemon juice (or both), a little dry mustard, salt, and perhaps a little fresh garlic and herbs. Heavy dressings such as Thousand Island, Roquefort, and Green Goddess should never come in contact with tossed Bibb, Boston, leaf lettuce, or Belgian endive.

There are two basic types of main-course salads: greens tossed with any number of ingredients and a dressing, and vegetable, fruit, meat, and seafood components that are combined with other ingredients and usually served atop greens. Needless to say, the possibilities are limitless, and for those who believe that preparing a fine salad is a veritable art, the challenge can indeed be very exciting. Composing salads involves a great deal more than merely throwing together whatever you can find and dousing it all with dressing. The smart chef begins by trying to produce a tasty version of the classics: the Caesar, chicken salad, spinach and fresh mushrooms with bacon, tomatoes stuffed with shrimp or crab meat, citrus fruits and onion rings, dandelion greens and tuna, Russian salad, and, of course, a mouthwatering chef's salad. Once you're satisfied with these accomplishments, you're then ready to experiment a little. You might add walnuts to your chicken salad, toss raw mushrooms and bacon chips with watercress instead of spinach, stuff artichokes in place of tomatoes with mayonnaised crab meat or curried scallops, or create a chef's salad with corned beef, smoked goose breast, or sautéed fish strips as the main ingredient. Your vinaigrette might not seem right for certain salads, so you reduce the vinegar and add a little chervil. And what's wrong with a sour cream and crushed fruit dressing? Try adding a few drops of lime juice and a pinch of salt to the mixture.

Once you've mastered the basic combinations as well as a number of dressings, you're ready to exert your expertise and invent new composed salads. Your first efforts might involve such seafoods as squid, mussels, oysters, or codfish, served individually with a vinaigrette or mixed with hard-boiled eggs, capers, onions, diced boiled potatoes, fresh parsley, and bound with homemade mayonnaise. No one loves anything better than shrimp salad, so you apply imagination and come up with shrimp and shredded cabbage, shrimp-stuffed cucumbers, or shrimp, orange sections, and walnuts tossed with sherry mayonnaise. With crab meat, why not add an oriental touch with the help of sliced water chestnuts, chopped green pepper, cold cooked rice, and a tangy soy sauce vinaigrette? And for an elegant lobster salad, try either mixing succulent chunks with diced chicken breast or combining the lobster with finely diced cucumbers, sliced raw mushrooms, and a fine Louis dressing.

A well-made chicken salad between fresh leaves of Bibb is always an appetizing sight at lunchtime, but adventurous individuals might add an entirely new dimension to the dish by mixing in bacon chips and a little tarragon and serving the salad stuffed in a mango or papaya. Beef salad can be incredibly bland, but when it's perked up with onion rings, capers, horseradish, a garlic-flavored vinaigrette, and served with escarole or chicory, it makes for memorable eating. The same applies to cold lamb, which, when marinated a few hours in oil and vinegar, onions, curry powder, Dijon mustard, rosemary, and parsley, goes perfectly with romaine or escarole with a few fresh basil leaves. Even sweetbreads poached in seasoned chicken broth and chilled can be combined with sliced cucumbers, celery, watercress, and a light vinaigrette to produce a main-course salad that's not only nourishing but radically different.

Perhaps the main-course salads that you see most these days are those built around fresh fruits and vegetables. Typical examples would include fruit chunks, nuts, and raisins on leaf lettuce topped with frozen yogurt; diced fruit and berries with sour cream and dill cupped in iceberg lettuce; mixed greens with raw mushrooms, wheat germ, alfalfa and bean sprouts, sesame and sunflower seeds, and some pimiento; blanched asparagus, broccoli and cauliflower florets, carrots, string beans, radishes, and any number of other crisp vegetables tossed with a few greens and a light vinaigrette or simply served on top of escarole or dandelion greens; and even such edible flowers as chrysanthemums, marigolds, nasturtiums, or violets, which, when mixed with Bibb lettuce, baby beets, and a well-seasoned light dressing, make for something truly unusual.

Devoting more attention to composed salads now that so many attractive fresh ingredients are available throughout the United States is a great way to add scope to your culinary repertory. Nutritious, tasty, generally slimming, and a challenge to the serious chef, main-course salads provide a pleasant change in anyone's eating habits and contribute an important dimension to our native cookery.

CLASSIC CAESAR SALAD

Carefully strip leaves from 2 stalks romaine lettuce, wash, and re-frigerate. In a small bowl mash 2 cloves garlic to a smooth paste with a pestle or spoon, add ¼ tsp. salt, dribble 3 tsp. fine olive oil, and blend thoroughly. Strain into small frying pan, heat slightly, add 2 cups unseasoned croutons, toss about 1 minute, and turn into a serving bowl. Squeeze 1 lemon (pits removed) into a small pitcher, boil 2 eggs exactly 1 minute, grate ¼ cup imported Par-mesan cheese into a serving bowl, and arrange everything on an attractive tray with cruet of olive oil, croutons, pepper mill, salt, and Worchestershire sauce. Chill dinner plates and arrange ro-maine leaves in large salad bowl. To prepare salad, pour 4 Tb. oil over romaine and toss twice with a salad fork and spoon, scooping leaves toward you in a slow roll. Add ¼ tsp. salt, ground pepper to taste, 2 more Tb. oil, and toss again. Pour on lemon juice, 6 drops Worchestershire sauce, and break in the eggs. Toss twice, sprinkle on cheese, toss again, add croutons, and toss twice more. To serve, arrange leaves on dinner plates, stems facing outward, and sprin-kle on croutons. SERVES 4–6.

CLASSIC CHEF'S SALAD

In a large salad bowl toss 1 cup each shredded cabbage, chicory, romaine, and watercress with 8 fresh basil leaves torn into small pieces. In spoke fashion on top of greens group 1 cup each ju-lienne strips of lean beef, tongue, and Swiss cheese; blanched cau-liflower and broccoli florets; enough cherry tomatoes to fill center. Cover and chill till ready to present, and toss with a vinaigrette or hot bacon dressing. SERVES 4–6.

CRAB MEAT SALAD LOUIS

For each individual serving, arrange two large artichoke bottoms atop a large slice of tomato resting on leaves of Bibb lettuce. Cover artichokes with fresh lump backfin crab meat, sprinkle on a little lemon juice, spoon on Louis dressing, and garnish with chopped hard-boiled eggs and pimiento strips.

BEEF SALAD

Tear into bite-size pieces the leaves from one stalk romaine plus a few leaves of chicory and/or escarole. Arrange in a large bowl. Add to greens 4 cups cold roast beef cut into 1-inch squares, 6 small new potatoes cooked and sliced, 6 hard-boiled eggs cut in half, 20 cherry tomatoes, 2 raw onions cut into rings, 1 Tb. capers, ¾ cup thinly sliced mushrooms, 2 Tb. chopped parsley, and 1 tsp. horseradish. Dress with a vinaigrette and toss gently but thoroughly. SERVES 4–6.

PEARS À LA RITZ

For each individual serving, peel two ripe Bartlett pears and level bottoms so they stand upright. With an apple corer remove stems and cores. Fill pears with cream cheese and set on Boston lettuce leaves. Melt ½ cup currant, guava, or Bar-le-Duc jelly and thin it slightly with 2 tsp. lemon juice. Let chill to thicken and pour over pears. Coat pears with blanched slivered almonds.

SALADE NIÇOISE

In a large mixing bowl combine 2–3 boiled sliced potatoes, ½ lb. blanched string beans, 1 chopped onion, and ½ cup vinaigrette. Arrange in a large salad bowl the leaves of 1 head Boston lettuce and 1 large sliced tomato. Add potatoes, string beans, onion, and 2 cans best-quality tuna packed in oil. On top place 8 strips anchovy fillets, 30 small black olives, 2 hard-boiled eggs cut into quarters, 2 quartered ripe tomatoes, and sprinklings of chopped chives and parsley. SERVES 4–6.

VEGETABLE SALAD

For one salad tear a medium-size leaf each of chicory, escarole, and romaine. Arrange on a large dinner plate. At each of four corners place two slices of cucumber, and in the center of greens place two rings of green bell pepper. On one ring arrange half a shredded carrot, and on the other two small canned beets, also shredded. Building toward the center add the following: 2 Tb. sliced raw mushrooms, 2 Tb. chopped celery, 1 Tb. sliced radish, 4 or 5 cherry tomatoes. Crown with alfalfa sprouts.

CHICKEN SALAD WITH BACON

In a large salad bowl mix 1½ cups each shredded romaine and escarole with 3 cups diced boiled chicken breast and leg, 1 diced avocado, 2 diced hard-boiled eggs, ½ tsp. salt, ground pepper to taste, and 1 tsp. lemon juice. When ready to serve, add ¾ cup fresh mayonnaise and mix thoroughly. Divide equally on chilled salad plates, sprinkle with crumbled bacon, and surround with tomato wedges. SERVES 4–6.

VINAIGRETTE

For about 1 cup, place in a screw-top jar 3 Tb. wine vinegar, 1 Tb. fresh lemon juice, 12 Tb. good olive oil, ¼ tsp. salt, ½ tsp. dry mustard, pinch of pepper, and 2 Tb. minced parsley and tarragon (optional). Shake vigorously for 30 seconds. (For Garlic Vinaigrette, add ½ clove mashed garlic.)

FRESH MAYONNAISE

For about 2 cups, beat in a round-bottomed bowl 3 egg yolks (brought to room temperature) for 3 minutes. Add ¼ tsp. dry mustard, ½ tsp. salt, a few grinds white pepper, and 2 tsp. lemon juice and beat another minute. Drop by drop add ½ cup top-quality olive oil, beating constantly till sauce has thickened. Slowly add 1½ cups more oil, stopping from time to time to beat so the sauce gradually absorbs all the oil. (If necessary, thin sauce with droplets of lemon juice.) Transfer to airtight jar and refrigerate. Mayonnaise keeps about 6 days under refrigeration.

Louis Dressing

For about 1⅔ cups, combine 1 cup fresh mayonnaise with ⅓ cup whipped cream, ⅓ cup chili sauce, 1 Tb. grated onion, and a pinch of cayenne.

Hot Bacon Dressing

In a skillet brown 6 slices bacon cut crosswise in julienne strips. Remove, drain, then stir-fry 2 thinly sliced scallions (including some tops) in drippings 5 to 8 minutes. Add ½ cup red wine vinegar, 2 tsp. catsup, ½ tsp. salt, a few grinds of pepper, and stir 5 minutes. Pour dressing over salad, crumble bacon on top, and toss. Makes about 1 cup.

Herb Dressing

Combine ½ cup safflower oil, ½ tsp. salt, ground pepper to taste, 1 Tb. minced chives, ½ tsp. parsley, and a 1 Tb. mixture of minced dill, tarragon, and chervil. Let stand at room temperature 3–4 hours, add ¼ cup wine vinegar, and stir thoroughly. Makes about 1 cup.

Yogurt Dressing

For 1¼ cups, mix 1 cup yogurt with 2 Tb. white vinegar, ½ tsp. sugar, ½ tsp. salt, ¼ cup skim milk, 2 Tb. minced chives, and a pinch cayenne. Cover and chill well.

SOME LIKE IT COLD

●●●

OF ALL the culinary splendors of this world, few approached the sumptuous array of classic French cold dishes in the Chambord dining room aboard my beloved S.S. *France*. I used to look forward to nothing more than the extravagance of making three or four transatlantic crossings a year for the sole purpose of eating, and I never failed to be struck with wonder at the mouth-watering preparations displayed ceremoniously at the foot of the grand staircase. *Canard à l'orange* glistening in a *chaud-froid* sauce; a pheasant in plumage surrounded by aspic-coated quail breasts stuffed with *foie gras* and mousses; a giant poached turbot decorated with tomato roses, radish tulips, and olive delphinia; spiny lobsters surrounded by stuffed tomatoes and eggs; miniature lamb chops masked in *chaud-froid* and adorned with vegetable florets; artistic hedgehogs fashioned from *foie gras,* truffles, and slivered almonds. The spectacle was always overwhelming and illustrated perfectly a maxim of the French food writer Robert Courtine: "True gastronomy centers on cold dishes, which are of a more uplifting subtlety and sensibility than the hot. You can't cheat with a cold dish. It is the final goal."

Although I could never hope to find duplication of the cuisine served on the legendary *France,* certain unusual cold dishes sampled throughout years of travel still serve to stimulate the adrenaline when thoughts turn to this type of food. I can remember vividly savoring a luscious iced lobster soufflé at Mark's Club in London one winter evening, a savory hare pie at Simpson's, and a chilled kedgeree of smoked fish at the Connaught Grill. On the Greek island of Hydra, I've sat with relatives for hours in the shade, sharing both cool *moussaka* and spinach and cheese pie, while on the sun-drenched terrace of the Gritti Palace in Venice, nothing ever tasted better than cold *risotto* bursting with scampi and other fresh seafood, *vitello tonnato* adorned with those miniature Italian black olives, or a platter of thinly sliced beef *carpaccio* annointed with olive oil and freshly ground pepper. Once, at the noble Brenner's Park Hotel in Baden-Baden, a spectacular cold lunch involved cold white asparagus with Westphalian ham served on a wooden plank, gull eggs stuffed with minced chives and radishes and topped with smoked salmon, and cold blue trout decorated with crayfish tails and twigs of dill. I can't imagine returning South during the summer without having such cold regional specialities as shrimp paste, shrimp remoulade, *daube glacé,* and quails in aspic. And as far as France is concerned, superlatives would have to include the chilled stuffed goose neck I tucked away one evening just south of Limoges, the Troisgros brothers' marinated raw fish at Roanne, and a suave onion tart downed with Gewürztraminer outside an inn secluded in the hills of Alsace.

What I do find sad is that when it comes to cold food, so few American cooks ever manage to veer from an all too familiar syndrome: cold fried chicken, baked ham and turkey, three-bean salad, deviled eggs, congealed salads, crudités, potato salad, and the like—the implication being, I judge, that guests never expect much more when cold fare is served. Heaven knows, I'm the first to proclaim the merits of a perfect Club sandwich, a still-juicy chilled lobster, a well-seasoned veal loaf or steak tartare, and a striped bass left to cool in its court bouillon. But why not, I ask, produce truly memorable meals from time to time by serving imaginative cold main courses that are somewhat out of the ordinary, eminently satisfying, and representative of creative effort? Curiously enough, many dishes that are normally served hot can be just as good or better when served cold (quails stuffed with *foie gras* or grapes, braised sweetbreads, pasta, chicken tarragon), and while I'd never advocate taking this to the extreme by wantonly plopping any chilled leftover on the table, I have learned that a little experimentation can produce some very appetizing results.

Cantaloupe Stuffed with Shrimp

2½–3   lbs. fresh shrimp
1   Tb. caraway seeds
4–6   small cantaloupes
        Juice of 1 orange
2   Tb. finely chopped dill
2   Tb. chili sauce
1   Tb. brandy
4   Tb. olive oil
        Salt and freshly ground pepper to taste
2–3   tomatoes, serrated-cut, seeds and pulp removed
4–6   black olives, sliced
¼   cup fresh mayonnaise
¼   cup whipped cream

In salted water with caraway seeds bring shrimp to a boil, covered. Remove from heat, let cool, then shell and clean all but 4 to 6 shrimp. Serrate lids off melons, remove seeds and strings, and cut out flesh in balls. Set aside 4 to 6 balls. Place shrimp, remaining melon balls, orange juice, dill, chili sauce, brandy, oil, and salt and pepper in a large bowl and mix thoroughly. Fill each melon with the mixture and replace lids upside down, fixing each at an angle with a cocktail stick. Place half a tomato on each lid, arrange artistically a reserved unshelled shrimp and melon ball inside each tomato, and finish with a few slices of olive. Place melon on a bed of ice. Mix mayonnaise and cream and serve separately. SERVES 4–6.

Cold Pasta and Chicken with Vegetables

½   lb. vermicelli or spaghetti
1   cup Garlic Vinaigrette dressing (see p. 164)
10   fresh mushrooms, sliced
1   cup broccoli florets, blanched
1   cup fresh green peas, blanched
12–14   cherry tomatoes
2   cups boiled chicken, boned, skinned, and cubed
⅓   cup pine nuts
⅓   cup fresh chopped basil

Cook pasta *al dente* in plenty of boiling water, transfer to a mixing bowl, add ⅓ of vinaigrette dressing, toss, let cool, and chill at least 3 hours. In another bowl place remaining vinaigrette dressing, add vegetables, and stir to coat thoroughly. When ready to serve, add chicken to pasta, toss, add vegetables plus chopped basil, and toss once more. SERVES 4–6.

VEAL AND HAM PIE

	Hot-water pastry (double crust, any standard recipe)
	Softened butter or lard
2	lbs. lean veal, cut into cubes
1	lb. smoked ham, cut into cubes
2	oz. beef bouillon
2	oz. brandy
1½	tsp. grated lemon peel
¼	cup finely chopped parsley
1	tsp. ground sage
1	tsp. summer savory
2	Tb. minced scallions
2	tsp. salt
	Freshly ground pepper to taste
4	hard-boiled eggs
1	egg yolk combined with 1 Tb. cream
1	envelope unflavored gelatin
2	cups cold chicken stock

Preheat oven to 350° F. Rub sides and bottom of large loaf pan with butter or lard. In a large mixing bowl combine veal, ham, bouillon, brandy, and seasonings and toss. Roll out ⅔ of the pastry about 20 inches long and 10 inches wide and fit carefully into the pan, removing excess from edges. Fill pan half full with meat mixture, arrange eggs in a row down the center, and add remaining meat mixture to within one inch of the top. Roll out remaining pastry and fit snugly on top. Decorate with leaf-shaped pastry cutouts and brush with egg wash. Vent steam with funnel. Bake 2 hours. Mix gelatin into stock, heat, and pour through funnel. Chill at least 6 hours and serve in thick slices. SERVES 4–6.

SOUTHERN *DAUBE GLACÉE*

1 3-lb. boneless rump or bottom round roast, trimmed of fat
1 2-lb. veal steak, trimmed of fat
2 pig's feet, well cleaned
5 qts. water
3 sprigs parsley
3 onions, coarsely chopped
2 stalks celery with leaves, coarsely chopped
1 clove garlic, finely chopped
2 bay leaves
1 tsp. thyme
2 whole cloves, pounded
1 tsp. cayenne
   Salt to taste
½ cup sherry

Place beef in a heavy casserole, add cold water to cover, bring to a boil, skim, reduce heat, and simmer 3 hours. In another large casserole place veal and pig's feet, add water plus all other ingredients except sherry, bring to a boil, reduce heat, and simmer 4 hours or till meat of pig's feet falls from bones. Transfer veal and pig's feet to a chopping board and mince meat. Strain stock, remove bones, and stir in sherry. Remove beef from casserole, place in a deep bowl, pour in stock, add minced meats and distribute evenly, cool to room temperature, then chill at least 6 hours and preferably overnight to set. To serve, turn out on a platter and carve in thin slices. SERVES 4–6.

GINGER CHICKEN

1   3½-lb. chicken, cut up
1½ oz. seasoned flour
2   tsp. ground ginger
2   oz. butter
3   tsp. peanut oil
1½ cups chicken stock
½   cup heavy cream
    Preserved ginger

Mix flour with ginger and dredge chicken in this mixture. In a large skillet sauté chicken in the butter and oil till golden brown. Remove chicken from skillet, add remaining flour to blend well with butter and oil, gradually add chicken stock, and bring to a boil, stirring. Return chicken to skillet, cover, reduce heat, and simmer about 5 minutes. Transfer chicken to serving platter, stir cream into sauce, pour over chicken, and chill at least 2 hours. To serve, garnish with thin slices of preserved ginger. SERVES 4–6.

SALMON CURED WITH DILL

3   lbs. fresh salmon, cleaned and scaled
4   Tb. crushed black peppercorns
    Large bunch fresh dill, washed and shaken dry
¼   cup kosher salt
¼   cup sugar

Cut salmon in half lengthwise and remove both the backbone and all small bones. With heel of hand, work ½ the crushed pepper into the sides of the salmon pieces. In a deep enamel or glass casserole place half the fish skin-side down and place dill on top. In a bowl combine salt, sugar, and remaining pepper and sprinkle mixture over dill. Top with other half of fish, skin-side up, cover with foil, and weigh down evenly with a heavy platter topped with a cloth-covered brick or a few cans of food. Refrigerate 2 to 3 days, turning fish over every 12 hours and basting it thoroughly

with the accumulated marinade. When ready to serve, remove salmon from marinade, scrape away dill and seasonings from center, and dry with paper towels. Carve slices ¼-
inch thick and serve with lemon wedges and mustard sauce.
SERVES 4–6.

CURRIED LAMB OR PORK WITH CUCUMBERS AND RED CABBAGE

½   cup olive oil
3   Tb. white vinegar
3   Tb. minced chives
1   tsp. dry mustard
1   tsp. salt
    Freshly ground pepper to taste
3½ lbs. cooked lamb or pork, cut into slivers
1   cup fresh mayonnaise
1   tsp. curry powder
3   cups cucumbers, peeled, seeded, and diced
    Salt
3   cups shredded red cabbage
    Leaves of romaine, washed and dried

In a deep bowl combine olive oil, vinegar, chives, mustard,
salt, and pepper, blend well, add lamb or pork, and let marinate at room temperature 1 hour, tossing from time to time.
In another bowl combine mayonnaise with curry powder.
Place cucumbers in a colander, sprinkle with a little salt, and
let drain 30 minutes. In a large bowl combine the marinated
meat, cucumbers, and red cabbage, toss lightly, and serve
atop romaine leaves lining a platter. SERVES 4–6.

THE SUMMER COOLERS

•••••••••••••••••••••••••••••

MY VERY first awakening to the virtues of cold soup occurred some years ago on a sultry summer day in New York. A respected gastronome invited me to lunch in a small restaurant where he introduced me to the distinct differences between a hot and cold Billi-Bi. At table there arrived a service wagon with two large copper pots, one steaming over a small flame, the other sunk deeply in ice. When the hot soup was served, the aroma of mussels permeated the immediate area, but, strangely enough, what I noticed upon sampling the soup was not so much the mussels as the taste of scalded cream. Then came the exact same soup but this time cold. At first I was aware primarily of the silky texture, but after a few spoonfuls, not only did the exquisite flavor of mussels begin to surge forth but every other ingredient was clearly identifiable. A total transformation had taken place, and there was no doubt in my mind that the cold soup was far more appealing and indeed more refreshing than the hot.

Thereafter I developed a virtual addiction to cold soups, and although I perhaps still crave them more during the summer months than anytime else, I've always gone out of my way to have good ones throughout the year. The cold cherry soup, for instance, I once prepared in Bucks County, Pennsylvania from a peck of fresh ripe cherries delivered one morning by a neighboring farmer still lingers in my mind as a sublime soup which, for some reason, I've never been able to reproduce successfully. Although there are many foods of the South that beckon me home when summertime arrives, none do I appreciate more than the wonderful fresh fruits, vegetables, and seafood with which to make cold apple soup, watermelon soup, gazpacho, shrimp bisque, strawberry puree, and even an exotic cold peach soup flavored with kirsch. When my family leaves in a car to vacation on the Carolina coast, we are never without two large Mason jars of freshly made vichyssoise kept chilled in a cooler, and once we've settled into the beach house, rarely is a lunch served that doesn't at least include a cup of some cold soup like watercress spiked with garlic, tomato seasoned with lots of fresh basil, or cream of summer squash redolent of mace and cloves.

Since there are not that many restaurants that bother to prepare cold soups, I've always had to search far and wide for truly memorable examples. Curiously enough, I recall only a few outstanding cold soups in the three-star restaurants of France—including La Tour d'Argent in Paris, where the veritable passion of owner Claude Terrail is not his legendary ducks but soups! On the other hand, how could I ever forget the chilled cream of lettuce soup served one summer by an expatriate friend on an herb-scented hilltop overlooking Toulon, or the ice-cold endive soup I once shared on deck of the S.S. *France* with a still-terrified young woman fleeing the tyranny of an ill-chosen spouse. Elsewhere, memories of cold soups are even sharper: a watercress, lemon, and al-mond soup at Lacy's in London, a cream of asparagus at Krogs in Co-penhagen, an inimitable madrilene sipped in the garden of the Ritz in Madrid, the Billi-Bi at Maxim's in Paris (where the soup was created), a delicate cream of cucumber atop the St. Francis in San Francisco, a cantaloupe soup at The Bakery in Chicago, and the famous Senegalese at the "21" Club in New York. These all made for rare gustatory ad-venture, and I simply find it incomprehensible that more serious res-taurants don't strive to offer something more inspired than a pitiful gazpacho prepared helter-skelter or tired vichyssoise that would make its creator, Louis Diat, shudder.

No doubt there are many admirable virtues to a steaming bowl of borscht or a hot lobster bisque or a thick onion soup crusted with Gruyère, but palatably speaking, hot soup that is normally served and swallowed rapidly rarely has the ability to pique the taste buds and appetite as effectively as a cold one that is sipped slowly, held momen-tarily in the mouth, and allowed to render flavors that have mingled and mellowed while being chilled. And indeed, nothing is more calm-ing on a hot summer's day than a cool cup of carefully made vichyss-oise or cream of avocado, a bowl of vegetable-fresh gazpacho placed in crushed ice, or an elegant goblet of jellied consommé topped with a lit-tle caviar. They can be enjoyed in the dining room, around the pool, or on the patio, and perhaps the most appealing feature of serving cold soups is the fact that with today's electric blenders and food processors, preparation is basically simple and work time is cut in half. And given the bounty of fresh ingredients with which we're blessed in the United States almost year-round, it's really a shame for enthusiastic cooks not to experiment and create delectable soups.

"Only the pure in heart can make a good soup," proclaimed Beethoven. Well, I know not to what extent the purity of one's heart influences the success and failure of soup making, but had this great man of music made reference instead to the purity of one's stock, he'd have been right on target. Succinctly put, nobody can ever be serious about producing great soups—hot or cold—without acknowledging the supreme importance of homemade stocks. Sure, there are a number of fine soups that don't necessarily depend on a stock base, but, generally, a soup is only as good as the stock with which it is made. Most cookbooks will tell you that canned stocks (i.e., broths, consommés, bouillons) make for adequate substitutes. They don't, not even when effort is made to improve them by adding other ingredients and seasonings. Most of the vichyssoise, for example, that you find in restaurants reeks of canned chicken broth, but in the kitchens of such respectable places as The Four Seasons and The Coach House in New York, Le Perroquet and Les Nomades in Chicago, and Commander's Palace in New Orleans (all of which serve superlative cold soups), it would be unheard-of to work with anything but homemade chicken, beef, and fish stocks. No doubt it takes time to produce fine stocks in the home, but in the long run they not only guarantee the very best soups possible but also prove much more economical than the canned varieties. Furthermore, stocks made in quantities can be frozen easily for future use.

The recipes that follow are classic, and each, served with a crisp salad, bread, cheese, and a chilled beverage, makes for a delightful lunch—or for that matter, light dinner. Once you've mastered these recipes, you might then want to try cold versions of soups such as oxtail, lobster bisque spiked with brandy, cream of carrot with marjoram, zucchini, apple-lemon, and tomato bouillon with basil. After that, why not a spicy, cold cream of fresh sorrel, or a dilled yogurt soup, or creations involving fresh plums, melons, raspberries, and apricots? Indeed, the possibilities for cold soups are endless, requiring no more than a good blender or food processor, homemade stocks, and a bit of imagination.

Beef Stock (Consommé)

4   lbs. beef bones, cut into 3-inch pieces
3   carrots, sliced
3   onions, sliced
1   pig's foot or veal knuckle
2   tomatoes, chopped
2   leeks, chopped
3   cloves garlic, chopped
2   ribs celery, chopped
1   turnip, chopped
1   tsp. thyme
8   sprigs parsley
1   bay leaf
4   cloves
8   peppercorns
4   qts. cold water
1   Tb. salt
2   egg whites plus shell

Preheat oven to 450° F. In a roasting pan, brown in the oven for 30 minutes the beef bones with half the carrots and onions, then transfer to an 8–10 qt. stockpot. Discard fat from pan, deglaze with a little water, and pour juices into pot. Add pig's foot or veal knuckle, remaining carrots and onions, and all other ingredients except salt and egg whites. If necessary, add more water to cover by 3 inches, bring mixture to a boil for 15 minutes, reduce to simmer, skim off scum, cover partly, and simmer 2 hours. Add salt and simmer another 3 hours, adding more water if necessary. Strain broth into a large bowl, cool, chill thoroughly, and remove fat from top. To clarify stock (and produce a delicate consommé), pour into a large saucepan, add the 2 egg whites plus shell, beat lightly, bring to a boil, and simmer 15 minutes. Strain broth through double thickness of cheesecloth. Yield: 2 quarts. (Double or triple proportions if you plan to freeze stock for future use.)

CHICKEN STOCK

3   lbs. chicken necks, wings, and backs
4   qts. cold water
2   carrots, sliced
2   onions, sliced
2   ribs celery, chopped
2   leeks, chopped
1   tsp. thyme
6   sprigs, parsley
4   cloves
8   peppercorns

Place chicken in an 8–10 qt. stockpot, add water, bring to a boil, simmer uncovered 30 minutes, and skim scum. Add vegetables and seasonings, simmer gently for 3 hours, strain through double thickness cheesecloth, and cool uncovered. Chill thoroughly in refrigerator overnight and remove all fat from top. Yield: 2 quarts. (Double or triple proportions if you plan to freeze stock for future use.)

FISH STOCK

1   carrot, sliced
1   onion, sliced
2   ribs celery, chopped
2   Tb. butter
    Salt to taste
2   cups dry white wine
3   cups water
2   tsp. lemon juice
2   lbs. washed lean fish bones (bass, scrod, cod, or flounder),
    tails, and heads
    Celery leaves
8   sprigs parsley
1   tsp. chervil
1   bay leaf
3   cloves
6   white peppercorns

In a large skillet sauté the carrots, onions, and celery in butter till soft and salt lightly. Add wine, water, and all other ingredients. Bring slowly to a boil, reduce heat immediately, and simmer gently no more than 30 minutes. Skim off scum and strain through double thickness of cheesecloth. Yield: 1 quart. (Double or triple proportions if you plan to freeze stock for future use.)

APPLE VICHYSSOISE THE FOUR SEASONS

4½	tart apples, peeled, cored, and quartered
	Juice of 1 lemon
1	cup dry white wine
2	cinnamon sticks
3	thin slices fresh ginger
5	Tb. sugar
1	Tb. applejack
¼	cup sour cream
1	cup beef consommé
1	cup heavy cream
½	tsp. kosher salt

Cut two quarters of apple into fine julienne, sprinkle with half the lemon juice, and set aside. Place remaining apple quarters, the wine, cinnamon, ginger, and sugar in a heavy saucepan, bring to a boil, cover pan, lower heat to medium, and cook 10 minutes or till apples are thoroughly cooked. Let cool, then remove and discard the cinnamon sticks and ginger. Place apples and their cooking liquid in a food processor or blender, add applejack and sour cream, and process till smooth. With machine running, pour in beef stock in a slow, steady stream, then pour cream in the same way. Blend in remaining lemon juice and salt. Place in refrigerator to chill thoroughly and serve in chilled bowls topped with raw julienned apple. SERVES 6.

COLD STRAWBERRY CREAM SOUP

3   cups fresh strawberries, washed and stemmed
1½   cups water
1½   cups white wine
½   cup sugar
2   Tb. fresh lemon juice
1½   Tb. cornstarch mixed in 1½ Tb. cold water
3   tsp. grated lemon zest
¼   cup sour cream

Slice all but 6 strawberries. Combine sliced berries, water, and wine and simmer in a covered saucepan about 10 minutes. Add sugar, lemon juice, and cornstarch, heat to a boil, and stir till thickened. Transfer mixture in two equal amounts to a blender, add grated lemon zest and sour cream, and blend till smooth. Cool, taste for sugar, and chill thoroughly. Serve in crystal soup bowls and top each portion with a whole strawberry. SERVES 4–6.

SENEGALESE

1   carrot, chopped
1   onion, chopped
1   rib celery, chopped
2   Tb. butter
1   Tb. flour
1   Tb. curry powder
4   cups chicken stock
    Paprika
½   Tb. almond paste
1   cinnamon stick
5   cloves
3   egg yolks, beaten
1   cup heavy cream, chilled
    Chutney

In a skillet sauté carrots, onions, and celery in the butter till soft, add flour and curry powder, and stir till well blended. Stir in chicken stock and bring to a boil. Reduce heat, season with paprika, add almond paste, cinnamon stick, and cloves and simmer about ½ hour. Add a little of the mixture to the beaten egg yolks, stir, add to mixture, and stir till slightly thickened. Strain through double cheesecloth, cool, then chill thoroughly. Before serving in chilled soup cups, taste for salt and blend in cream. Garnish each serving with a little chutney. SERVES 4–6.

GAZPACHO

2	large tomatoes, peeled and seeded
1	large green pepper, seeded and sliced
1	large Spanish onion, sliced
1	large cucumber, peeled and sliced
1	clove garlic, peeled and halved
½	cup mixed herbs (parsley, basil, tarragon, and chives)
½	cup olive oil
¼	cup red wine vinegar
3	Tb. lime juice
¼	tsp. Tabasco
1½	tsp. salt
4	cups beef consommé
½	cup dry bread croutons
¼	cup chopped parlsey

In a blender or food processor fitted with steel blade, puree one-half the vegetables along with one-half the garlic, mixed herbs, half the olive oil and vinegar. Transfer mixture to a large bowl, add lime juice, Tabasco, salt, and consommé and mix thoroughly. Chill soup at least 2 hours and adjust seasoning. Rub skillet with remaining garlic, add remaining olive oil, and sauté croutons till brown. Chop remaining vegetables. Pour soup into chilled bowls, add chopped vegetables to each bowl, and garnish with parsley. SERVES 4–6.

BILLI-BI

6   doz. unshelled mussels, scrubbed in cold water
4   cups fish stock
1   cup dry white wine
2   carrots, sliced
3   onions, chopped
3   ribs celery, chopped
¾   lb. mushrooms, chopped
½   cup chopped parsley
¼   tsp. white pepper
       Salt to taste
1½   cups light cream, scalded

In a deep, heavy pot combine mussels with fish stock, white wine, vegetables, and seasonings. Bring slowly to a boil, reduce heat, cover, and simmer about 4 minutes or till mussels open (discard any that don't). Set aside and allow to cool. Remove mussels and reserve for another use. Strain broth through double cheesecloth into a clean pan, bring to a rapid boil, and cook till reduced by half. Lower heat, stir in cream, cool, then chill thoroughly. Adjust seasoning. SERVES 4–6.

COLD BORSCHT

6   cups beef stock
5   beets, peeled and grated
1   carrot, sliced
2   onions, chopped
1   Tb. sherry
1   Tb. vinegar
1½   cups sour cream
       Freshly ground black pepper to taste
       Salt to taste
3   beets, lightly cooked, cut in julienne and chilled
2   cucumbers, peeled, seeded, cut in julienne, and chilled
       Fresh dill, chopped

In a large pot pour beef stock, add grated beets, carrots, onions, sherry, vinegar, 1 cup of the sour cream, and black pepper. Bring to a boil, reduce heat, and simmer gently 20–30 minutes. Strain through double cheesecloth, cool, then chill thoroughly. Taste for salt. Divide julienne beets and cucumbers among chilled soup plates, add soup, and garnish each portion with dollops of remaining sour cream and chopped dill. SERVES 4–6.

JELLIED CONSOMMÉ WITH CAVIAR

1   envelope unflavored gelatin
4   cups beef consommé
    Fresh American sturgeon or salmon caviar

In a saucepan soften gelatin in 1 cup of the consommé, heat slightly, and stir till gelatin is completely dissolved. Pour into a 3-qt. baking dish, add remaining consommé, stir thoroughly, then chill 5–6 hours or till firm. To serve, cut consommé into cubes, spoon into large crystal goblets, and top each portion with caviar. SERVES 4–6.

PEARL BYRD FOSTER'S LIME GLACÉ

6   cups chicken stock
1   medium onion, sliced
2   stalks celery (leaves included), chopped
5   cloves garlic, crushed
3   sprigs parsley
3   tsp. unflavored gelatin
8   Tb. fresh lime juice, strained
3   drops Tabasco
1   cup heavy cream, whipped
2   Tb. candied ginger, chopped

Pour chicken stock into a large pot, add onions, celery, and garlic, bring to a boil, reduce heat, and simmer 1 hour. Drop parsley to wilt in stock, remove and transfer to blender with 1 cup of the stock, blend well, and return to pot. Stir mixture well, then pour through a fine sieve into a large bowl, pressing with back of spoon to get all liquid. Dissolve gelatin in ¼

cup water, add to hot liquid, and stir till dissolved completely. Cool to room temperature, stir in lime juice and
Tabasco, and chill till thickened. Serve in icy-cold glass cups
or bowls topped with generous dollops of cream. Garnish
each portion with 1 tsp. candied ginger. SERVES 4–6.

VEGETABLE
ARISTOCRAT

●●●●●●●●●●●●●●●●●●●●●●●●●●●

GENERALLY NO one on earth exercises more patience and self-control than the dedicated gastronome yearning for foods available only certain times of the year. On the whole, I take nature's careful rationing in stride, knowing that year-round there are at least ample quantities of fresh salmon and oysters, country ham, caviar and champagne to carry me through the most frustrating times when an ephemeral delicacy I crave is absent from the markets.

Somehow I manage to wait calmly for summer's ripe, tough-skinned tomatoes, lima beans, raspberries, Elberta peaches and Pecos cantaloupes; for autumn's succulent wild game, sensuous persimmons and Beaujolais nouveau; and for winter's fresh *foie gras* and truffles. Where my defenses almost give way, however, is shortly after Christmas when thoughts turn to fresh asparagus. Ah, *les asperges, die Spargeln, gli asparagi!* Whatever the language, asparagus signifies bliss. I make periodic phone calls to friends in Southern California to learn whether or not the green beauties have shown up yet in supermarkets, and I do everything but bribe the owners of speciality food shops in an effort to be notified the instant the first fresh supply arrives, toward the end of February or early March. Why not settle for canned asparagus? Well, let's just say that as far as I'm concerned, canned asparagus is to fresh as cosmetic surgery is to true beauty.

For most people, the arrival of spring is heralded by the appearance of lilacs and daffodils, the sound of the cuckoo, and the awakening of the vine, but for me nothing signifies nature's rebirth like the first fresh asparagus. Lightly boiled and buttered, steamed and christened with hollandaise, tucked into omelettes, blended into salads, pureed into soup, or dipped cold into a tingling vinaigrette, this aristocrat of vegetables has the same earthy subtlety as truffles and morels, the versatility of crayfish and caviar, and the mystery and delicacy of *foie gras*. Asparagus can be pencil-thin or fat as a banana, dark green to lavender to ivory, and sweetly mellow or spicily acidic. All true asparagus lovers have their preferences as to size, color, and taste, but I doubt there's one who, obsessed with consuming as many spears as possible before the season ends, would ever hesitate to eat whatever example might be served—so long, that is, as the fragile vegetable has been neither overcooked nor maligned by some alien sauce or adornment.

Given the choice, I'd most likely opt for the type of giant lavender Italian asparagus to which I was introduced years ago by none other than Charles Ritz at his famous hotel in Paris. On the other hand, I swoon over the rare opportunity to savor the celestial whites grown underground in Belgium, Holland, and Germany, the green Lau: 's and pink Argenteuil from France, or the English Suffolks. When some considerate soul cares enough to bring me a supply of the extraordinarily thin green shoots that are indigenous to New England and best eaten raw, I create a special occasion. Just let me hear of a restaurant that happens to be serving wild asparagus (the species I know best is called "Jersey grass"), and I'm the first to call and request that an order be kept aside. As for my blessed mainstay—the luscious green asparagus of California—my refrigerator is never without a couple of bunches from early March to late May, and I think nothing of paying as much as six bucks a pound for jumbo stalks, even in April.

Historically, the popularity of asparagus can be traced as far back as the ancients—and possibly even further in the Orient. The Romans had a particular fondness for the wild variety; Juvenal found nothing more delectable for dinner that "a plump kid with more of milk in him than blood, some wild asparagus, lordly eggs warm in their wisps of hay together with the hens that laid them, and grapes, pears, and apples to end with." Asparagus was considered a delicacy on any feast table in Renaissance Italy and France, and Louis XIV prized this member of the lily family so much that when his gardener at Versailles, Quintinie, perfected a system whereby it could be produced year-round, the king bestowed a title on him. For over a century the town of Schwetzingen has been respected as the asparagus capital of Germany, but had Elector Karl Theodor not taken extraordinary measures to cultivate his massive castle garden in the late eighteenth century, it's quite possible that these famous white *Spargeln,* nurtured beneath the earth, might never have existed. As for America, asparagus was as much appreciated by generations of settlers as chowder, maple syrup, coleslaw, and apple pie—so much so, in fact, that by the late nineteenth century one of the most fashionable dishes in upper social circles was "ambushed asparagus" (tucked into cut-out rolls with an offbeat version of hollandaise and preferably served with green-pea pancakes and Bermuda potatoes *en robe de chambre*).

To suggest that Europeans demonstrate toward asparagus a reverence that no longer exists in the United States would be something of an understatement. To be sure, most Americans enjoy having this vegetable from time to time, but, curiously enough, very few think of it as anything more than a casual side dish that makes a nice change from salad or beans. Europeans, by contrast, show the same enthusiasm for fresh asparagus as for such other luxury greens as cardoons and arugula, making a big to-do over the stalks when they first appear in early spring and celebrating the season by holding asparagus festivals. Although the giant *Spargeln* are featured in restaurants all over Germany and Switzerland during April and May, the center of activity is still Schwetzingen, a few kilometers from Heidelberg. Not even at the castle restaurant do they cook the white shoots in champagne as Karl Theodor always preferred, but it's not out of the ordinary to meet chefs in town who insist the only way to maintain purity is by using mineral water.

Asparagus lovers the world over flock to Malines in Belgium to sample what many connoisseurs consider to be the finest whites anywhere. In Holland, both the regions of Zeeland and Limburg have festivals throughout May and June, but since the Dutch fear nothing more than the possible consequences of publicizing their limited treasure of white asparagus, rarely is the subject even mentioned in guidebooks and brochures. Very fine Italian asparagus is cultivated around Genoa, but, come springtime, dedicated enthusiasts know the best green *asparagi* are at Pescia near Montecatini in Tuscany. And there's no better example of the lavender-tipped white variety than that served every way imaginable in the restaurants of Ravenna. France is the only country I know that has both an asparagus society based on membership (the Confrérie de l'Asperge) and an asparagus museum (at Argenteuil). But then only in France do you find sophisticates (mainly in April at the Hotel de l'Univers at Argenteuil) who will spend hours on end debating the distinct differences between such varieties as Lauris, Argenteuil, Candes, Laon, and Marmande.

Given the wide variety and quality of asparagus grown in this country (the well-known French chef, Jean Troisgros, has pronounced

American asparagus the finest in the world), it's a shame more restaurants don't make the effort to celebrate this distinguished vegetable. Unfortunately, few Americans will ever have the opportunity to sample fresh white asparagus on home territory for the simple reason that unlike fifty years ago, when plenty of whites were cultivated in California, the Northwest, and the Midwest, the little that is produced today in California is either consumed in the region or processed for canning. On the other hand, we should all be proud of our glorious green asparagus: the Martha Washington and Washington species that grow in profusion in Pennsylvania, New Jersey, and New England; the thin, dark varieties cultivated throughout the South and Midwest; and, above all, the superb California jumbos so esteemed by aficionados.

In addition to being simply a delicious vegetable, asparagus is also beneficial to sound health and ideal for those trying to take off weight with as little misery as possible. Although the white variety raised underground contains very little vitamin C due to the absence of chlorophyll, both white and green asparagus are relatively high in vitamin A, riboflavin, calcium, phosphorus, thiamine, niacin, and protein. The agent asparagine acts as a gentle stimulant to kidney function, the high percentage of water (about 93 percent) helps to normalize the fluid balance of the body and increase hemoglobin in the blood, and the fibrous texture provides an excellent source of roughage. Since eight asparagus stalks contain no more than about twenty calories, dieters can feast with abandon, relieved to learn that this is one green vegetable as flavorful by itself as when dressed with butter or sauce.

While fresh green asparagus is widely available in this country from March to early summer, without a doubt the finest stalks are those found during April and May. After this time asparagus begins to lose its fresh, pungent flavor, and once it begins to blossom, it's virtually tasteless. When shopping, look for fully green, firm, crisp stalks that have moist cut ends and closed, compact tips. I prefer fat asparagus not only because it always seems more juicy but also because it's easier to handle and less is wasted when peeled. Whether you prefer thick or thin, remember always to select asparagus of the same size to assure even timing in cooking and an eye-pleasing presentation. When markets mix sizes in bundles, insist on being allowed to pick and choose as you please.

There are many schools of thought about preparing asparagus for cooking. Some people prefer simply to bend the stalks until they break to separate the tender tips from the tough ends; others use a potato peeler to cut away the exterior of the butts and remove scales that might contain sand; and still others peel the ends with a knife and soak the stalks to remove dirt. I'm against the breaking technique since there's plenty of moist, edible flesh inside the butt. Nor do I like to remove the scales, which can be easily cleaned by thorough rinsing and which I find attractive. Usually a potato peeler works fine on thin stalks, but to shave off the hard outer flesh on the butts of jumbos (graduating the cut upward from the base), nothing does the job better than a small, sharp paring knife.

As for cooking asparagus, there's only one absolute, steadfast rule: do not overcook. Nothing on earth looks or tastes worse than a limp, soggy, overcooked asparagus. Many enthusiasts prefer to protect the delicate tips by steaming the stalks upright in either an asparagus steamer or inverted double boiler, but I still get the best results by plunging asparagus (loose or tied in bundles, depending on the quantity) into a skillet or kettle of boiling, salted water, setting the side of the vessel containing the tips slightly off the eye of the heat, boiling slowly until barely tender, and draining on a clean napkin or towel. Perhaps the best test for judging whether or not asparagus is adequately cooked is to lift it gently with a fork after about four or five minutes. If it bends slightly, it's done; and if the butts have been peeled properly, the entire stalk is edible.

Much has been said and written about the correct way to eat boiled or steamed asparagus. But I, for one, couldn't imagine eating asparagus—with or without sauce—any other way but with my fingers.

Nothing is more glorious than asparagus served either *au naturel* with a little butter and lemon or with a classic hollandaise, mousseline, or maltaise sauce. On the other hand, since this versatile vegetable can be used to enhance any number of preparations, what more exciting idea than to hold your own spring asparagus festival at home and compose an entire eight-course menu featuring this verdant aristocrat? Portions, of course, should be small, and unless you have adequate staff, guests should be limited to those close friends who'd enjoy dining informally and, when necessary, lending a hand in the kitchen. The recipes that follow could be utilized for any occasion, but to produce all eight dishes for a single meal not only would pay homage to a great delicacy but could also be lots of fun. As for the asparagus ice cream, those who might accuse me of excess fantasy should be relieved to know that its creator was none other than Monsieur Escoffier.

MENU
Fried Asparagus Cocktail Appetizers
Cream of Asparagus Soup
Open-Face Asparagus Omelette
Fillets of Sole with Asparagus and Almonds
Aromatic Cold Asparagus
Stir-Fry Asparagus and Beef
Asparagus Rolls with Ham and Monterey Jack
Asparagus Ice Cream

FRIED ASPARAGUS COCKTAIL APPETIZER

1½   lbs. asparagus, peeled, rinsed, and dried
1½   cups peanut oil
1   whole egg, beaten
1   cup fine bread crumbs
      Salt

Heat oil very hot in a skillet, adding more, if necessary, to cover thickest part of asparagus. One by one, dip asparagus into egg, roll in bread crumbs, and fry 1 minute on each side, making sure not to crowd the pan. As each spear finishes cooking, drain on paper towels, salt to taste, cover lightly, and serve hot. SERVES 4–6.

CREAM OF ASPARAGUS SOUP

1½   lbs. asparagus, peeled, rinsed, and cut into ½-inch dice—2-inch tips reserved
3   Tb. butter
¼   cup shallots or onions, minced
1   clove garlic, minced
6   cups chicken stock
1   cup heavy cream
2–3 Tb. arrowroot (optional)
      Salt and cayenne to taste

In a skillet sauté diced asparagus, shallots, and garlic in butter till limp. Steam asparagus tips 3 minutes in 1 cup chicken stock, strain stock into sautéed asparagus, and set tips aside. Add remaining stock to asparagus and simmer 8–10 minutes. Put asparagus through blender and pour through a fine sieve. Add cream and optional arrowroot, stir, and heat but do not boil. Add tips, season to taste, and serve in hot tureens with cheese biscuits or rye crisps. SERVES 4–6.

OPEN-FACE ASPARAGUS OMELETTE

1½   lbs. asparagus, peeled and rinsed
3   Tb. butter
1   Tb. parsley, finely chopped
1   Tb. chives, finely chopped
     Salt, freshly ground pepper, and nutmeg to taste
12   eggs
4   Tb. heavy cream
1   lemon, quartered

Cook asparagus till barely tender, drain, and cut on the bias into thick slivers. Melt butter in a skillet, add asparagus, herbs, and seasonings, and sauté lightly. Break eggs into a bowl, add cream, and beat till blended. Pour mixture over asparagus in skillet, and raise edges of omelette with a fork till eggs are set. Place a round serving platter over skillet, and turn out omelette bottom-side up. Garnish the dish with lemon wedges. SERVES 4–6.

FILLETS OF SOLE WITH ASPARAGUS AND ALMONDS

1   lb. asparagus, peeled and rinsed
5   tomatoes
1   Tb. vegetable or peanut oil
2   tsp. garlic, finely chopped
1   tsp. tarragon
    Salt and freshly ground pepper to taste
8   fillets of sole or flounder
    Flour for dusting
6   Tb. butter
¾   cup slivered almonds, blanched and browned

Cook asparagus till barely tender and set aside to drain. Skin tomatoes and chop coarsely. Heat oil in a skillet, add tomatoes, garlic, tarragon, and salt and pepper, and sauté lightly. Transfer mixture to a serving dish, arrange whole asparagus on top, and place in warm oven. Dust sole fillets in flour, season lightly with salt and pepper, and, in another skillet, brown quickly in butter on each side. Arrange fillets on top of asparagus and tomatoes, toss almonds in pan sole was cooked in, and sprinkle almonds over fish. Serve very hot. SERVES 4–6.

AROMATIC COLD ASPARAGUS

1½ lbs. thick asparagus, peeled and rinsed
⅓   cup top-grade olive oil
1   cup onion, chopped
½   tsp. thyme
    Pinch powdered fennel
2   bay leaves
    Zest of 1 lemon cut into strips
½   tsp. peppercorns
½   cup white wine or vermouth
¼   cup wine vinegar
2   cups water
½   tsp. salt
    Chopped chives

In a saucepan sauté about 10 minutes in olive oil the onions, garlic, herbs, and lemon strips. Add peppercorns, wine, vinegar, water, and salt, and simmer slowly, covered, about 20 minutes. Arrange asparagus in oval sauté pan or flameproof casserole, pour on the marinade, bring to a boil, and simmer covered about 10 minutes or till asparagus is tender but not overcooked. Remove asparagus and arrange on platter. Reduce liquid by half, pour over asparagus, and chill thoroughly before serving sprinkled with chopped chives. SERVES 4–6.

STIR-FRY ASPARAGUS AND BEEF

Marinade

1   Tb. light soy sauce
1   Tb. dry sherry
½   tsp. sugar
1½   Tb. cornstarch dissolved in 2 Tb. water
1   Tb. peanut oil

Sauce

1   Tb. light soy sauce
1   Tb. oyster sauce
2   tsp. cornstarch dissolved in 3 Tb. water and 2 tsp. peanut
     oil

1   lb. flank steak
1   lb. asparagus, peeled and rinsed
2   cups peanut oil
1   quarter-sized slice ginger, peeled and chopped
1   clove garlic, peeled and smashed
½   tsp. salt
½   tsp. sugar
1   Tb. dry sherry
⅓   cup water

Mix marinade and sauce. Cut meat into thin strips and marinate in refrigerator at least 30 minutes. Cut asparagus on the bias into 1½-inch pieces, leaving tips intact. Heat oil until very hot in a wok or large skillet, scatter in the beef, toss about 15 seconds till whitened, transfer to a plate, and reserve for another use all but 2 Tb. oil. Add ginger and garlic to wok or skillet, press into oil, scatter in the asparagus, and toss briskly about 1 minute. Add salt, sugar, and sherry and stir well. Add water, even out the ingredients, cover, and steam for 1 minute. Uncover, add beef, and toss contents rapidly. Add sauce and stir till meat and vegetables are smoothly glazed with sauce. SERVES 4–6. (Adapted from Irene Kuo's *The Key to Chinese Cooking:* Knopf, 1977.)

ASPARAGUS ROLLS WITH HAM AND MONTEREY JACK

12–15	thick asparagus, peeled, rinsed, parboiled 5 minutes, and drained
½	lb. boiled or lightly cured ham, thinly sliced
½	lb. Monterey Jack cheese, thinly sliced
8	Tb. butter

Place 3 asparagus on top 1 slice ham, then place 1 slice cheese plus 1 Tb. butter to cover asparagus. Wrap ham carefully around asparagus and secure with a miniature skewer or toothpick. Prepare other packets in like manner. Grease bottom of small casserole or baking pan with 2 Tb. butter, arrange packets in vessel, place 2 crisscrossed slices of cheese on top each packet, and dot each with remaining butter. Bake in a 400° F oven for 20 minutes or till tops begin to crust. Baste once before serving very hot. SERVES 4–6.

ASPARAGUS ICE CREAM

½	lb. asparagus tips, thoroughly rinsed
1½	cups sugar
10	egg yolks
1	qt. whole milk, boiling

Parboil asparagus tips 3–4 minutes, drain, and blend to a paste in electric blender or food processor. In a saucepan work sugar and egg yolks with a wooden spoon till mixture becomes thick and draws out in ribbon form. Little by little dilute with boiling milk and stir over moderate heat till mixture coats withdrawn spoon (do not allow to boil). Set asparagus paste to steep 30 minutes in milk. Transfer mixture to a stainless steel mixing bowl and stir over ice till very cold. Place in refrigerator till ready to serve in stemmed goblets. SERVES 4–6.

DRESSING FOR DINNER

●●●

OF ALL the foods we've come to associate with the holidays, certainly none is more misunderstood and abused than the stuffing served with the traditional roasted turkey. No doubt some cooks take as much pride in "the fixings" as in the turkey itself, but, unfortunately, far too many people, confronted with the necessity of stuffing a large fowl, do no more than haphazardly mix a mound of white sandwich bread with onions, celery, a bit of seasoning, and water, the inevitable result being a soggy, bland dressing that would be virtually inedible without the camouflaging benefits of giblet gravy.

Equally distressing is the fact that so few Americans ever attempt to stuff anything other than a turkey for their festive dinner. Surely no one enjoys a great turkey feast any more than myself (if, that is, the stuffing has been treated with the same respect as the golden bird), but from time to time nothing comes as a more welcomed change or solicits the acclaim of guests more than some other fowl, meat, or fish with an imaginative dressing prepared with interest and care. A fine country ham, a fat juicy goose, a noble crown roast of pork, a brace of pheasant, even a large pike or striped bass—all make for adventurous eating and all lend themselves beautifully to a wide variety of mouth-watering stuffings.

Historically, the use of stuffings and forcemeats to add flavor, stretch meat, correct fattiness or dryness, or make a main dish out of minor ingredients can be traced back at least as far as the Romans, who, according to one source, were particularly fond of jugged pigeon stuffed with figs as well as quail dressed with a mixture of liver, mushrooms, breads and grapes. Although the Roman occupation of Gaul most assuredly had some influence on the various stuffed foods recorded from the Middle Ages in France (the centuries-old Parisian restaurant, Le

Tour d'Argent, for example, specialized in plum-stuffed cranes in the fifteenth century), nowhere did the practice of stuffing foods catch on more quickly than in England. From the fourteenth century through the eighteenth century, what characterized English "high cooking" more than anything else were the exotic forcemeats and dressings that graced the banquet tables. Saddles of mutton were stuffed with kidneys and herbs; huge carp and salmon swelled with either a fennel or tarragon bread stuffing or a panada (bread dressing soaked in milk) enriched with thyme, chives, and ground fish; whole pigs doubled in weight from the addition of apples, onions, and suet; and at one seventeenth-century festival, the stuffed dishes carried ceremoniously into the great hall involved nothing less than a cygnet, turkey, pig, kid ("with a pudding in his belly"), goose, sea bream, haunch of venison, and leg of mutton. Little wonder that during the eighteenth century (the golden age of English cookery) the world looked upon the British Isles as the most gastronomically extravagant nation on earth, and little wonder that during the following century the infamously rich dish known as quails *à la financière* (stuffed with liver forcemeat and truffles, glazed with a Madeira-enriched *demi-glace* sauce, and served on croutons) made its debut not in France but at the court of Queen Victoria.

In regional America the stuffings might not be so exotic as those of our ancestors, but some are nevertheless worthy of the attention of anyone seriously interested in developing new ideas in the kitchen. Two of the most popular dishes in New England are cod stuffed with a breaded oyster dressing and haddock filled with minced clams, onions, and crumbed crackers. In the Upper Midwest, the heroic pike is most often served with a stuffing of bread, apples, mushrooms, eggs, and herbs, while on the West Coast seafood connoisseurs love nothing more than a large rex sole made even more corpulent by a mixture of Olympia oysters and shredded Dungeness crab. In Bucks County, Pennsylvania I've enjoyed more than one pheasant dressed with chestnuts and juniper berries, as well as the Pennsylvania Dutch speciality of duck stuffed with highly seasoned mashed potatoes. And in my native South, the variety of good stuffings found from the Carolinas to Louisiana is enough to make any estranged rebel long for home: roast quail puffed with oysters and sage; flounder, Spanish mackerel, red snapper, pompano, and red fish stuffed with everything from shrimp to oysters to crabs.

Whichever viand you plan to stuff with whatever dressing, there are a few general tips you might do well to follow:

• • • Rich stuffings go best with the more bland fowls, meat, and fish, whereas light stuffings should be used for heavier foods.

• • • To avoid food poisoning, never mix stuffing till ready to use, and never stuff a bird, roast, or fish till ready to cook. Equally important, always remove stuffing after the meal and refrigerate separately.

• • • Contrary to what many cookbooks say, the use of any raw pork product in a stuffing or forcemeat is only asking for trouble. To taste a stuffing for seasoning, always sauté beforehand till well cooked.

• • • In estimating the amount of stuffing to prepare, a good rule of thumb is ¾ cup per pound of fowl, meat, or fish and 1 cup per pound if you choose to cook extra stuffing separately.

• • • Always spoon stuffing in lightly, allowing plenty of space for expansion while cooking, and don't forget that all stuffed foods require extra cooking time.

• • • By far the best bread to use for bread stuffings is homemade, day-old bread or freshly baked corn bread. Overly soft commercial bread that is not toasted usually produces a soggy, heavy dressing when mixed with liquids. As for bread crumbs, the term "dry" refers to bread dried in the oven, whereas "soft" indicates two- to four-day-old bread that has been either soaked or browned in butter. Most commercial bread crumbs are perfectly acceptable for stuffings.

• • • To cook extra stuffing, spoon into a lightly greased pan and bake uncovered for approximately one hour.

Basic Corn Bread Stuffing for Roast Turkey

There are turkey stuffings, and there are turkey stuffings, but none, I hold, is quite as celestial as the one on which I was weaned and which, in fine Southern tradition, my mother still prepares with absolutely no regard for measurements. "I can give you all the basics," she instructed, "but if you insist on measuring the ingredients, you'll just have to figure out the amount yourself. Remember one thing, though: don't forget to toast the bread and simmer the vegetables very slowly for at least one-and-a-half-hours." The following recipe, for the body cavity, is the agonizing result of repeated testing and represents, I pray, a good approximation of the original. The recipe for dressing the neck cavity was inspired by James Beard. Both make enough stuffing for a 12–15 pound turkey with enough left to fill an 8-inch pan.

Body Cavity

4	cups chopped celery
2	cups minced onions
	Chicken or turkey broth (fresh or canned) to cover
1	stick butter
7	cups toasted and crumbled bread
7	cups crumbled fresh corn bread
1	Tb. salt
2	tsp. freshly ground pepper
2	tsp. sage or poultry seasoning
1	cup finely chopped parsley
5	eggs, beaten

Place celery and onions in a large saucepan, add chicken or turkey stock to cover plus stick of butter, simmer very slowly about 1½ hours, and let cool. In the meantime, combine in a large bowl the toasted bread and corn bread, pour vegetables and liquid into bread mixture, add seasonings, parsley, and eggs and mix thoroughly with hands till texture is smooth (adding more broth for greater moisture).

Additional ingredients might include one or two of the following:

4	cups fresh oysters, whole or chopped
4	cups clams, whole or chopped
2	cups sliced mushrooms, sautéed
2	cups chestnuts, pecans, almonds, or filberts, roasted and chopped
2	cups black olives, chopped
2	cups fresh whole cranberries, cooked
½	cup Bourbon

Neck Cavity

2	lbs. sausage meat
1½	tsp. salt
1	tsp. thyme
1	tsp. Tabasco
1	tsp. ground coriander
1	tsp. freshly ground pepper
¾	cup pine nuts
½	cup finely chopped parsley

Combine sausage meat with other ingredients, mix well, cook over medium heat till brown (stirring occasionally and breaking up with a fork), and drain off excess fat.

SAUSAGE AND PRUNE STUFFING FOR CROWN ROAST OF PORK

One of the incontestably spectacular American dishes is a regal crown roast of pork which, when filled with a bold stuffing, makes for a truly stylish feast. Although traditional stuffings would include such variations as apples and onions or chestnuts and kumquats, the one below, which reflects both Scandinavian and American Midwestern tastes, is particularly delicious. The recipe yields enough stuffing for an 8-9 pound roast (about 20 ribs).

2	lbs. sausage meat
½	cup diced onions
½	cup diced celery
½	cup cooked and chopped prunes
1	cup bread crumbs, soft
2	Tb. light brown sugar
½	cup chopped parsley
½	tsp. sage
½	tsp. cinnamon
1½	tsp. salt
	Freshly ground pepper to taste
1	egg, beaten
¼	cup chopped apricots

In a large, heavy skillet cook sausage meat (breaking up with a fork) till brown, drain on paper towels, and reserve 3 Tb. fat. In same skillet sauté onions and celery till golden. Transfer sausage, onions, and celery to a large mixing bowl, add remaining ingredients, mix thoroughly, and check seasoning. Fill center of crown roast with stuffing during last hour of baking. Garnish with chopped apricots.

TANGERINE AND YAM STUFFING FOR ROAST DUCK

Not only is duck now readily available in most markets, but it also lends itself to any number of fruit, vegetable, or rice stuffings. Forget the overworked orange, cherry, and wild rice dressings, and try something imaginative and very American like a tangerine and yam combination. Yield: enough stuffing for a 5–6 pound duck.

⅓   cup minced scallions
⅓   cup blanched and diced carrots
3   Tb. butter
1½ cups cooked, peeled, and mashed yams or sweet potatoes
1   egg, beaten
1½ cups bread crumbs, dry
¼   cup finely chopped parsley
2   tangerines, separated, plus some finely grated rind
   Sprinkling of rosemary or thyme
   Dash of salt
   Freshly ground pepper to taste
1   Tb. brandy

In a skillet sauté scallions and carrots in butter till tender. Beat egg into yams till fluffy, add scallions, carrots, and all other ingredients, mix thoroughly, and check seasoning.

COLLARD GREENS AND APRICOT STUFFING
FOR BONED BAKED HAM

Most likely the reason that both the English and American Southerners love ham so much (both plain and stuffed) is because they produce some of the finest examples in the world. Yorkshire, Suffolk, and Westmorland hams have nourished generations of discerning Britishers, while in the United States the country hams of Virginia, North Carolina, Tennessee, Kentucky, and Georgia are prized. The following recipe (which makes enough dressing for a boned 10–12 pound ham) celebrates both cultures in that the collard or mustard greens are indigenously Southern and the apricots an almost predictable English ingredient in any ceremonial stuffing for ham. Kale, watercress, cabbage, or even celery could easily be substituted for the collard or mustard greens, depending on personal tastes.

4	slices bacon
½	cup minced scallions
½	cup minced celery
½	cup minced bell pepper
½	cup minced parsley
2	cups coarsely chopped spinach
2	cups coarsely chopped collard or mustard greens
1½	cups pitted and halved apricots
	Tabasco to taste
¼	tsp. marjoram
¼	tsp. cumin
½	tsp. salt
	Freshly ground pepper to taste

In a heavy skillet fry bacon till crisp, drain on paper towels, crumble, and pour all but 3 Tb. fat from skillet. Add scallions, celery, and bell pepper to skillet and sauté over medium heat till soft. Stir in all other ingredients including crumbled bacon, reduce heat to simmer, and cook about 20 minutes or till all vegetables are soft. Stuff into boned cavity of ham.

EGGPLANT AND PINE NUT STUFFING FOR
BONED ROAST LEG OF LAMB

Although the French stuff their *gigots* with everything from kidneys to truffles to gigantic cloves of garlic and the English pride themselves on ducal joints of lamb and mutton packed with apricots, currants, fresh mint, and any variety of nuts, Americans have never really given much thought to stuffing a handsome boned leg of lamb. Naturally a well-seasoned garlic bread dressing helps produce a simple but satisfying dish, but since I've always had personal reason to associate lamb with Greek cookery, I'm particularly fond of this stuffing designed for a 6-pound joint.

3   Tb. olive oil
1   medium-sized eggplant, peeled and cubed
1   onion, finely chopped
1   clove garlic, minced
¾   cup bread crumbs, dry
2   Tb. finely chopped parsley
2   tsp. lemon juice
¼   cup pine nuts

In a large, heavy skillet sauté eggplant, onion, and garlic in olive oil about 5 minutes or till tender. Add bread crumbs, parsley, lemon juice, and pine nuts and continue cooking over medium heat, stirring, another 5 minutes. Stuff into boned cavity of lamb.

SHRIMP AND CRAB MEAT STUFFING FOR
BAKED STRIPED BASS

Whether or not it is true that the first viand stuffed by Pilgrims was not a turkey but a large cod, it's for sure that Americans have always prepared a staggering variety of fish bursting with clams, shrimp, oysters, crab meat, mussels, lobsters, anchovies, fruits, vegetables, cheese, you name it. The recipe for shrimp and crab meat stuffing which I discovered some years back in the *Cotton Country Collection*, published by the Junior Charity League of Monroe, Louisiana is, in this slightly modified version, one of the best I know for a 4-4½ pound bass. It would make an equally delicious stuffing for a large red snapper, pike, or flounder.

4   Tb. butter
1   onion, minced
2   ribs celery, finely diced
¼   green pepper, finely chopped
1   doz. fresh shrimp, chopped
¼   cup chopped fresh mushrooms
½   lb. lump crab meat
    Pinch thyme
1   small bay leaf
1   Tb. Worcestershire sauce
¼   lb. browned and finely chopped almonds
½   cup heavy cream
1   cup bread crumbs, dry
    Salt and freshly ground pepper to taste
3   oz. sherry

In a large, heavy skillet sauté onions, celery, and green pepper in butter till soft. Add shrimp and mushrooms, cover momentarily to produce liquid, uncover, and continue cooking still shrimp are barely pink. Add all other ingredients, stir thoroughly, cook 5 more minutes, and stuff into cavity of bass.

DESSERT COOKIES
WITH A PEDIGREE

••

I STATE, without explanation or apology, that the one gastronomic trait I do not have in common with my fellow Americans is a passion for rich desserts. When I'm invited to dinner at a private home, I can hardly enjoy the appetizer and main course for fear of what cloying wedge of cake or pie might be served to wreck totally what's come before. I find it incredible in fine restaurants to hear people (who, more often than not, are already overweight) exclaim about how they can't eat such and such since they want to save room for some massive, overly sweet concoction described at the bottom of the menu or displayed on a trolley. And just the idea of popping into a pastry shop off the street and knocking off a mid-afternoon cream puff or piece of cheesecake is enough to still my appetite for two days. When inspired, I will taste a blackberry cobbler or take a spoonful of chocolate mousse or break off a morsel of homemade fruitcake, but, quite frankly, I can't imagine *ever* consuming an entire portion of pecan pie or coconut cake.

This is not to say, however, that I simply hate sweets, for I do indeed crave something at the end of any meal to fill up that legendary tooth—even after a cheese and fruit course. And what I do enjoy are a few homemade cookies—fresh, light, elegant cookies to be nibbled casually with coffee, perhaps a digestive liqueur, and good conversation. Unfortunately, most Americans view cookies as mere snacks, which is not surprising when you consider those packaged abominations which children and adults alike have been conditioned to devour at any hour of the day or night and which I haven't had the courage to sample in years. I, on the other hand, consider fresh cookies an intelligent addition to a well-orchestrated lunch or dinner, a short coda that doesn't necessarily make or break the opus but that certainly contributes the finishing touch.

Of course, the custom of offering tiny, light confections in place of heavy desserts has been practiced for decades in many of the great restaurants of Europe, and I doubt there's a single American traveller to France who would fail to be impressed with the mouth-watering array of *petits fours* and *friandises* served with coffee at all the legendary three-star citadels. If the idea works in these places, why, I ask, not at least try to apply more of this same sensible approach to our own eating patterns? Americans, naturally, tend to snicker at something so seemingly simple and prosaic as a cookie, but take it from one who regularly bakes his own supply of delicacies, a few well-made cookies not only provide an eminently satisfying alternative to those rich desserts but also do lots less damage to the digestive track and waistline than a ludicrous slab of apple pie or strawberry shortcake.

Although I am rarely without tins of homemade chocolate-chip cookies or ginger snaps, there are certain other cookies that I associate automatically with special occasions and that, at least in my own mind, couldn't be any more American in nature. All (including the cheese biscuit) are appropriately light and delicate, and, when arranged artistically on an attractive platter, illustrate perfectly how the humble cookie can be elevated to distinguished gustatory heights. One suggestion: When you make these cookies, make plenty, for they keep well when stored in airtight containers and always seem to disappear faster than you anticipated.

JELLY TREATS

3   sticks butter, softened
1   cup sugar
4   egg yolks
4   cups plain flour
    Currant or mint jelly

Preheat oven to 325° F. Cream butter and flour with an electric mixer, add egg yolks, mix, add flour, and mix thoroughly. Roll batter into small balls with hand, place on a cookie sheet about 1½ inches apart, press thimble or fingertip in center of each, and bake about 10 minutes or till done. Remove from oven, place dot of currant or mint jelly in holes, and continue baking about 10 minutes or till slightly brown. Let cool till jelly is hard. Yield: about 100

Nutty Fingers

4   sticks butter, softened
10 Tb. sifted powdered sugar
5   cups flour
2   cups chopped nuts
2   tsp. vanilla extract
    Dash salt
    Powdered sugar, sifted

Preheat oven to 350° F. Cream butter and sugar with an electric mixer, add flour, mix, add nuts, vanilla, and salt, and mix thoroughly. Take small pieces of dough and form into finger shapes, place on a cookie sheet about 1½ inches apart, and bake about 30 minutes or till lightly brown. Let cool on paper towels and roll in sifted powdered sugar. Yield: about 75.

Sugar Cookies

4   sticks butter, softened
1½   cups sugar
1   egg
4   cups plain flour
1   tsp. vanilla extract
1   tsp. almond extract
     Red or green cherries

Preheat oven to 350° F. Cream butter and sugar with an electric mixer, add egg, mix, add flour and flavorings, and mix thoroughly. Drop small bits on a cookie sheet about 1½ inches apart, press a red or green cherry into each cookie, and bake 10 to 15 minutes or till barely browned around edges. Cool on paper towels till cherries have hardened. Yield: about 100.

BENNE COOKIES

1   cup benne (or sesame) seeds
1½   sticks butter, melted
1½   cups light brown sugar
1¼   cups plain flour
¼   tsp. baking powder
¼   tsp. salt
1   tsp. vanilla extract
1   egg

Heat oven to 300° F. and toast benne seeds on a cookie sheet
10 to 15 minutes, stirring. Remove from oven and increase
heat to 325°. In a large mixing bowl combine butter, sugar,
flour, baking powder, salt, vanilla, egg, and cooled seeds and
mix thoroughly. Drop batter by ½ teaspoons onto a greased
foil-lined cookie sheet and space about 1½ inches apart. Bake
15 to 20 minutes or till evenly browned (if pale in center and
puffed, the cookies are not ready), watching constantly to
avoid burning. Carefully peel from foil and cool on paper
towels. Yield: about 85.

MINT SURPRISES

2   sticks butter, softened
1   cup sugar
¼   cup brown sugar
2   eggs
1   tsp. water
1   tsp. vanilla extract
3   cups flour, sifted
1   tsp. soda
½   tsp. salt
     Solid chocolate mints

Preheat oven to 375° F. Cream butter and sugars with an
electric mixer, add eggs, water, and vanilla, and mix. Blend
in flour, soda, and salt, mix well, and chill at least 2 hours.
Place about 1 teaspoon dough in palm of hand, press a mint

in center, and fold dough up around mint. Place on a greased cookie sheet about 1½ inches apart and bake 10 to 12 minutes or till slightly brown. Cool on paper towels. Yield: about 55.

LEMON BARS

¼ cup powdered sugar
⅛ tsp. salt
1 cup flour
1 stick butter, softened

Preheat oven to 350° F. Place all ingredients in a bowl, mix thoroughly, place mixture in a 9″ x 9″ baking pan, and bake 20 minutes. In the meantime, mix together:

1 cup sugar
½ tsp. baking powder
⅛ tsp. salt
2 eggs, slightly beaten
2 Tb. lemon juice
   Confectioners' sugar

Remove pan from oven and pour on lemon mixture. Return to oven, bake 20 minutes, and cool. Sprinkle with confectioners' sugar and cut into 24 bars.

FRUITCAKE COOKIES

1½ cups flour
¼   tsp. soda
½   tsp. salt
½   tsp. cinnamon
½   stick butter, softened
½   cup brown sugar
2   eggs
1   cup sherry
1   tsp. sherry extract
3½ cups chopped nuts
3   slices candied pineapple, chopped
1   cup candied cherries, chopped
1   cup dates, chopped
¼   lb. white raisins
¼   cup crystallized orange and lemon peel, chopped

Preheat oven to 300° F. Combine flour, soda, salt, and cinnamon in a bowl and set aside. Cream butter and sugar with an electric mixer, beat in eggs, and mix well. Combine dry ingredients and sherry alternately with the butter mixture, add sherry extract, stir in nuts and fruit by hand, and mix well. Drop mixture by heaping teaspoons on a greased cookie sheet about 1½ inches apart and bake about 20 minutes. Yield: about 85.

CHOCOLATE MACAROONS

½   lb. unsweetened almond paste, cut into thin slices
½   cup sugar
4   oz. semisweet chocolate, melted
3   egg whites, unbeaten

Preheat oven to 325° F. Place almond paste in a bowl and gradually knead in sugar. Add chocolate, mix till well blended, add egg whites in small amounts, and mix to form a smooth, thick paste. Place mixture in a pastry bag and onto a buttered baking sheet squeeze 1½-inch rounds about

1½ inches apart. Bake 25 to 30 minutes or till macaroons are just firm. Yield: about 24.

CHEESE BISCUITS

2 sticks butter, softened
½ lb. extra strong New York State Cheddar cheese, finely
   grated
¼ tsp. salt
   Dash cayenne pepper
2 cups plain flour
   Pecans

Preheat oven to 375° F. Combine butter, cheese, salt, and cayenne pepper in a large mixing bowl and mix till thoroughly blended. Add flour and knead till mixture is firm and smooth. Roll dough in palms of hands into balls the size of large marbles, place on a cookie sheet about 1½ inches apart, and bake 10 minutes. Remove from oven, press a pecan into the center of each biscuit, return to oven, and continue baking 20 minutes more or till slightly brown. Yield: about 75.

IV

SERIOUS
EATING

RAW ELEGANCE

●●●●●●●●●●●●●●●●●●●●●●●●●●●●●●●●●●●●

EVENTUALLY THE time comes for the ultimate gustatory treat; steak tartare. I know you've been meaning to try it for years, but you just never got around to ordering it in restaurants or making it at home. Why? Perhaps you found the idea of eating raw meat in public a little too showy, a bit too much like the smart aleck faking a passion for Chinese sea slugs or the jerk neophyte sucking on a fish head from his *bouillabaisse*. On the other hand, maybe you've been intimidated by the false assumption that steak tartare is a dish intended only for epicures. Or . . . . maybe you've just been squeamish. Whatever, it's ridiculous to stall any longer; you're not only missing out on one of the glories of great eating, you're also denying yourself a possible cure-all for lethargy, obesity, hangovers, and maybe even sexual impotence.

To the uninitiated, steak tartare is no more than a simple serving of chopped raw beef that's been seasoned, mixed with onions, mustard, capers, anchovies, and God knows what other ingredients, and served with a raw egg yolk sunk in the middle. Aficionados (of which I'm proud to consider myself one) know that a properly concocted steak tartare is a subtle, complex dish that can never be thrown together haphazardly, and whose perfection depends on the freshness and leanness of the meat, a time-tested balance of impeccable ingredients, and a deft hand at mixing. (The French and Belgians, adventurous eaters who've been downing raw meat for centuries, are as fastidious about the preparation of steak tartare as the selection of fine wines.) There's no excuse for anybody's having to eat bad steak tartare, not when it's so easy to prepare at home. So first, let me show you exactly how to go about making it.

1. Go to a dependable butcher and buy a fresh, lean piece of sirloin (steak or top), a rump roast, or top round roast weighing about 2 pounds. If you want the butcher to grind it for you, make sure he removes every suggestion of fat, that he wipes the meat well with a clean cloth, and that he grinds it twice (medium blade) in a clean machine. If you prefer to prepare the meat yourself at home, trim and wipe as above, cut it into workable pieces, run it twice through a hand grinder or grind it for a few seconds in a food processor (*never* use a blender, which yields a miserable mush), or, for ideal loose texture, chop it on a well-scrubbed chopping board with two heavy razor-sharp knives, slicing the meat rapidly with both hands until it reaches a smooth (but not silky) consistency. Squeeze a seeded lemon wedge over the meat, and shape it into a large patty. Wrap the patty tightly in clear plastic (not aluminum foil, which doesn't seal properly), and refrigerate until you are ready to use it.

2. Shortly before mixing, make ready the following basic ingredients:

   1   small onion, very finely chopped
   2½   tsp. fresh parsley, finely chopped
   1½   tsp. English or Dijon mustard
   1½   tsp. salt
   1   tsp. freshly ground pepper
   2   fresh raw egg yolks
   3   Tb. Cognac

3. Spread the chopped meat on the chopping board and blend in the onions with two forks, one to sprinkle gradually the onions evenly over the surface, the other to press them down into the meat. Fold the meat in from the edges to the center, spread out again, and mix in two tablespoons of the parsley. Fold again, spread, add mustard, salt, pepper, and egg yolks, fold again, spread, add Cognac, fold once more, then work the ingredients thoroughly into the meat, pushing the tines of one fork steadily downward in the center of the patty while simultaneously bringing up more meat from the edges with the other. (Don't be rough. This final blending should last no longer than thirty seconds for the desired light, almost fluffy, texture. If you keep pressing the meat too long after the ingredients have been added, you'll end up with a heavy mound.) Now form the meat into oval-shaped patties, carefully smooth out all surfaces with either a dinner knife or the handle of a fork, sprinkle on top of each the remaining parsley, and eat as a main dish with a few crisp fresh vegetables (quickly steamed or blanched), a little black bread, and a fine bottle of red wine. No more. SERVES 2.

As for optional embellishments, the following breakdown should be taken into serious consideration:

Acceptable	Passable But Déclassé	Criminal
2 drops freshly squeezed garlic juice	Chopped egg yolks	Chopped pickles
3 dashes Tabasco	Worcestershire sauce	Catsup
Pinch imported paprika	Chopped anchovies	Mayonnaise
2 tsp. olive oil	Chopped mushrooms	American mustard
1 tsp. finely chopped dill	Diced green peppers	Heavy cream
	Capers	Random herbs
	Chives	Soy sauce
	Cayenne	Parmesan cheese
	Fresh caviar	Chopped olives

Of course, steak tartare has not always been this same tasty sophisticated dish you'll soon learn to perfect. In fact, long after raw meat was supposedly first consumed simply as strength-giving fare by the fierce Tartars of Genghis Khan, the steak began to be appreciated throughout Europe, not so much for its epicurean merits as for its revitalizing quality. Mrs. Beeton, Brillat-Savarin, the Edwardians, even present-day British tug-of-war teams have all endorsed the meat as an extraordinary source of energy, a truly invigorating pick-me-up capable of restoring heaven knows what in man.

While I'm sure modern medicine would refute claims for steak tartare as an aphrodisiac food, devotees are firm believers in its strange powers and couldn't care less what all the learned doctors think. Skeptics will tell you it's all psychological, but the truth remains that after consuming a hearty amount of raw meat you always experience an indescribable uplift, a joyful internal eruption that prompts you to try to accomplish the impossible, to combat any odds. And, after all, it does stand to reason that when you digest meat full of pure, unadulterated protein, iron, niacin, and vitamin B_{12} (much of which is otherwise lost during the cooking process), the chemical reaction in the body is going to be almost as pronounced as what a victim of pernicious anemia receives from iron injections. Now, I'm not about to try to prove for sure that a steady diet of steak tartare would solve the problems of chronic lethargy and impotence, but were I in a position to embark on such a seemingly logical campaign, I'd begin by demonstrating the effect raw meat has on my beagle. It's no news to any canine lover that you normally never give domesticated dogs fresh uncooked meat or bones, either of which can send them into a wild frenzy—especially if they detect simultaneously a sexual scent. Anybody who cares to doubt this might be further interested to know that one piece of advice given by some professional dog trainers to owners with sluggish pets is to increase the protein in Bowser's diet. Again, I have no intention of drawing any irrational conclusions, but it might give those in doubt about their sexual prowess food for thought.

Considering the American obsession with obesity and small waistlines, it's truly astonishing that not one of those cookbook wizards has ever come on big about steak tartare as the ideal dietetic food. What's so marvelous about reducing on a diet of steak tartare (an eight-ounce patty of raw ground meat contains only a little over 400 calories) and, say, salads composed of endive, raw mushrooms, and any number of other fresh vegetables, is you're not only eating delicious food that quickly satisfies hunger but, more important, what you're digesting is nutritionally sound. In addition to all the vitamins, minerals, and protein present in both the steak and its embellishments, there's also a healthy amount of that vital substance known as salt. And, as one food historian, Reay Tannahill, has tried to remind us, "When a human being perspires, he loses some of his natural body salts. These have to be replaced by the food he eats. Raw meat is the best provider; cooked meat is less good, because salt is usually lost in the cooking process." Any way you look at it, steak tartare makes lots of sense for anyone trying to knock off pounds painlessly, indeed a lot more sense than all those terrifying, humiliating, criminal diet plans that leave you feeling like a wilted asparagus and not looking much better.

Still another unsung merit of this wonder dish is its potential as a hangover remedy. James Beard likes to relate how, during the days of Prohibition, well-heeled New Yorkers with heavy heads from bootleg liquor swore by raw meat as the supreme cure. In Germany, it's common in beer halls to see all-night sluggers order a platter of raw chopped beef and onions before facing the dawn, and, come to think of it, my very first steak tartare was virtually fed me years ago during a Paris restaurant's closing hour by the same villainous French student who introduced me to Pernod. Of course, no therapy on God's green earth can actually dispel all the miserable consequences of too much booze, but to this day I know of nothing that cushions the blow any better than a hefty serving of raw meat.

Naturally, there will always be people who recoil in horror from the idea of eating steak tartare, convinced, now and forever, that any meat which is not charred to a crisp is unsafe for human consumption. (And, curiously enough, these are usually the same ones who never think twice about downing meats reeking of preservatives or fruits glistening with artificial coloring.) Well, sensible precaution is one thing, fanaticism is another, and, as I discovered when I decided to look into the facts of the matter, even some of the top medical brains associated with the USDA in Washington seem nothing less than obsessed with pointing out to the public all the salmonella (surface bacteria on meat), bovine cysticerosis (beef tapeworm), taxoplasmosis (a sometimes fatal parasitic disease), and Lord knows how many other possible consequences of eating raw beef. After listening to the good doctors rave about why they'd never put an ounce of uncooked meat in their mouths (convictions backed by absurdly weak evidence), I began to check out all this mess in David Belding's authoritative *Textbook of Parasitology*. The results of my research should not only serve to assure consumers about the reasonable safety of steak tartare but should encourage a few specialists in Washington to check the books from time to time. To record but a couple of the truths I dug out:

> Chances of acquiring the disease [taxoplasmosis] from undercooked mutton and beef appear to be slight. Epidemiologic evidence does not support the idea that meat-eating is the principal source of human infection since the incidence of positive dye tests is about the same in vegetarians and meat eaters. . . .
> Bovine cysticercosis may reach five percent in countries where human infection is common. Its incidence throughout the world varies up to thirty percent: United States of America, 0.4 . . . Yugoslavia, 30.

As for salmonella, I have the word of none other than the USDA's chief of the microbiology staff of the meat and poultry inspection program, that while theoretically it's always possible for any government-inspected meat to contain some bacteria, the incidence in American beef would be so low as to practically negate the possibility.

"No country in the world has as stringent a meat-inspection program as we do," he insisted, "and that stamp on the outside of beef carcasses means the meat is virtually safe for human consumption, even in its raw state. Half the country now prefers beef cooked rare, so we're forced to take every measure humanly possible. Now I'd never recommend that people eat raw pork or chicken because contamination of these products is still the most difficult to control. But beef is safe, and so long as it's handled properly by both butchers and consumers, there's no reason for anyone to worry about eating steak tartare."

One point of debate among tartare lovers revolves around which cut of meat is most suitable. Most restaurants serve chopped fillet, and while there's no doubt this is the leanest and tenderest beef available, it's also true that the flavor cannot compare to that of sirloin and a few less expensive cuts. Personally I prefer sirloin or top round, but I might add that some of the best steak tartare I've eaten was made with rump and, on one occasion, with extremely lean chuck. Naturally, it's all a matter of personal taste, but what matters most in the long run is whether the meat is completely fresh, of choice grade (prime contains too much fat), and well trimmed of all surface fat.

You should never make steak tartare from the packaged hamburger found in the cases of supermarkets. Not only is this chopped meat full of fat; it's also been exposed to who knows how many hands and perhaps to a dirty meat grinder.

Although mixing a tartare is fun to watch or bring off yourself, a grand performance requires considerable skill and experience. For years I've studied the artistic technique of a veteran restaurant captain I know and have yet to duplicate successfully the feathery raw wonder he produces with two forks. Some experts prefer to work the patty with only one fork, while others use simultaneously a fork in one hand to add ingredients and a dinner knife in the other to gradually scrape the mixture to a smooth texture. I've known people who swear by wooden spoons, rubber spatulas, chef's knives, and I must confess that on one occasion (when a waiter stupidly abandoned the perishable dish to go do something or other) I didn't hesitate to dash to the rest room, scrub thoroughly, dash back, grab the meat and other ingredients off the serving table, and unabashedly mix the steak tartare with my hands. It was delicious.

So forget any silly notions which previously may have held you back. Order your raw beef when the inclination hits you, eat, and enjoy. Before long, you'll be curious to try a steak tartare made with lamb or horsemeat, and not long after that, who knows, you might even share my present longing to taste a little well-seasoned raw buffalo meat.

AMERICAN CAVIAR

●●

FRESH BELUGA malossol caviar is one of those hallmarks of the good life for which—so far—there simply is no substitution. For those who prize the luxury, it's right up there with crown sable, Rolls-Royce, and Tiffany silver. Fresh, unprocessed truffles may be the most expensive food on earth, but the roe taken from the giant beluga sturgeon of the Caspian Sea could also be sold by the karat. To compare its aroma, flavor, and texture with that of all the cheap pasteurized imitations accepted by far too many people as caviar is like comparing vintage Krug Private Reserve Champagne with cold duck. Since fresh beluga malossol can cost up to $450 for fourteen ounces in specialty food shops (not to mention a cool fifty bucks an ounce in fine restaurants), it's hardly surprising that most Americans will live a lifetime and never enjoy even their first taste. I suppose I'm one of the few who can truthfully say he has had his fill of the delicacy on more than one occasion, but, then, I'm one of the happy few who know that a First-Class ticket aboard the *Queen Elizabeth 2* still entitles you to unlimited quantities of Russian and Iranian caviar for five blessed days. Beluga, osetra, sevruga, sterlet—the roe of these four species of Caspian sturgeon may vary in size and color, but all signify the world's finest caviar.

"Isn't it fascinating?" mumbles Dafne Engstrom in her slight Swedish accent, gazing intently at a tiny black fish egg between her fingers, then squeezing it to release the oil inside, and finally licking her fingers. "Every year it gets better, and one of these days there'll be plenty for everyone." What she is referring to, standing there with me before a dozen different containers in her bright San Francisco kitchen, is not beluga or osetra or sevruga but American caviar made from the roe of sturgeon fished from the Columbia River in Oregon. Other containers hold golden caviar from the whitefish of the Great Lakes, and still others display large oval berries of reddish orange salmon caviar.

Slowly we taste, rolling the eggs around in our mouths, munching down, waiting for an aftereffect at the top of the throat, and nibbling on dry Swedish crisp bread. I am stunned into euphoria by the gray black sturgeon—no fishy aroma, small loose eggs that are just firm enough because of careful salting, mellow in flavor, with a pleasant finish that hints of the sea. It's an incredibly close resemblance in taste and texture to imported sevruga. Next to this fresh produce, a bottled, pasteurized lumpfish caviar dyed black (the cheap sort found even in supermarkets) is downright disgusting. The mysterious golden white-fish is relatively mild, a bit hard, clean-tasting, intriguing. One container of salmon eggs has an engaging aroma, but I find the caviar a bit too pungent; another is delightful on every count. The spoon plunges into more dark sturgeon, this one having been refrigerated a number of weeks. Still no offensive odor, and the eggs are tight, but what a difference in flavor! "It could be yeasty by now," explains Dafne, "but don't forget this roe came from a different sturgeon, and we possibly added too much salt to that batch."

A few days later I'm in New York sampling Mario Garbarino's American caviar, most of which comes from sturgeon caught in the Arkansas River in Oklahoma. The first bite, spooned from a large plastic barrel just in from the airport, is pleasantly salty, but the consistency of the eggs is a little soft, too gooey. Then comes a tin with beautiful, medium-sized black- and rust-colored roe, the source of which he refuses to reveal. The eggs are loose, firm, faintly salty, delicious, but when I taste this caviar again at home in three days, the aroma is fishy. In the deli section of a large department store I purchase small jars of fresh sturgeon and salmon caviar produced by a highly respected food purveyor. The black is unpleasantly oily and bland, but when I find the same product in a delicacy shop, I find it to be in top shape; the red at both places is a little deflated but in no way cloying or strong.

Next, a chef calls to say he's sending over some sturgeon he has just received through a local distributor from a producer in the state of Washington. Name, address, and phone number unknown. I test. No aroma whatsoever; tiny, sticky eggs that burst the second they're touched, most likely from overcuring; a salty but interesting flavor with the help of lemon juice, but dull without. When I learn that a sample has been sent to one of New York's most celebrated French restaurants, I call the chef for his opinion. "It looks like caviar," he says, "but it really doesn't taste like caviar."

And so goes the exciting but maddeningly frustrating quest to discover all there is to know about the embryonic stages of what may be developing into a major American industry. Years ago in the Napa Valley, the future of California wines couldn't have been more obvious to me; today the role American caviar is bound to assume in our gastronomy is equally evident. As was true in the beginning of the development of our wonderful wines, however, the caviar business is just blooming, desperate for organization, standardization, and promotion. Ten years back, people snickered at the suggestion that this country could eventually produce some of the world's finest wine; I predict that ten years from now, American caviar not only will be a popular, eminently affordable delicacy but will also have put a big dent in the market for the imported product. Whether the overall quality will ever equal that of Russian beluga remains to be seen. But if the handful of enterprising, energetic individuals currently struggling to make a dream a reality succeed even halfway in their efforts, we have something special to look forward to. Although production is still relatively low and consistency in quality uneven, American caviar (sturgeon, salmon, whitefish) is now available in many fine food shops all over the country. The price of the very best sturgeon? Anywhere from half to a quarter that of imported beluga. And I can assure you that, at its best, our caviar is already on a par with Iranian sevruga.

What's ironic about all this is that, unbeknownst to all but the most ardent aficionados, during the nineteenth century much of the caviar in Europe was imported from no less a place than the United States. Up to 100,000 pounds annually were collected from the sturgeon teeming in the great inland lakes and virtually all the large rivers, especially the Hudson. The American caviar industry was centered in the East, but even as far west as San Francisco large quantities of the delicacy were produced for export year after year. Then (as, to some extent, now), Americans had little taste for the salty black roe. Pots of fresh caviar and caviar sandwiches were given away free with nickel beer in New York saloons just to induce thirst. However, overfishing and industrial sprawl eventually put an end to the local sturgeon supply, as it did to our great lobster industry, and by the time of World War I, the action had shifted to the Caspian, the world's largest saltwater lake. For decades, Russian and Iranian caviar was relatively plentiful and sensibly priced, but, to round out the irony, by the 1960s it was discovered that not only were the waters from the Caspian to Astrakhan (the center of the Russian caviar industry) gradually evaporating but also that the royal sturgeon were being killed off throughout the sea by increased industrial pollution.

Today some experts insist that production remains reasonably healthy and that the future of fresh beluga is assured by the ever-soaring prices that make the delicacy available only to the privileged few. Others are convinced that, even with the advances being made in artificial breeding, the day is quickly coming when Russian and Iranian caviar will be no more than a memory. Whatever the outcome, one thing is for sure: there will never be a surfeit of imported caviar, and the already prohibitive prices are hardly likely to go down.

The resurgence of the industry in this country was brought on in the early seventies primarily by a Swedish couple in their forties, Mats and Dafne Engstrom. The depleted supply of crawfish in their native land, where crawfish are a staple, and the abundance of this delectable crustacean in California promped the Engstroms to set up office in their San Francisco home and establish a small production plant up in Sacramento. They began shipping tons of live crawfish abroad, as well as quantities of Pacific salmon, under the name California Sunshine, Inc. Later, they made the surprising discovery that the waters of the Columbia River in Washington and Oregon and the Sacramento River in California were alive with big, healthy sturgeon, the precious roe of which were being simply discarded or thrown to the cat by sport and commercial fishermen. "One day a fisherman brought me a set of roe attached to this tough membrane, the skein," says Dafne, "but we didn't know what to do with it. I spoke with chefs and food experts. I browsed through books in Russian bookstores. I called the Russian Embassy and the Consulate. I read everything I could get my hands on that mentioned caviar. Eventually, through trial and error, I perfected the technique of separating the eggs by rubbing the skein gently through a screen. I learned, too, about the importance of curing the roe with only pure salt, but there are so many other steps to correct processing—you just can't imagine."

Since California law strictly prohibits commercial fishing of sturgeon in the state's waters in order to protect the relatively small supply, the Engstroms next assembled a small but reliable group of suppliers in Oregon, Washington, and Canada and were soon distributing a few hundred pounds a year of "Tsar Nicoulai" black caviar to a handful of luxury restaurants in San Francisco and New York. This was followed by their endeavor to produce fresh golden caviar from the roe of white-fish, then a very small amount of red from the delectable Pacific coho salmon. Experts, lucky enough to sample all three, raved. Marketing of the more desirable (and more expensive) sturgeon caviar is still limited due to short seasonal supply of roe from up north, but the Engstroms' inexpensive "Tsar Nicoulai" golden caviar is quickly finding its way to more and more outlets throughout the country. "And we're just begin-ning with the fresh red salmon," informs Dafne. "The source is plenti-ful, but we're a small operation and have to take things step by step. I refuse to market anything that so much as resembles that dreadful pasteurized salmon caviar you see everywhere on shelves, and fresh salmon roe is not the easiest to work with."

Spurred on perhaps by the Engstroms' innovations, other producers began to materialize fast after discovering that rivers throughout the country are once again full of some dozen species of hefty sturgeon (not including, alas, the large beluga). From Van Nuys, California, came Say-Co; from Myrtle Beach, South Carolina, it was Atlantis; from New Jersey, Romanoff; from New York, Poriloff, Iron Gate, and, most im-portant of all, Aquamar. Like the Engstroms, Mario Garbarino was initially involved with other luxury food products (European mush-rooms, *foie gras,* and truffles) when he founded Aquamar in the early seventies, but then it happened. "My wife and I were vacationing in her home state of Oklahoma when I found out about all the sturgeon in the Arkansas River. Of course the locals thought I was crazy when I asked if they could get me some 'fish eggs,' but before long I made all the contacts, and, after learning a processing technique from an expert in Iran, I showed the fishermen how to process exactly what I wanted. Soon I discovered sources in the Northeast, the Midwest, and the deep South."

By the mid-seventies, Garbarino was supplying cruise ships with three thousand to five thousand pounds of fresh American sturgeon caviar a year. In 1980 he succeeded in selling his product to fine restau-rants, food shops, and a couple of domestic airlines. And now he's managed to place Aquamar in every Neiman-Marcus store around the country. "One day I'll distribute maybe thirty thousand pounds of fresh sturgeon," he insists proudly, aware that sources in the East are far better than those out West. "And after that, it will be up to seventy thousand or eighty thousand pounds," he continues, peering over papers and boxes and cans in his miniscule, cluttered storefront office far uptown on New York's First Avenue. "Our first golden whitefish caviar is now available, though I must say I don't believe this variety can ever be in the same class as the sturgeon—no matter who produces it."

Exactly where does all the roe come from? Which species of sturgeon and salmon yield the finest roe? Just how is the caviar processed? Getting answers to these questions is no less difficult than trying to learn the formula to Coca-Cola or figuring out why a Steinway performs as it does. Most producers will admit that they separate the roe from the skein by sieving through a screen, but from that point on secrecy on every level of operation is as tight as that in Astrakhan. No one has any intention, for instance, of revealing how much salt is added to turn the roe into precious caviar, and very few producers will give any hint whatsoever as to what species of sturgeon they're having most luck with, much less where that sturgeon is located. Should roe be removed while the fish is alive, or should it be killed and bled first? Are the sturgeons of the Mississippi and Hudson as desirable as those found in New England and Northwestern rivers? Can roe be oversalted for preservation, then water-washed with success? And what about the know-how of all those nameless fishermen who've been given the responsibility of processing the caviar at the many unidentified locations? Answers to these questions are not exactly volunteered by either producers or government agencies, and when there are responses, they tend to stand in conflict with all other opinions. "No sir, I'm not talking," says Dafne Engstrom. "We've worked too hard to reach this point of success without having to worry about others coming out to deplete the small supply of Western roe and duplicate our processing technique."

Amid all this mystery, of course, is the consumer, eager to sample the new caviar yet determined to find a product that is delicious, dependable, and fairly priced. Over a period of months I must have tasted close to fifty different fresh caviars from all parts of the nation, some truly exceptional, others good but not distinguished, and a few pretty awful. Since personal reaction to this sort of food tends to be much more subjective than usual, I held a number of tastings to solicit the opinions of all types of people: those who had enjoyed imported beluga and sevruga all their lives; those who had always hated caviar; and those who had literally never tasted the first egg. The results were amazing, with the so-called pros disagreeing almost brutally, the skeptics accustomed to cheap pasteurized glop experiencing a revelation, and the neophytes downing any and all roe like peanuts. "This can't be American!" "It's so much fresher tasting and less salty than the imported." "For the price, it's incredible."

Almost without exception, all three varieties of the Engstroms' caviar captured top honors in blind tastings, but there were always some who preferred a given tin of Aquamar sturgeon or a certain spoonful of Poriloff's salmon or even a couple of well-made pasteurized products. These individuals, as I saw it, represent the public, which means that even if the domestic caviar being marketed is still inconsistent in quality, most people generally like what they're tasting. Conclusion: The consumer must insist upon sampling before buying, letting his palate be the only guide.

There's no argument among purists that the best way to savor any fresh sturgeon caviar is either *au naturel* or perhaps on a little toast or dark bread with a few drops of lemon juice—and preferably with a small glass of iced vodka or flute of champagne. On the other hand, now that all varieties of caviar are more plentiful and affordable, it seems a shame not to begin experimenting in the kitchen. The simplest and most discreet possibilities might include caviar mixed into scrambled eggs, omelettes, pasta, seafood salads, potato salad, or a soufflé; or caviar stuffed into hard-boiled eggs, cherry tomatoes, *croustades* or profiteroles; or caviar used to enhance open-face sandwiches of shrimp, smoked salmon or sturgeon, chicken, and cucumber. More interesting would be caviar incorporated into mousses and terrines; lukewarm sauces such as hollandaise and Béarnaise with caviar served over asparagus and broccoli; shredded chicken breast salad with a caviar vinaigrette; or miniature cream puffs stuffed with caviar cream and glazed with aspic. "What about caviar in salads of sweetbreads, crawfish, or brains?" one chief I know dreams aloud. "Or any number of seafood ceviches with caviar. Or tortellini stuffed with caviar in an Alfredo sauce. Or quail eggs Benedict with caviar? Really, this is a whole new dimension in cooking to be explored."

Many feel that the major problem with fresh caviar is not so much the way it is produced as the way it is handled by retailers and consumers alike. It is true that the longevity of any caviar is partly dependent on the amount of salt added, but even a highly salted product must be refrigerated continuously from source through distribution channels to consumer. Due to its low oil content, whitefish caviar freezes beautifully. Unfortunately, however, if either sturgeon or salmon caviar is frozen, the berries burst and the quality deteriorates dreadfully. As with the expensive imported products, American red and black caviar stored in airtight containers at a constant temperature of twenty-eight to thirty degrees Fahrenheit (caviar freezes only at twenty-six degrees) remains in good shape from one to two weeks. Dafne Engstrom has also discovered that if opened fresh caviar is covered snugly on top with a sheet of plastic wrap before being recapped, its quality can hold up to a month under ideal refrigeration. I don't like to keep any fresh caviar around for over a week. When purchasing, ask not only how long the caviar has been stored and at what temperature but also for a sample. If the berries are firm, clean, and loose, and the taste slightly salty and in no way fishy, you've got a good product. If the caviar is mushy, oily, and strong, walk out.

There can be no doubt that the American caviar industry is still in a state of incubation and that numerous obstacles will have to be overcome before we have an abundant amount of a consistently first-rate product. But there can also be no doubt that progress is being made fast. Already there seems to be enough red and golden caviar on the market to satisfy the present demand, and even the more prized sturgeon caviar is reasonably available to those willing to spend about one hundred dollars a pound. That the supply of the black delicacy can only increase becomes pretty obvious when you listen to producers like Garbarino alluding to all the new sources of roe and the Engstroms describing the aquaculture techniques they're learning from Sergei Doroshov, Russian defector and marine biologist at the University of California at Davis. "We're building our own sturgeon farm," Mats says, "so that we can induce sturgeon in private waters to produce eggs within four to six years instead of the fifteen to twenty it takes in nature. The Russians are already trying to raise fish in hatcheries, but in a country where the temperature ranges from zero to sixty degrees, there's no way spawning can remain constant. In California we have an average of sixty degrees year-round. If eventually we could perfect the technique whereby the sturgeon are relieved of their eggs by Caesarean section rather than by killing them, the fish could produce for decades."

Increased production of caviar, of course, is one thing; a quality product is another. There most surely will be hundreds of others coming to capitalize on the success of people like the Engstroms and Garbarino, but how many will match the efforts of these pioneers to attain a high standard of excellence? "I'm often asked if my domestic caviar will ever stand up to the imported beluga," says Mario Garbarino.

"Well, I sell both varieties, but I try not to think in those terms—even though I have located some roe in the South that is very similar in size and taste to that of the beluga. What I do know is that there is already some delicious, sensibly priced fresh American caviar on the market for the first time in decades and that a few of us are determined to make it even better."

As for myself, I'll certainly never turn down a mound of fresh beluga, but neither will I miss any opportunity to savor as much of the domestic delicacy as possible.

The following recipes utilizing the new American caviar were created by chefs at some of the country's finest restaurants. The dishes illustrate only a few of the many ways that fresh domestic caviar can be incorporated in our ever-developing style of cooking.

OYSTERS WRAPPED IN SPINACH LEAVES ON GOLDEN CAVIAR
(Restaurant Jean-Louis, Washington, D.C.)

2   doz. small fresh oysters (preferably Maine belons)
2   doz. impeccable spinach leaves, rinsed
1   cup vinaigrette dressing made with hazelnut oil
    Freshly ground pepper to taste
16 oz. golden caviar

Shuck oysters and transfer their juices to a large saucepan. Bring liquid to a boil, add oysters, poach 5–10 seconds, and transfer to a mixing bowl. In another large saucepan, poach spinach leaves in boiling salt water 5 seconds and dry on clean towel. Add vinaigrette dressing to oysters, toss oysters lightly, add freshly ground pepper to taste, then wrap each in a spinach leaf. On each of four large dinner plates place five small portions of caviar around plate and one in center. Position wrapped oysters atop caviar. SERVES 4 as appetizer or light lunch.

Red and Black Caviar Meat Puffs

(La Caravelle, New York City)

2	cups all-purpose flour
4	eggs, separated, yolks beaten
	Pinch sugar
	Freshly ground pepper to taste
8	oz. beer
½	lb. boneless beef sirloin strip
12	oz. red caviar
12	oz. black caviar
2	oz. onions, finely chopped
	Chopped parsley for garnish

In a mixing bowl add beaten yolks, sugar, and pepper to flour and mix well. Add beer and mix again. Whip egg whites stiff, fold into mixture, and let set 1 hour. Flatten sirloin as thin as possible—⅛″ thick—with a rolling pin and cut into 12 even pieces. Place a spoonful of red caviar atop 6 slices of beef, then a spoonful of black on remaining 6 slices. Sprinkle a few chopped onions on top of each. Fold sides around the mixture, close tightly, and roll very gently with hands into balls. Dip each ball into batter, coat evenly, and deep-fry in peanut oil 5–6 minutes. Drain well and present sprinkled with chopped parsley in a clean linen napkin nestled in an attractive basket. SERVES 4–6 as an appetizer.

New Potatoes with Black Caviar

(Stanford Court, San Francisco)

12–14	very small red waxy potatoes (1 lb. or less)
4–5	cups rock salt
½	cup sour cream
	Oil for deep frying
3½–4	oz. black or golden caviar

Preheat oven to 450° F. Wash and dry potatoes, arrange on bed of rock salt in a shallow baking pan, and bake 30–35 minutes. Remove potatoes from oven and slice in half. Scoop out pulp with a melon-ball cutter or small spoon, mash slightly in a small bowl, and keep warm. Heat oil to 375 ° F in a large saucepan, drop potato shells in oil, and fry till golden brown and crisp. Drain well on paper towels. Fill shells with mashed potato, top with a spoonful of sour cream, and add a teaspoon or more of caviar. Serve as an appetizer on thick salad plates atop hot rock salt. SERVES 4–6.

HORSERADISH FLAN WITH FENNEL SAUCE AND RED CAVIAR
(*Le Perroquet, Chicago*)

3	eggs
1½	cups heavy cream
	Pinch nutmeg
	Salt and white pepper to taste
¾	oz. fresh horseradish, grated
⅓	stick unsalted butter
½	cup thinly sliced fennel bulb
⅓	stem fennel, including a few leaves, roughly chopped
3	Tb. roughly chopped onions
3	Tb. roughly chopped mushrooms
3	Tb. dry white wine
¾	cups chicken stock
1–2	Tb. butter
3	drops Pernod
12	oz. red caviar
	Fennel leaves for garnish

Preheat oven to 325° F. In a stainless steel bowl stir eggs lightly with a whisk, then add cream, stir, and strain through a sieve into another bowl. Add salt, pepper, nutmeg, and horseradish and stir. Ladle batter into 4–6 buttered 2-oz. savarin molds or ramekins, stirring batter before each ladling. Place molds in a baking pan and add enough boiling water to pan to rise half-way up sides of molds. Place in oven and bake till slightly puffed: 8 minutes for savarin molds, 15 minutes for ramekins. Remove from oven and let sit in water.

In medium-size, covered skillet steam vegetables about 5 minutes. Add wine and reduce slightly, uncovered. Add chicken stock and cook about 5 minutes more. When vegetables are tender, transfer mixture to a blender or food processor, reduce to a puree, and strain into clean skillet. Add butter plus Pernod and blend well. Roll a film of sauce around bottom of 4–6 dinner plates and unmold flans into center of plates. If cooked in savarin molds, fill center with caviar; if ramekins, spoon mound of caviar on tops. Garnish sides of plates with fennel leaves. SERVES 4–6 as appetizer.

BAY SCALLOPS WITH GOLDEN CAVIAR, PASTA AND BLACK CAVIAR SALAD
(The River Café, Brooklyn, New York)

1	lb. bay scallops
	Salt and freshly ground pepper to taste
2	oz. golden caviar
1	oz. black caviar
2	oz. dry white wine
2	oz. light fish stock
2	oz. heavy cream
2	oz. fresh mayonnaise
2	oz. olive oil
½	oz. white wine vinegar
1	Tb. chopped parsley
4–6	oz. fresh fettucine, cooked *al dente*
2	tomatoes, peeled, seeded, and diced
1	oz. tiny capers, washed well

Season scallops lightly with salt and pepper and place in a stainless steel or enamel skillet with the wine and stock. Bring to a simmer, then remove scallops from liquid and let them cool. Reduce liquid to 2 oz., add cream, stir, strain, and let cool. Place mayonnaise in a stainless steel bowl and whisk in oil and vinegar. Whisk in strained cream mixture, add parsley, and stir. In a small bowl mix together pasta, golden caviar, and 2 oz. of the sauce. Place pasta salad equally in middle of 4 large dinner plates and top each portion with ¼ oz. black caviar. Mix scallops with tomatoes, capers, and remaining sauce, and taste to determine if more pepper is needed. Surround each pasta salad with equal portions of the mixture. Serve at room temperature to 4.

DISCOVERING GREAT AMERICAN CHEESES

••

A WEDGE of well-aged Crowley with a sturdy Petite Sirah. A slice of tangy Nauvoo Blue with a spot of Ficklin or Woodbury. A nugget of Nisqually Goat with a luscious Late Harvest St. Jean. Sound baffling? Well, let me explain that I'm referring to cheeses and wines, and, to be more specific, to certain extraordinary *American* cheeses and wines which might be unfamiliar to most people but which you just might begin to think about serving at the end of a great meal in place of rich cakes, mounds of heavy pastries, and all those overly sweet cordials.

Surely it can be said that nothing characterizes the gastronomic revolution in America more than our determination and ability to draw upon foreign and regional traditions with the prospect of eventually developing a refined cuisine that is distinctively our own. Already incorporated in our ever-evolving style of eating are native varieties of cured ham, pasta, mushrooms, snails, oysters, smoked fish, caviar, hitherto unknown greens and fruits, milk-fed veal, even fresh *foie gras,* and slowly making their way to the national table are any number of regional specialities that have been reinterpreted and given new flair. We now produce our own mineral waters, concoct our own exotic aperitifs, and utilize many of our well-known spirits in the creation of new dishes. Twenty years ago people sneered at any wine label that was not printed in France; today even the most prestigious French producers are racing to California to buy acreage.

Inconsistent, however, with all this gustatory exploitation is the nation's general unawareness of the many wonderful natural cheeses being made in the United States. All make a mockery of those innocuous, plasticized, processed disasters stacked high in supermarkets, and some equal or excel many of the imports in both quality and price. So far, few of our speciality cheeses are widely available outside the regions where they are produced, but regular distribution is increasing as steadily as the number of new cheesemakers, and even now the curious gastronome need do no more than drop a short line or make a quick phone call to receive delivery in a matter of days. Granted that many of these fresh cheeses are essentially imitations of foreign originals (Swiss, Gouda, Feta, and so forth), I've learned while traveling about that the more innovative American producers are making impressive efforts to develop certain styles of cheese that could one day be as indigenous to the United States as our already legendary Liederkranz, Monterey Jack, and Colby.

Why, you might ask, go to the trouble of acquiring domestic speciality cheeses that can cost as much as the imports when the counters of supermarkets, delis, and food shops are overflowing with every foreign cheese from French Brie and double creams to Danish Samsoe to English Double Gloucester? The first reason, I propose, is simply because these premium fresh cheeses exist, many of which provide a taste experience that is altogether different from that of the imports. Second, the probability of domestic cheeses being in better shape and containing fewer additives and preservatives than foreign products is almost assured due to fast delivery from the source. And third, just the idea of introducing a few well-made American cheeses with some of our finer wines at the dinner table seems a lot more interesting (and, yes, downright patriotic) than serving something like an underripe, pasteurized Port du Salut with an all too familiar, exorbitantly expensive Bordeaux.

Curiously enough, fine domestic cheeses have been made in various regions of the country ever since the earliest days of our history, the result primarily of immigrants trying to duplicate the favorites they left behind. Most of the small cheesemakers have been long forgotten, victims of twentieth-century mass production and processing, but some did survive to make important contributions to our gastronomy. What ardent turophile is not familiar, for example, with how the Swiss Emil Frey, attempting to reproduce his native Bismarck Schlosskäse, created a cheese in Monroe, New York that his boss would name Liederkranz after the choral club where it was first introduced? Also during the nineteenth century the Scots dairyman David Jacks developed a cheese in Monterey County, California that was to assume his last name (minus the "s") coupled with that of the nearest shipping point. The formula for Brick—the semisoft, pale yellow, nutty beauty similar to

Limburger—was worked out in Wisconsin by John Jossi in 1877, only to become one of the most popular American originals in the Midwest. And who could fail to mention Colby and Herkimer, the first developed in the late nineteenth century by the Steinwand family in Colby, Wisconsin, and the second a celebrated Cheddar named for the small market town in Herkimer County, New York.

Of equal importance in our cheesemaking history are not only those small producers and distributors who once created or popularized great cheeses but also those who continue to combat the almost overwhelming odds against the commercial giants who all but monopolize the market. With regard to the best blue cheeses, I refer to how Nauvoo began its distinguished evolution in 1937 when Oscar Rohde (father-in-law of the present owner, Bill Skully) discovered what could be accomplished in limestone caves along the Mississippi near Nauvoo, Illinois, or how the proprietors of Maytag Dairy Farms worked in close coordination with Iowa State University back in 1941 to develop the exquisite blue they produce today. Celso Viviani's son and grandson, Pete and David, still turn out the same Sonoma Jack their predecessor perfected fifty years ago at the Sonoma Cheese Factory in Sonoma, California, and Pierce Thompson continues at the Marin French Cheese Company in Petaluma, California to make Brie and Camembert in the style originated by his great-grandfather in 1865. I refer to Randolph Smith, owner of Crowley Cheese Factory in Healdville, Vermont, who, along with his wife and son, patiently handcraft the rare Colby first kneaded by the Crowley family 1824; to Jack Ayers at Sugarbush Farm aging his distinctive Cheddars in the sheds of an old farmhouse high above Taftsville, Vermont; and to the Demeter family in Lena, Illinois hand-packaging their sumptuous Bries and Camemberts and coming up with such successful new American creations as the double cream Sno-Belle (intimately referred to by most of us as Snow Cheese).

Tillamook, Teleme, Husker, Cache Valley, Calef, Old Heidelberg, Camosun, Schloss, Kentucky Trappish, Mossholder—these are but a few speciality cheeses that have been produced in thirty-five states over the past few decades, yet remain virtually unknown to all but those who live in the particular regions. Add to this the better, unprocessed imitations of foreign cheeses, some of which actually surpass the originals in quality and others which have begun to take on new identity. Consider goat cheese, for one, which for centuries has been a veritable staple in the diets of Europeans but only recently halfway appreciated in the United States. Anticipating the newly educated American palate, Daniel Considine was perhaps the first to make goat cheese for wide distribution on his farm in south-central Wisconsin, followed by Clayton Rawhouser in Winger, Minnesota (who created both a goat's milk Cheddar and a goat's milk Colby), Gail LeCompte in Lebanon, New Jersey (Chevreese cheese), Jere Linda Sayer in New Providence, Iowa (Capricorn), Laura Chenel in Sonoma, California, and David and Jeanne Greatorex in Kapowsin, Washington (soft Nisqually Capri and hard Capricese). At the edge of the Blue Ridge Mountains in Crozet, Virginia, Owie Bloemers was determined to duplicate the delicious Gouda she so admired while living in her husband's native Holland, but the unpasteurized, handmade Farmstead cheese she developed from local Grade A cow's milk turned out to be even better than the original. "There is no other cheese like it," says Owie. "It's a Virginia product, and it's an Albermarle County product. Here the climate, the red dirt, and the grasses the cows eat are different from those in Holland. Maybe one day this will be called simply Virginia cheese."

One word about buying and caring for these fresh cheeses which, don't forget, are biologically alive and continue to develop—unlike those inert supermarket corpses: Whether you order by mail (which for most people will be necessary a while longer) or purchase in a shop, make every effort to get cheese at the peak of its flavor. With firm, aged cheeses like Cheddar, Tillamook, and Colby you shouldn't encounter many problems, and on the packages of such soft-rind products as Brick, Liederkranz, Old Heidelberg, and Bierkäse there is usually a pull date and directions pertaining to the various stages of ripeness (I never hesitate to open packages in a shop and inspect the cheese). When ordering blue cheeses by mail, make it clear that you want your dessert cheese aged and creamy, not dry and crumbly (at Maytag, you should request "extra aged"), and when ordering soft flor rinds like Brie, Camembert, and Sno-Belle, state that you'd prefer a soft, ripe cheese and not one that's firm and chalky in the center (Sno-Belle in gold wrapping, for example, is riper than that in silver). If you do end up with an underripe Brie or Sno-Belle, simply remove all wrapping, rewrap the uncut cheese loosely in wax paper (*not* foil or plastic), place in the bottom of the refrigerator, and check the ripeness from day to day. Ideally, the white surface of the flor rinds (which is completely edible) should be taking on a slightly brownish tint and feel quite soft to the touch. To stop the process, wrap tightly in plastic. Remember, finally, that any ripe fresh cheese can be wrapped in plastic, frozen, and thawed slowly for twenty-four hours on the lowest shelf of the refrigerator.

Serving cheese with wine after the main course or salad permits numerous possibilities. Quite often the dry white or red wine served with the meal is perfectly acceptable also with the cheese, though matching a particular sweet wine with a particular cheese is not only always intriguing but adds a special touch. In any case, effort should be made never to overwhelm a delicate wine with an assertive cheese, and vice versa. A chewy, tannic Petit Sirah is capable of taking on satisfactorily the pungent Liederkranz or Old Heidelberg, but to pit this big red against a creamy Sno-Belle or elusive Nisqually goat would not only deny the wine its full potential but discredit the cheese. If as many as three distinctly different cheeses are offered on the same board (with three different knives, of course), it would be wise to make available both a dry and sweet wine with the appropriate glasses. Some form of bread should always be passed, but to play it safe with those like myself who generally prefer their cheese without bread, it's a good idea to set a salad fork when special pronged cheese knives are not being used. It goes without saying that all fine cheeses should be served close to room temperature.

Blue with port, sherry, or a noble Cabernet; goat with a sweet botrytised Chardonnay, Late Harvest Riesling, or zesty Chenin Blanc; Jack or Tillamook with a young Pinot Noir or light, fruity Zinfandel; Brick or Bierkäse with a gutsy Muscat—any combination is possible, and all make essential contributions to the development of a critical palate. Although it's true that certain American cheeses and wines seem to have a natural affinity, it's also true that nothing is more subjective than a choice of wine for a specific kind of cheese. What's most important is that throughout our country are some beautiful cheeses capable of adding magnitude to any meal, purely American products which are playing an intricate role in the gastronomic revolution and which are just waiting to be discovered by adventurous food lovers.

DOMESTIC SPECIALITY CHEESE MAIL ORDER

Listed here by region are the names, addresses, and phone numbers of producers and distributors of the finest speciality cheeses made in America. Included also are some, though not necessarily all, of the fresh cheeses kept in stock. All companies will either ship direct from the factory or supply the names of local outlets where the cheeses are more readily available. Be sure to inquire about prices and shipping policies, both of which can vary from region to region.

EAST

Crowley Cheese Factory
Healdville, Vermont 05147
802-259-2340
(Colby)

Sugarbush Farm
Woodstock, Vermont 05091
802-457-1757
(Aged Cheddar, Sage Cheddar, Green Mountain Blue,
Green Mountain Jack)

Vermont Country Store
Weston, Vermont 05161
802-824-3184
(Aged Cheddar, Sage Cheddar, Smoked Cheddar)

Plymouth Cheese Corporation
Box 1
Plymouth, Vermont 05060
802-672-3650
(Granular Cured Cheddar)

Calef's Country Store
Barrington, New Hampshire 03825
603-664-2231
(Aged New York and Vermont Cheddar,
Sage Cheddar, Smoked Cheddar)

Dean & DeLuca
121 Prince Street
New York, New York 10013
212-254-7774
(Goat, Monterey Jack, New York and
Vermont Cheddar)

Washington Market
162 Duane Street
New York, New York 10013
212-233-0250
(Chenel Raw Goat, Brie, Sno-Belle,
Fresh White Cheese)

Richter Bros., Inc.
801 Washington Avenue
Carlstadt, New Jersey 07072
201-935-6850
(Sonoma Jack; String; Brie; Camembert; Schloss;
Tillamook; New York, Wisconsin, and Vermont Aged
Cheddar, Colby, Edam, Gouda)

Phillips Lancaster County Swiss Cheese Center
433 Centerville Road
Gordonville, Pennsylvania 17529
717-354-4424
(Six varieties of natural Swiss)

Georgetown Wine and Cheese Shop
1413 Wisconsin Avenue, N.W.
Washington, D.C. 20007
202-333-8822
(Monterey Jack, Maytag Blue, Brick, New York and
Vermont Aged Cheddar, Sage Cheddar, Tillamook,
Teleme, Fresh Cream Cheese, Bierkäse, String,
Goat, Asiago)

SOUTH

Landsdale Farm
Route 2, Box 288A
Crozet, Virginia 22932
804-823-2348
(Farmstead Raw Milk Gouda)

Early's Honey Stand
Route 2, Box 100
Spring Hill, Tennessee 37174
615-486-2230
(Tennessee Cheddar, Monterey Jack, Aged Swiss)

Martin's Wine Cellar
3827 Barone Street
New Orleans, Louisiana 70015
504-899-7411
(Fresh Cream Cheese, Blue, Monterey Jack,
Colby, New York Cheddar, Bierkäse, Swiss)

Jamail's
3114 Kirby Drive
Houston, Texas 77098
713-523-5535

(Over one-hundred domestics including Goat,
Herkimer, Blue, Brie, Camembert, Teleme,
Tillamook, Brick, String, Bierkäse, Smoked
Gouda, Monterey Jack, Liederkranz, Sno-Belle)

MIDWEST

Maytag Dairy Farms
Route 1, Box 806
Newton, Iowa 50208
515-792-1133
(Blue, Brick, Raw Milk Cheddar, Swiss, Edam)

Nauvoo Milk Products, Inc.
P.O. Box 188
Nauvoo, Illinois 62354
217-453-2213
(Blue, Aged Cheddar, Baby Swiss)

Kolb-Lena Cheese Company
301 West Railroad Street
Lena, Illinois 61048
815-369-4577
(Brie, Sno-Belle, Old Heidelberg, Camembert,
Swiss, Blue, Colby, Feta)

Steve's Cheese
Route 2
Denmark, Wisconsin 54208
414-863-2397
(Blue, Aged Cheddar, Colby, Edam, Brick,
Farmer's Cheese, Swiss)

Gibbsville Cheese Company, Inc.
Box 152, Route 3
Sheboygan Falls, Wisconsin 53085
414-564-3242
(Aged Cheddar, Colby, Monterey Jack, Two-Tone—
Colby and Monterey Jack)

Wisconsin's Best
723 East Alfred Street
Weyauwega, Wisconsin 54983
414-867-3185
(Aged Colby Longhorn, Aged Wisconsin Cheddar)

The Big Cheese
Skyway Level, IDS Crystal Court
Minneapolis, Minnesota 55402
612-823-7269
(Colby, New York and Wisconsin Aged Cheddar,
Monterey Jack, Co-Jack—Colby and Monterey Jack)

San Francisco International Cheese Imports
1908 Innes Street
San Francisco, California 94124
415-648-5252
(Sonoma Jack, Aged Cheddar, Teleme, Oregon Blue,
String, Nisqually Capri Goat, Capricese Goat)

Oakville Grocery
1555 Pacific Avenue
San Francisco, California 94109
415-885-4411
(Chenel Goat, Nisqually Capri Goat, Capricese
Goat, Tolibia Blue, Oregon Blue, Kentucky
Raw Milk Cheddar, Sonoma Jack, Teleme, Cabot
Aged Cheddar)

Marin French Cheese Company
7500 Red Hill Road
P.O. Box 99
Petaluma, California 94952
707-762-6001
(Brie, Schloss, Camembert)

The Cheese Factory
Pleasanton, California 94566
415-846-2577
(Five varieties of Jack, Teleme, String, Blue,
Colby Longhorn, Old-Fashioned Cream Cheese,
Swiss, Aged Cheddar)

Tillamook County Creamery Association
Box 313
Tillamook, Oregon 97141
503-842-4481
(Tillamook)

MOUSSE, BEAUTIFUL MOUSSE

●●●

How could I ever forget that particular lunch I shared with Jovan Trboyevic at Le Perroquet in Chicago? Having agonized through still another unsettling trip aboard a particularly monstrous manifestation of the Wright Brothers' folly, I was eager for some decent, light sustenance once my calm had been at least partially restored. Aware of my fragile state of mind and jittery stomach, Jovan once again proved his genius for orchestrating *the* appropriate meal. Chatham oysters poached in white wine and anointed with a light butter sauce, home-cured goat cheese, chocolate truffles, and a '70 Château Carbonnieux were singular experiences, to be sure; but the meal's tour de force was a simple, warm, main-course duck liver mousse served in a miniature porcelain skillet with fresh mushroom "sticks" and a feathery sauce made with veal stock, tomato, and sherry vinegar. This creation was consumed in no more than three or four bites, but what subtle perfection, what bliss, what eminent satisfaction. Given other circumstances, I might have opted for a more traditional main course of lamb chops or fish stew or rack of veal, but on this occasion, nothing could have made more sense or yielded more soothing pleasure than that beautiful mousse.

Mousse is a light, smooth concoction, either sweet or savory, composed of eggs, cream, and one or more pureed ingredients. The mousse originated in France in the Middle Ages, and no country has contributed more to the evolution of this dish than France. Whether the Normans introduced it to the English is debatable, but by the fourteenth century, the *moyse* or *mouse* (particularly that made with apple) was one of the most popular preparations in Britain. Although this ancient dish is similar in texture to the familiar soufflé, pudding, custard, and flan, it was only with the advent of modern blenders and food processors capable of doing all the necessary grinding and pureeing in a matter of seconds that mousses began to catch on in the United States. There was always, no doubt, chocolate mousse—that same rich preparation found in all French bistros but, curiously enough, never so much as mentioned by Escoffier in his lengthy consideration of more than fifty different mousse varieties. But today, as a result of the titanic impact of *la nouvelle cuisine* on American cooking styles and eating habits, fluffy cold and hot mousses composed of everything from seafood to meats to vegetables to exotic fruits are being seen more and more. So far only the most sophisticated restaurants in this country have elevated mousses beyond the dessert menu, but before long, mousses served as appetizers, vegetables, side dishes, and main courses (especially at lunchtime) will surely play an integral role in the development of American cookery.

Already in the United States certain chefs are producing mousses that are every bit as impressive as those created by their European confrères. In Los Angeles, the mousseline of white fish with truffle sauce at L'Ermitage is being imitated and modified all over town— with and without success. Customers at La Maisonette in Cincinnati beg for the exact recipe for the mousse of ham and *foie gras*. Gastronomes visiting New York enjoy debating the merits of The Four Seasons' mousses of crab meat, bay scallops, duck livers, and trout with leeks; Roger Fessaguet's mysterious *mousseline de volaille grande-mère* at La Caravelle; Francine Scherer's mousse of chicken and sweetbreads at Soho Charcuterie; and Larry Forgione's tangy duckling mousse at The River Café. And in Chicago, the talk of epicures is what Jovan Trboyevic can possibly come up with as sucessors to his sensational mousses of sea urchin, fennel, turnip, parsnip, and kiwi served at Le Perroquet and his private restaurant, Les Nomades. "The thing to remember about mousses," Jovan told me, "is there must be logical contrast in both taste and color: carrots, turnips, and broccoli, say, for a three-vegetable mousse with tomato-saffron cream sauce, or a pungent mushroom mousse with a beautiful but subtle pimiento sauce, or a mild mousse of capon with a colorful and assertive basil sauce. There's more to a great mousse than just pureeing anything you have on hand. There is an important chemistry to be understood."

Although one of the most delightful ways to end any meal is with a lovely iced mousse made from fresh berries, melon, chocolate, nuts, coconut, or any other dessert ingredient, why not also consider serving mousse either as an appetizer or as the principal focus of the meal? The following recipes illustrate only a fraction of the existing possibilities. The mousses intended to be served as desserts should be obvious enough; the others lend themselves to any number of occasions: the molded salmon in aspic as either a luncheon main course or a dinner appetizer; the Blue Cheese as either an appetizer or savory; the artichoke as a main course or side vegetables. Most of these mousses are a cinch to prepare; several require a little more time and effort; and all can be modified easily by an imaginative chef. Whichever ones you choose will lend a gracious touch to any meal and add an exciting new dimension to your American cookery.

BLUE CHEESE MOUSSE

1	envelope unflavored gelatin
3	Tb. cold water
½	lb. blue cheese, room temperature
2	oz. cream cheese, room temperature
1½	tsp. Worcestershire sauce
	White pepper to taste
2	eggs, separated
¾	cup heavy cream
	Parsley or watercress

In a small bowl sprinkle gelatin over water, let soften, stir over simmering water till dissolved, and let cool. In another bowl combine cheeses and whip with an electric beater till mixture is smooth. Stir in Worcestershire, pepper to taste, egg yolks, and gelatin. In another bowl beat egg whites till stiff and gently fold egg whites and whipped cream into cheese mixture. Transfer mixture to a lightly oiled 1-quart mold and chill at least 6 hours. Turn mousse out onto a serving platter and garnish with parsley or watercress. SERVES 4–6.

Cold Ham Mousse

1   envelope unflavored gelatin
½   cup Bourbon
½   stick butter
¼   cup flour
1   cup hot milk
½   tsp. nutmeg
     Cayenne pepper to taste
     Salt to taste
2   egg yolks
½   cup heavy cream
2   cups cooked ham, chopped finely in a blender or food processor
     Orange slices and watercress

In a small bowl sprinkle gelatin over 3 Tb. of the Bourbon, let soften, and stir over simmering water till dissolved. In a heavy saucepan melt butter, add flour, and stir over low heat about 2 mintues. Add milk gradually and stir till mixture is thick. Add nutmeg, a few grains of cayenne, salt, and remaining Bourbon and stir thoroughly. In a small bowl mix eggs with heavy cream, stir in a little hot sauce, then add mixture to sauce. Stir over low heat till well thickened, add gelatin and chopped ham, and blend thoroughly. Transfer mixture to a 1-quart lightly greased mold and chill at least 6 hours. Dip mold quickly into hot water, turn out onto a platter, and garnish with orange slices and watercress. SERVES 4–6.

Molded Salmon Mousse in Aspic

6   cups fish stock
2   parsley sprigs, ½ bay leaf, ⅛ tsp. thyme tied in cheesecloth
2½ lbs. salmon steak
3   Tb. gelatin
½   cup white wine
    Dill sprigs
    Strips of lemon peel
1   pitted black olive
¼   lb. smoked salmon, cut into small pieces
¾   cup minced onions
½   stick butter
    Salt, white pepper, and lemon juice to taste
1   cup heavy cream, lightly beaten
    Carrot rosettes

Place fish stock and herb bouquet in a large enameled saucepan, bring to the simmer, and poach salmon for 8–10 minutes or till it flakes. Remove fish from stock, skin and bone it, and set aside to cool. Strain stock into a large bowl, chill, remove fat, and clarify by simmering with 2 egg whites plus one crushed shell. In a small bowl, sprinkle gelatin over white wine, let soften, add to hot stock, and stir till gelatin is dissolved. Let aspic cool, line a 1-quart decorative fish mold with a thin layer of aspic, and chill till set. Dip dill sprigs, lemon peel, and black olive into aspic and decorate the gills, tail, and eye of the mold. Chill till decorations are set, add another layer of aspic, let set, and continue process till aspic is about ¼-inch thick. Flake salmon into a bowl and add smoked salmon. Sauté onions in butter till soft, add 2 cups of the aspic, simmer 5 minutes, and add to salmon. In a blender or food processor puree salmon mixture in batches, transfer to a large bowl, add salt, pepper, and lemon juice, and fold in cream. Pack mousse into the mold, pour on a thin layer of aspic, cover, and chill at least 6 hours. Dip mold quickly into hot water, turn out mousse onto a large serving platter, and decorate sides of platter with carrot rosettes. Pour remaining aspic around mousse, adjust carrot rosettes, and chill till aspic is set. SERVES 4–6.

Artichoke Mousse with
Curried Mayonnaise

1   envelope unflavored gelatin
3   Tb. cold water
2   9-oz. packages frozen artichoke hearts
    Juice of 1 lemon
½   cup mayonnaise
1   cup sour cream
½   tsp. salt
½   tsp. white pepper
    Curried Mayonnaise: Blend 1 tsp. curry powder in 1 cup
    fresh mayonnaise

In a small bowl sprinkle gelatin over water, let soften, stir over simmering water till dissolved, and let cool. Cook artichoke hearts according to package directions in lightly salted water with the lemon juice. Drain and chop coarsely. Place artichokes, gelatin, ½-cup mayonnaise, sour cream, and seasonings in a blender or food processor, puree, pour into a lightly oiled 5–6 cup mold, and chill at least 6 hours. Dip mold quickly into hot water, turn out onto a serving platter, and serve with curried mayonnaise. SERVES 4–6. (Note: Spinach, mushrooms, broccoli, or celery root can be substituted for the artichokes.)

Peach Rum Mousse

1   envelope unflavored gelatin
3   Tb. light rum
3–4   ripe peaches, peeled, pitted, and halved
¼   cup superfine sugar
      Juice of 1 lemon
1–2   drops almond extract
¼   tsp. salt
½   cup heavy cream, whipped
2   egg whites
      Rum

In a small bowl sprinkle gelatin over rum, let soften, stir over simmering water till dissolved, and let cool. Place peaches, sugar, lemon juice, almond extract, salt, and gelatin in a blender or food processor, puree, and transfer to a mixing bowl. Fold in whipped cream and chill mixture till it just begins to set. Whisk egg whites till stiff, beat half into mixture, then fold in the remaining half. Transfer mixture to a lightly oiled 4–5 cup mold and chill at least 6 hours. To serve, spoon a little rum over each portion. SERVES 4–6.

LEMON MOUSSE WITH RASPBERRY SAUCE

1	envelope unflavored gelatin
2	Tb. white wine
⅓	cup lemon juice
1½	Tb. grated lemon rind
3	eggs, separated
½	cup sugar
1	cup heavy cream, whipped
1	10-oz. package frozen raspberries, thawed and drained (juice reserved)
⅛	cup sugar
1	Tb. lemon juice
1	Tb. kirsch

In a small bowl sprinkle gelatin over white wine and let soften. Add lemon juice and grated lemon rind and stir over simmering water till gelatin is dissolved. In another bowl beat egg yolks with 3 Tb. of the sugar till mixture ribbons, slowly add gelatin mixture, and stir. In another bowl beat egg whites till foamy, add remaining sugar, and beat till meringue holds soft peaks. Add whipped cream to egg yolk mixture and fold in half of meringue. Add cream mixture to remaining meringue and fold together. Chill mousse at least 2 hours. In a blender or food processor combine remaining ingredients and puree. Strain puree to remove seeds and add enough reserved raspberry juice to thin slightly. To serve, spoon mousse onto plates and add sauce on the side. SERVES 4–6.

CANTALOUPE MOUSSE

1   large cantaloupe
⅓   cup gin
2   Tb. superfine sugar
    Pinch salt
¼   cup heavy cream, whipped

Cut off top third of cantaloupe, remove seeds, and scoop out enough balls to measure 2 cups. In a bowl place balls with 2 Tb. of the gin, toss, and chill. Scoop remainder of the flesh from shell and top and puree in a blender or food processor. Slice bottom off melon so it will stand upright and chill the shell. In a bowl combine the puree with remaining gin, sugar, and salt and fold in whipped cream thoroughly. Cover mixture with foil and place in freezer till firm, stirring from time to time. Transfer mousse to the shell and arrange melon balls over it. SERVES 4–6.

GAME IS THE NAME

●●●

ALTHOUGH BRILLAT-SAVARIN, that masterful eighteenth-century
French philosopher of the table, was never very far from some form of
exciting gastronomic adventure, it seems that nothing impressed him
more than the succulent wild game to which he was treated on his first
visit to American shores. On one occasion, in Connecticut, the eminent
epicure and a Yankee companion had felled a number of small partridges, a half-dozen gray squirrels, and a magnificent wild turkey.
Once the catch made its way into the kitchen of the host, a gentleman
farmer by the name of Bulow, the dextrous French visitor wasted no
time turning out partridge *en papillote*, squirrel simmered in court
bouillon spiked with Madeira, and a roasted turkey which was *"char-
mant à la vue, flatteur à l'odorat, et délicieux au goût!"*

Whether or not Brillat-Savarin was in the position to slip a few slices
of truffle under his turkey's skin (the classic French method), I don't
know, but truffle or no truffle, you can rest assured that the taste and
texture of that wild fowl was a far cry from those characterless corn
oil-injected birds found in American supermarkets today. You can also
count on the probability that the freshly killed partridges and squirrels
were juicy and flavorful, the ideal fare for a cold winter meal. Of
course this type of wild game, in addition to numerous other varieties,
was as much a staple of the American diet in the eighteenth and nineteenth centuries as chicken, pheasant, partridge, deer, quail, grouse,
elk, woodcock, bear, buffalo—all were once plentiful in both markets
and restaurants, so much so that eventually hunting quotas had to be
introduced to assure that our finest animals and birds did not altogether disappear from our fields and woodlands.

Today controls on most species are stricter than ever, and those who enjoy wild game must consider it a delicacy. No doubt there is still enough available in season (generally from October to March) to allow outdoor enthusiasts to stock their freezers, and even out of season a sufficient quantity is produced on game farms to keep large-city purveyors, speciality butcher shops, mail order outlets, and restaurants in good supply. With the reasonable availability of wild game in the United States, therefore, I find it both curious and sad that most Americans seem to have lost whatever passion we once had for these exotic meats and fowl. Naturally when the supply of any foodstuff is limited over a long period of time, its popularity is bound to dwindle, but even so, how many people today take advantage of the opportunities to savor a brace of young quail, an aromatic venison pâté, a roast pheasant stuffed with tarragon and crushed berries, or a rich jugged hare stewed in its own blood?

Contrary to popular belief, wild game is now available in quite a few restaurants in the United States (through I consider it nothing less than disgraceful that many restaurants are either ignorant about the acquisition and preparation of game or simply content to forget about this fare in favor of exploiting the public's obsession with beef steaks and prime ribs, tasteless battery ducks swimming in syrupy sauces, and overcooked veal cutlets oozing with mozzarella cheese). I've enjoyed delicious roast quail with sautéed artichoke bottoms and "dirty rice" at Brennan's in Houston, braised South Dakota pheasant and Montana elk at the American Restaurant in Kansas City, wild boar at Maxwell's Plum in New York City, a memorable ragoût of venison at the Bakery in Chicago, and a succulent buffalo steak (which, by the way, is lower in cholesterol and higher in protein than beef steak) at Stonehenge in Ridgefield, Connecticut. Rosellini's Other Place in Seattle (which probably serves more game than any other restaurant in America) offers game-farm fresh pheasant, quail, chukar partridge, guinea hen, and grouse, as well as such exotica as bear, antelope, and mountain sheep. At The Fort outside Denver, Don and Nancy Krohn pride themselves on both their buffalo sausage and steaks ("Buffalo steak outsells beef steak two to one," says Nancy, "and our customers come from all over the world."). Habitués of "21" in New York know that they can always be served either a brace of quail, baby pheasant, mallard duck, wild boar, or the venison steak with a special game sauce for which the restaurant is justly renowned. And at The Four Seasons in New York, both the fall and winter menus include quail roasted with sage and fried grapes, medallions of venison with chestnut puree, possibly the most flavorful stuffed baby pheasant this side of the Atlantic, and, occasionally, an exemplary buffalo steak.

Most experts agree that although the majority of Americans will most likely never prefer partridge or grouse to the traditional holiday turkey or ham, the popularity of wild game is nevertheless gradually increasing. "We're selling more game than ever before," I was told by Jerry Stein at Iron Gate Products in New York, perhaps the largest purveyor of game in the country. "Without doubt it's catching on, and one reason is that with the sophistication of modern transport and freezing processes, we can supply a customer with anything from chukar partridge to snow grouse to Muscovy duck all year long on a few days' notice. In addition to our suppliers in this country, we have wild game coming in from Scandinavia, New Zealand, Canada, all over. And let me tell you this, except for certain birds like quail and wild duck (which, because of their delicate juices, should be bought fresh), frozen game is actually better than fresh for the simple reason that freezing breaks down tissue and thus helps to tenderize. Ninety percent of all game sold in this country is frozen."

Needless to say, unless a sportsman presents you with a pair of fresh pheasant or a few quail, you have to acquire your game either from a speciality butcher shop or write one of the mail-order outlets located in various areas of the country. Game fresh from the field can be delectable, especially if it's young and has been cleaned impeccably and handled properly. Some connoisseurs, however, approach such a gift with a certain degree of apprehension, and I must admit that after hearing about rabbits infected with tularemia, fowl suffering from Newcastle disease, and venison that's become rancid due to overexposure to air, I personally feel a little better knowing the game I eat has passed government inspection. In most states it is illegal to sell wild game that hasn't undergone regulatory inspection, and from what I've learned, there are very few butchers today willing to dress, hang, and prepare any type of game that doesn't bear a stamp of approval. Fortunately, most birds and animals raised on preserves are killed young and frozen immediately, so what you find in the market should be of the finest quality.

There are three categories of wild game: large furred (venison, bear, boar, buffalo); small furred (rabbit, hare, squirrel); and feathered (pheasant, partridge, turkey, goose, duck, woodcock, grouse, pigeon, quail, dove). Although venison was once so common in this country that it was referred to simply as "meat," today the term applies only to the flesh of antlered animals (deer, reindeer, antelope, elk, moose). The old (and questionable) custom of hanging venison till it was practically putrefied (supposedly for the sake of superior flavor) has all but disappeared in the United States, and now most deer meat that is bought in fine butcher shops is usually tender, juicy, and not excessively gamy. Meat from older animals, however, can be tough and strong in flavor, so if you or your butcher have any doubts, the traditional solution is to leave it for at least twenty-four hours in a marinade of ½ wine, ¼ each of vinegar and water, fresh garlic, thyme, bay leaves, salt, pepper, and an onion studded with a few cloves. Venison, which makes not only excellent steaks and roasts but also delectable pâtés and burgers, should always be larded or barded when roasted (with strips of fat salt pork either run through or wrapped around the meat) and should never be overcooked unless it's incorporated in a stew or ragoût. Bear and boar are generally marinated and prepared like venison, but buffalo meat, which tends to be tough, requires long marinating. (The Horse and Hound Inn in South Salem, New York, marinates its buffalo for two weeks in corn liquor steeped with hickory nuts.)

The variety of small furred game most prized by hunters and connoisseurs alike is hare—preferably the large jackrabbit and snowshoe. Most Americans seem to have no qualms about eating jugged hare in England and *civet de lapin* in France, but once back home, no way. Perhaps it's because our worship of the bunny rabbit doesn't apply on foreign soil; maybe the fancy language of menus helps to transform our mental patterns; or, most likely, it's due to the fact that Europeans know a lot more than we do about preparing this type of game. In any case, both hare and wild rabbit are delicious when cooked properly. Since the meat of hare is dark, a bit tough, and fairly gamy, it's best when marinated for a day or two, then either braised or stewed. Young rabbit, on the other hand, is light meated, finely textured, and tastes something like chicken. So tender is the meat of cottontail, brush, and marsh rabbits that knowledgeable Southerners love it fried for about twenty minutes in hot oil or sautéed in bacon fat and served with a sour cream sauce. And the same is true for squirrel (one of the few species of wild game that still abounds all over the country). Young squirrel is tender, delicately flavored, and a gastronomic delight when either rubbed with dried sage and broiled or fricasseed with Bourbon. Although squirrel meat that is older tends to be tough, it is nevertheless a key ingredient for that sublime concoction known throughout the South as Brunswick stew—when, that is, the dish is authentic. Perhaps the finest tribute to the gray squirrel came a few years back when I was told by the great French chef Paul Bocuse that he simply didn't understand why more Americans didn't value the subtle taste of this plentiful animal.

No doubt the most popular game in this country is the feathered variety, with pheasant, quail, and duck heading the list. Today the American pheasant is a crossbreed of several varieties, including the English ringneck and the Mongolian pheasant, and both the showy, colorful male and the less exotic female are prized for their densely packed, white-meated breasts. Roast pheasant under glass, pheasant steamed in a clay pot, pheasant in cream, pheasant pie, pheasant braised with juniper berries and sauerkraut—these are all classic dishes that can transform an otherwise ordinary meal into a memorable feast. Quail is the most abundant of all game birds in the United States, and although natives of Oklahoma and the Southwest consider a brace of valley, spotted, or desert quail the absolute ultimate in palatal satisfaction, Southern sportsmen insist that there is no species quite like the bobwhite. Wild duck roasted rare with green olives remains one of the great gastronomic dishes served at epicurean dinners, and anyone who's ever appreciated a well-prepared mallard, canvasback (which feeds on the wild celery along the Chesapeake Bay shoreline and is rare) teal, or widgeon is quick to point out the radical differences between these juicy, flavorful birds and the fatty, overcooked, bland domestic version served in every "Continental" restaurant from coast to coast.

Much of the same can be said for both wild goose and wild turkey as compared with their domestic cousins. To be sure, any fresh goose makes for a nice change from the traditional turkey, and at Christmas nothing gives me more pleasure than stuffing the one I get on Long Island with prunes, apples, and walnuts and serving it with a natural or wine gravy. But compared to a very young brant or white-fronted wild gander, a domestic goose is not only incredibly fatty but quite impractical when you're trying to feed more than four persons. The noble American wild turkey that so fascinated Brillat-Savarin still thrives in the East (though, alas, no longer in Connecticut) and the lower Midwest, but, unfortunately, it is one of the most difficult birds to acquire from markets even during the cold months (probably because so much wild turkey is smoked to satisfy the year-round demands of epicures). Again, however, if you're determined to serve this extremely lean and succulent bird instead of the supermarket variety, check with your specialty butcher well in advance and in all likelihood he'll track one down for you.

Other varieties of feathered game which enjoy limited but ever increasing popularity in the United States are pigeon, dove, partridge, woodcock, and grouse. Although the dark meat of pigeon and dove can be delicious if not overcooked, these are relatively small birds that can be dry and tough when not well barded with bacon and braised slowly (or "smothered"). The same holds true with partridge which, due to its stubborn texture, should be marinated, then turned and basted frequently during the roasting. I've never eaten an American partridge that could equal those served during the first days of the season in England and France (French restaurant menus list young partridge as *perdreau*—masculine—and older ones, ungraciously, as *perdrix*—feminine), but the chukar partridge (originally imported from the Himalayas and now native to the Northwest) can make for memorable dining when marinated and cooked properly.

While woodcock and grouse are widely distributed throughout the country, their appeal so far seems to be limited to sportsmen, for neither is easy to come by on the commercial market. In France, the rich, dark meat of woodcock, as well as the cooked entrails on toast, is possibly prized by gastronomes over that of all other game birds, while in England and Scotland the most coveted of all game is young Scotch grouse, fat from the tender and aromatic shoots of heather on which it feeds and the bird which makes August 12, "The Glorious 12th," into a very important day for huntsmen eager to begin the grouse season. Unfortunately, the United States Department of Agriculture forbids the importation of any fowl from Great Britain due to the supposed risk of Newcastle disease, but, nevertheless, connoisseurs agree that such domestic varieties of grouse as ruffed, spruce, sharptailed, and even sage (which feeds on sage buds and can thus be strong in flavor) often prove to be exceptional delicacies if they are young and tender (proof of which is clean claws and soft breast-bone tips) and either braised or roasted.

Like venison, most feathered game should be wrapped in either bacon or fat salt pork to prevent drying out during the cooking process. To rid marine birds of their possible fishy flavor, either soak in salt water overnight or insert flavor-absorbing fruits and vegetables (onions, apples, celery, garlic) into the cavity to remain during cooking and later discarded. Interchangeable flavorings which generally complement game birds are wine, brandy, gin, tarragon, onions, leeks, acidulous grapes, and such tart wild berries as juniper, gooseberries, currants, and lingonberries. There are two distinct schools of thought about whether or not to marinate wild fowl for additional tenderness and flavor. No doubt if you're working with an older partridge or grouse, which in all likelihood is very ripe, placing the bird in a marinade for a few hours not only improves the texture of the meat but also softens the gamy flavor. But in most cases (and definitely when the bird is young), I find that marinating such birds as duck, goose, and pheasant does no more than destroy delicate natural flavors and quite often turns the meat into a flaccid mess.

Age determines how wild fowl should be cooked, and if there is any doubt that a bird is young or prime, a moist-heat method or roasting in foil is always advisable. Most light-fleshed fowl (pheasant, quail, guinea hen, turkey) is cooked fairly well done, while, ideally, dark-meated feathered game (duck, goose, grouse, pigeon) should be roasted till brown on the outside but rare and juicy within. Small birds like quail, woodcock, and dove are often good wrapped in grape leaves, then skewered and roasted or broiled. If there is occasion to acquire these birds undrawn, try first cooking the entrails, then chop them finely, sauté in butter, and serve on toast fried in butter or natural fat. In any case, don't forget that small bird livers should always be reserved for later use in pâtés, stocks, soups, ragoûts, and any number of unusual dishes.

As to the best ways to serve wild game, remember that all sauces and accompaniments should not detract from but rather complement the natural flavors of the meat. Traditionally, a roast haunch or rack of venison is served with a highly seasoned black pepper–gooseberry jelly sauce, a puree of chestnuts, and fresh watercress, whereas a saddle of venison usually requires no more than a regular black pepper sauce, chestnuts braised with Brussels sprouts, possible a little mild currant jelly, and steins of ale. Roast shoulder of boar is beautifully enhanced by a sauce of current jelly with orange zests, mustard, and wine vinegar, as well as by generous servings of buttered noodles and fried apples. For both roast hare and rabbit, use either a simple mustard sauce or one made from pan drippings, sour cream, and seedless grapes, and serve with noodles or boiled potatoes and broiled seasoned tomatoes.

Generally I feel that game birds, delicious in themselves, gain nothing from being smothered with other flavors, just as I'm in total accord with those who believe that after a while the traditional accompaniment of sweet sauces and wild rice becomes a monumental bore. Not only does delicate fowl not need the type of heavy, syrupy sauces with which you're usually confronted in restaurants, but nothing does a greater injustice to fine wine—which goes so perfectly with game birds—than sharp sweets. If a sauce is in order, prepare either a light one of pan drippings, wine or brandy, seedless grapes, and possibly a few truffles, or a smooth *velouté* made with chicken broth, cream, and tarragon. A chestnut dresing or rice pilaf with chopped giblets goes very nicely with pheasant, guinea hen, and partridge, but for something truly sensational serve the fowl with either sauerkraut or cabbage studded with spicy slices of garlic sausage, braised endive, and sautéed hominy cut into squares. Appropriate accompaniments to wild duck, goose, and turkey (all served with a wine gravy) are turnips, kale, wild rice, spiced fruits such as apricots or crab apples, and an orange and onion salad with rosemary vinaigrette. With quail, dove, and pigeon, try steamed cucumbers, pureed parsnips, seedless white grapes, curried rice, whole baked garlic cloves, and chopped giblets atop toast fried in butter. The English love to serve grouse with exotic berries, preserved quince, and the like, but I must say one of the most imaginative items I ever tried was toast fried in fat and spread thinly with a fine natural American Blue cheese.

With a little effort, wild game can indeed be found from coast-to-coast, and from all indications it is already enjoying renewed popularity in both restaurants and gastronomic circles. Throughout the last half-century, most Americans lost their taste for wild game simply because it was virtually unavailable. Today we once again have adequate supply and, in all likelihood, the day is quickly approaching when, with our ever-increasing obsession with fine food, many of us simply won't settle for an ordinary turkey when we can have a haunch of venison, a golden gander stuffed with apples, prunes, and walnuts, or even the same succulent wild turkey that Brillat-Savarin traveled 3,000 miles to savor. And who knows, once we're again accustomed to serving and ordering the more standard varieties of wild game, we may begin to develop an interest in something truly compelling like wild mountain goat!

Roast Saddle of Venison
with Black Pepper Sauce

1   6–7 lb. saddle of venison
1   clove garlic, cut
    Softened butter
    Crushed thyme
    Freshly ground pepper
    Salt

If venison is prime, marinate 2–3 days in refrigerator, turning every 4 hours when possible. If young, either lard with
fresh pork fat or bard with fat salt pork or bacon. Preheat
oven to 500° F. Rub saddle thoroughly with garlic, butter,
thyme, and pepper. Place on a rack in a shallow pan and
roast 30 minutes, basting frequently. Reduce heat to 350°
and continue roasting till meat thermometer placed into
thickest part of meat registers 130°. Remove from oven, salt
to taste, and let stand 15 minutes on a hot platter before
carving. Carve in long, thin slices parallel to spinal column.
Serve with Black Pepper Sauce. SERVES at least 6.

BLACK PEPPER SAUCE
4   Tb. butter
1   carrot, chopped
1   onion, chopped
3   sprigs parsley
1   bay leaf
¼   cup marinade liquid (strained) or wine vinegar
3   cups beef stock or bouillon
10   peppercorns
½   cup red wine

In a skillet sauté vegetables in butter till soft, add parsley,
bay leaf, marinade or vinegar and simmer till reduced by
one-third. Add stock or bouillon, bring to a boil, reduce heat,
and simmer 1 hour, covered. Add peppercorns, simmer 5
minutes longer, and strain sauce into a saucepan. Add red
wine and simmer 20 minutes more. Correct seasoning.

BRAISED PHEASANT WITH
SAUERKRAUT AND SAUSAGE

1	lb. salt pork, thinly sliced
5	lbs. fresh sauerkraut, washed and drained
2	cloves garlic, finely chopped
18	juniper berries
	Freshly ground pepper
2	4-lb. pheasants
2	onions, studded with 2 cloves
	Parsley sprigs
5	Tb. each butter and oil
2½	cups chicken stock
2	garlic sausages

Preheat oven to 350° F. Line a deep braising pan with strips of salt pork, arrange half of sauerkraut in a layer on top of pork, add garlic, 12 juniper berries, and pepper to taste. Place onion with parsley sprigs in cavity of each pheasant, truss the birds, and brown in butter and oil in a large, heavy skillet till golden. Transfer pheasants to bed of sauerkraut and cover with remaining sauerkraut, 6 juniper berries, pepper to taste, and chicken stock. Bring mixture to a boil, cover pan tightly, transfer to oven, and cook 1½ hours. Add sausages halfway through cooking. To serve, arrange pheasant on top of mound of sauerkraut and garnish with sliced sausage and parsley. SERVES 6.

ROAST WILD GOOSE WITH APPLE,
PRUNE, AND WALNUT STUFFING

1	12- to 14-lb. wild goose, giblets reserved
	Salt and freshly ground pepper to taste
1	Tb. dried sage
	Apple, prune, and walnut stuffing*
8	slices thick bacon
	Flour
1	cup strong giblet stock

Preheat oven to 325° F. Salt and pepper goose inside and out, rub sage thoroughly throughout cavity, add dressing, and either truss or skewer bird. Bard breast with bacon slices, place in roasting pan breast-side up, and roast approximately 2 hours. Remove bacon, increase heat to 450°, and continue roasting till golden brown. Transfer to heated platter. Skim fat from pan juices, add 1 Tb. flour, and stir till smooth. Add stock slowly, stirring constantly, bring sauce to a boil, reduce heat, and taste for seasoning. SERVES at least 6.

* *APPLE, PRUNE, AND WALNUT STUFFING*
1   cup port wine
½   lb. extra-large pitted prunes, washed and drained
½   cup seedless raisins, washed and drained
1   lemon, thinly sliced and seeds removed
1   onion, chopped and sautéed till soft in 1 Tb. butter
1   large sour apple, peeled and coarsely chopped
1   cup coarsely chopped walnuts
½   tsp. mace
    Salt and freshly ground pepper to taste
2   Tb. lemon juice, strained
½   cup minced celery, tops included
2   cups bread crumbs

Soak prunes and raisins in wine and refrigerate overnight. When ready to cook, add lemon, simmer in a large saucepan till tender, and drain thoroughly. Chop prunes, raisins, and lemon, add all other ingredients but celery and bread crumbs, and toss. Correct seasoning. When ready to stuff bird, add celery and bread crumbs and toss. Stuff loosely.

Quail Stuffed with Oysters

6   quail
18   large fresh oysters, shelled
     Butter, melted
2   cups cornmeal
1   lemon, cut into 6 slices
     Salt and freshly ground pepper to taste
6   strips bacon

Preheat oven to 450° F. Wipe each quail inside and out with a damp cloth. Dip oysters into melted butter, then into cornmeal, and stuff three into each quail. Add a lemon slice to each cavity, salt and pepper to taste, tie or skewer birds with wings and legs close to body, and bard each with a strip of bacon. Place birds on a rack in a shallow roasting pan and roast for 30 minutes. Remove bacon, baste quail with pan juices, and return to oven for another 5 to 10 minutes, basting once. Serve on buttered toast. SERVES 6.

Jugged Hare

1   5–6 lb. hare
2   cups red wine
1   tsp. salt
     Freshly ground pepper to taste
½   tsp. thyme
½   tsp. powdered bay leaf
3   onions, minced
½   lb. lean bacon
3   Tb. flour
1   bouquet garni (parsley, thyme, bay leaf, 1 clove garlic)
18   small whole onions, sautéed in butter 5 minutes
18   small mushrooms, sautéed in butter 5 minutes
¼   cup heavy cream

Cut hare into eight pieces. Prepare marinade by mixing wine, salt, pepper, thyme, bay leaf, and 1 minced onion in a large bowl and marinate hare in refrigerator, covered, 1 or 2 days, turning frequently. Preheat oven to 350° F. Cut bacon into squares, brown in a heavy casserole, set aside, and sauté remaining 2 minced onions in bacon fat till soft. Add 3 Tb. flour and cook slowly, stirring constantly till golden brown. Dry pieces of marinated hare thoroughly, add to roux, and brown them, stirring constantly. Add strained marinade and the bouquet garni to casserole, cover, and simmer 1 hour. Add bacon lardons, whole onions, and mushrooms. Cover, transfer casserole to oven, and cook about 45 minutes. Shortly before serving, remove bouquet garni, skim off any fat, and thicken sauce with heavy cream. Serve in a deep dish and garnish with toast points fried in butter. SERVES at least 6.

BUFFALO STEAK WITH WILD RICE DRESSING

1   cup wild rice
2   cups water
1   tsp. salt
1   lb. ground buffalo chuck
½   cup finely chopped onions
½   cup sliced mushrooms
5   Tb. oil
6   slices cubed French bread, crusts removed
1   cup hot beef stock or bouillon
¼   tsp. sage
    Freshly ground pepper to taste
6   buffalo T-bone or rib steaks
    Salt
2   cups red wine
6   Tb. butter

Wash rice, cover with water, add ½ tsp. salt, bring to a boil, cover, and cook over low heat about 45 minutes. Drain well. Preheat oven to 350° F. In a skillet brown ground buffalo, onions, and mushrooms in 2 Tb. of the oil. Place bread in bowl, cover with stock or bouillon, and let stand till soft. Stir in rice, meat mixture, remaining ½ tsp. salt, sage, and pepper. Place in a greased 2-quart casserole, cover, and bake for 1 hour. In remaining oil pan-broil buffalo steaks quickly in two heavy skillets over high heat, transfer to a heated platter, and salt them. Deglaze skillets with the wine, add butter, stir thoroughly, and pour over steaks. Serve with dressing and fresh cranberries. SERVES 6.

REGAL ROASTS

●●●●●●●●●●●●●●●●●●●●●●●●●●●●●●

THE NEXT time you're contemplating a truly festive American dinner, why not forget all about turkeys, capons, baked hams, and other such supermarket staples? Why not even put aside the idea of serving prime ribs of beef or rack of lamb, always viable alternatives but dishes that have become as popular year-round as steak. Instead, I submit, really go all out, conjure memories of a glorious past when a feast was really a feast, and prepare the types of baronial joints of meat that nourished our ancestors and that make a mockery of the more pristine eating habits of the late–twentieth century. Set a lordly table for at least twelve to fifteen, uncork your best Cabernets, and, if nothing else, prove that there's noble justification for our reputation as incurable meat-eaters.

Up until the turn of the century, chefs and homemakers all over Europe and America could hardly conceive of a grand dinner that did not include a spectacular chine of beef, a baron of lamb, a whole leg of veal or mutton, a haunch of venison, or a highly decorative suckling pig. Not only were these giant roasted meats eminently more succulent than the comparatively puny examples served by succeeding generations, but they were also far more economical since the leftovers could be turned into savory stews, meat loaves, hashes, curries, raised pies, and any number of other dishes. Over the centuries, such famous cookbook authors as Robert May, Hannah Glasse, Amelia Simmons, Mrs. Beeton, Fannie Farmer, and even Escoffier always devoted considerable space to the purchasing and preparation of large joints, but today just try to find even a recipe for this type of fare in the plethora of cookbooks flooding the market.

Of course, I'm not suggesting that anyone go so far as to attempt turning out a peacock in plumage, a stuffed swan, or a sirloin of buffalo. But rest assured that during the Middle Ages throughout northern Europe, and especially in England, there was hardly a beast of the field or bird of the air that didn't merit a fine turn on the spit for special occasions. Note, for example, only a few entries on the bill of fare of a dinner given for the English Archbishop Nevill during the reign of King Edward IV: "roo rost poudred for mutton" (roe deer spiced like mutton), "capons with whole geese rost," "pastels (haunches) of venison rost," "cony rost" (rabbit), "herenshaw rost" (young herons), "pecocke with gylt" (in plumage), "signettes rosted" (baby swans), and "porke rost." In the sixteenth century, the English developed the roasting of meat to a fine art, and by the following century it was usual to find the sort of jubilant fare once served a large party by a certain Mr. Constable, rector of Cockley Clay in Norfolk: "a leg of veal larded with six pullets," "a pheasant with six woodcocks," and chines of beef, venison, mutton, veal, and pork "supported by four men."

In eighteenth-century France, the great chef Menon normally included a separate course of some eight different "rosts" when orchestrating a fashionble meal. Back in England, we need only study the 1787 diary of countryman James Woodforde to realize the importance of roasted meats on the daily table: May 22, roasted chine of mutton; May 28, small roasting pig; June 21, roasted saddle of mutton, and so forth. So popular, in fact, were these large cuts that by the nineteenth century a carving school had been established in Soho where the upper-class ladies of London could receive instruction on how to deal correctly with the huge joints. "The rich supported vast households," writes Elizabeth Ayrton in *The Cooking of England,* "and the joints that they roasted were as large as the animals would provide or their spits could carry. A large joint always roasts better than a small one because its size allows time for the outside to be properly crisped, while the inside is just cooked enough but quite undried. The roasts of our ancestors, varying from perhaps 30 pounds (a livery piece) to 6 pounds, were carved to give the best slices to those of highest rank. A piece of the crisp outside, seasoned and 'frothed' (basted until crisp) and 'tasting of the fire,' with several slices from the middle—pink, juicy, and slow cooked—made a perfect portion. . . ."

The pilgrims to America celebrated the first Thanksgiving in 1621 by roasting plenty of venison, duck, and goose (no turkey!), and from that date until the twentieth century, the history of American gastronomy seems to revolve around our forefathers' love of meat. Before the invention of the stove in the nineteenth century, no kitchen was complete without a cavernous fireplace fitted with a roasting-spit, and even after the enclosed stove became an accepted piece of household equipment, Americans still enjoyed nothing more than roasting sizable quantities of everything from pig to bear to elk. One congressman from puritan Massachusetts, for instance, preserved the menu of a White House meal given by Thomas Jefferson, composed of nothing less than "rice soup, roasted rounds of beef, turkey, mutton, ham, loin of veal, cutlets of mutton, fried eggs, fried beef, and a pie called macaroni." Reflecting on a particular family meal, a Wisconsin writer recalled tables stretching "vast and white, crammed with two or three roasts and a dozen relishes and vegetables for an ordinary supper—and Aunt Dell moaning that she had nothing in the house." And in her *Home Cookery* of 1853, Mrs. J. Chadwick began her directions for preparing "Alamode Beef": "Take a nice piece of rump of beef weighing about twelve pounds. . . ." In the South, of course, almost any social occasion was cause to barbecue at least fifty or sixty pounds of pork, or haul out a thirty-pound country ham aging in the loft. As the West developed, it was common for pioneers to roast a whole side of beef, a leg of mutton or venison, or a couple of tender baby goats.

I'm convinced we never ate so well as in those expansive days, and, although big-scale barbecues are still staged for very special outdoor events throughout the South and Texas, I find it sad that today's supermarket technology and dietary cultists have encouraged most people to forget all about the hefty roasted meats that once adorned any august table. From time to time we're exposed to a gigantic whole round of beef sliced thin behind the counter of some suburban cafeteria, or a succulent leg of veal being carved on a silver trolley in a fancy French restaurant. Carnivores of the first chop can't make it through the year without at least one pilgrimage to Simpsons-on-the-Strand in London for roasted saddles of Southdown mutton, haunches of venison, whole suckling pigs, and hips of Scotch beef ("Rare please, carver, with the fat left on!"). Paul Bocuse may be world famous for his innovative *nouvelle cuisine*, but about the only way I'd now make a special trip to his restaurant in southern France is if he would promise to duplicate the roasted baron of Charolais beef he carved not long ago at a hotel reception in Paris. I'm afraid the age is over when luxury liner passengers were presented the sort of roasted oxen that graced the First-Class saloon of the *Aquitania* (the term "steamship roast" is still used to designate a large joint), but let me assure you that the chef aboard the *Queen Elizabeth 2* still thinks nothing of roasting legs, shoulders, and eight-rib racks of lamb, oversize turkeys and ducks, thirty-pound hams, double Angus sirloins, ribs of beef, and entire beef filets—twice a day. A tour through these kitchens is almost a gastronomic return to Elizabethan times.

Are there home chefs, you ask, who today actually entertain in this fashion? Not many, to be sure, but when someone like New York's Janet Yaseen (whose husband, Roger, happens to be the American president of the prestigious Confrérie de la Chaîne des Rotisseurs) decides to prepare a truly spectacular dinner, everything revolves around a magnificent roast. At one such occasion for twelve guests I attended, the menu was as follows: ramekins of cold mussels with fresh chive mayonnaise, an eighteen-pound baron of lamb with truffle and Madeira sauce, wild rice, a coarse puree of leeks with heavy cream, a fine puree of carrots with orange peel, goat cheese with honey and raspberry sauce, a rich walnut torte, and, to wash everything down, rare bottles of Beaulieu Vineyard's '68 Private Reserve Cabernet Sauvignon.

"I just don't understand," exclaimed Janet when I asked her why more people don't make the effort to serve large roasts. "There's no comparison between the flavor and aroma of a big, fresh, custom-cut joint and those small cellophane-wrapped pieces of meat in supermarkets. You know, today everybody gets thrilled about potatoes and carrots fresh from the ground or a whole fish presented on a platter or a brace of pheasants. But most people seem no longer to have any feeling for the animalness of meat. Perhaps it's because so much has been ground and hashed and chopped and processed to the point of absurdity, or maybe innovations like the *nouvelle cuisine* have managed to make us forget the entire wonderful range of the food experience. Well, serious gastronomes still get an exciting shiver when they see meat resembling the basic animal. For those who really care about what they eat, there's no more compelling sight than a beautiful, aromatic, sensuous baron of lamb or hip of beef."

Since so few standard cookbooks provide directions for the preparation, cooking, and carving of large joints of meat, you might well wonder how I came up with the recipes that follow. Simple: I consulted professional chefs and butchers, especially the nationally famous Lobel brothers, who not only operate the finest retail meat market in New York City but also are the authors of four books on meat. Supermarket butchers were generally knowledgeable and helpful, but, unlike the custom butchers, far too many suggested cooking methods which, upon testing, produced meat that was too well-done for my taste. As far as I'm concerned, to overcook these exceptional roasts is nothing less than criminal—and that includes both the veal and pork. (Those who still fear trichinosis in pork should know by now that the trichina parasite is destroyed at a temperature well below 150° F.) Remember that one advantage of serving large roasts is that the very size allows for a juicy interior even though the exterior might be well-done and crisp. The timings I indicate should yield medium-rare beef, lamb, and venison, and medium veal and pork. If you prefer otherwise, or have doubts about your oven temperatures, use a sophisticated meat thermometer. Any oven that can accommodate a twenty-pound turkey will take these roasts comfortably.

There are two cardinal rules for cooking these cuts of meat in the oven. First, they must be roasted in an open pan—which at least approaches spit roasting. (If covered, the meat is baked, not roasted, and the results in texture are altogether different.) Second, when boneless, the meat must be elevated enough so that the heat circulates evenly around it. Other than that, the chef is at liberty to experiment with all sorts of dredgings, basting ingredients, stuffings, sauces, gravies, and accompaniments. "Since you're working with such a basic item," says Leon Lobel, "the possibilities for being creative are endless. Just the way you score the fat or carve or modify the sauce or garnish the platter can add a personal touch that transforms an otherwise forbidding hunk of meat into a culinary triumph." On the other hand, never fail to keep in mind that nothing should detract from the roast itself, that appetizers and desserts should be relatively simple, and that even such traditional accompaniments to beef as horseradish and English mustard should be used in discreet quantities.

Any private butcher, given proper advance notice, should be able to furnish these roasts—and often at a savings of from 25 percent to 35 percent of normal retail cost. Also keep your eye open at supermarkets, where whole top rounds of beef sometimes go on sale and where, when the prices of pork and lamb are reduced, the butcher will usually cut to order at little extra cost. Wherever you shop, you'll certainly be paying less for the beef, lamb, and veal than for smaller cuts that involve more labor and processing, and the savings will become even more evident when you utilize any delicious leftovers.

"Since the time when the first cook roasted the first piece of meat," write the Lobel brothers in their *Meat Cookbook,* "those members of the tribe, clan, troop, and community who devoted themselves to making food more pleasurable and tastier have been held in special regard as the keepers of charismatic gifts—gifts given to one to share with many." I doubt that many of us would relish the charred leg of mastodon prized by primitive man, but even with all our gastronomic prowess, there's still no dish to highlight a celebration like a regal roast that's been carefully selected, lovingly prepared, and ceremoniously presented.

BARON OF LAMB

Have butcher prepare an 18-lb. baron of lamb (saddle plus two legs), trimming excess fat and scoring in a crisscross pattern. Preheat oven to 450° F. Blend thoroughly ¼ cup olive oil, juice of 1 lemon, ½ grated onion, 1 tsp. dried ginger, 1 clove crushed garlic, and ½ tsp. each salt and freshly ground pepper. Bring lamb to room temperature, rub thoroughly with mixture, and let stand at least 2 hours. Wrap center loin end in double foil, position lamb on a rack in a large open roasting pan, reduce heat to 325°, and roast approximately 1¼ hours, basting frequently. Remove foil, increase heat to 350°, and continue roasting about 20 minutes, basting once. Remove from oven, transfer to carving board garnished with plenty of fresh watercress, parsley, or mint leaves, and let stand 15 minutes. Pour surplus fat from pan, pour rest of juices into a saucepan, add 1½ cups beef stock or bouillon and 2½ Tb. Cognac or Madeira. Bring to a boil, stirring, adjust seasoning, and pour sauce into a sauceboat. To serve, remove two fillets from saddle and carve in strips on the bias; carve thin slices from rump; and slice legs downward from fat.

Serve sauced meat with red currant jelly and mint sauce, grilled tomato halves with bread crumbs seasoned with garlic and oregano, small white beans, a coarse puree of leeks with heavy cream, and a fine French claret or American Pinot Noir.

HALF HIP OF BEEF

Have butcher prepare and score upward the surface fat on a 17-lb. half sirloin with bone. Preheat oven to 475° F. Bring beef to room temperature and sprinkle lightly with flour well-seasoned with freshly crushed black pepper, powdered English mustard, and a little nutmeg. Position meat fat-side up in a large open roasting pan and place in oven. After 10 minutes reduce heat to 350° and roast approximately 2¼ to 2½ hours without basting. Remove from oven and transfer to carving board. Pour surplus fat from pan, add 1½ cups brown stock or bouillon to pan residues, bring to a boil, and stir, scraping bottom of pan. Reduce heat, simmer gently to reduce gravy slightly, adjust seasoning, and strain into a sauceboat.

Serve meat with gravy, freshly grated horseradish, English mustard, small roasted potatoes, tiny buttered carrots, and boiled cabbage tossed with sautéed apples, onions, and cinnamon. A fine ale goes well.

WHOLE TOP ROUND OF BEEF

Have butcher prepare a 15-lb. whole top round of beef, tying securely and neatly. Preheat oven to 450° F. Bring beef to room temperature and dust with 2 Tb. dried and pounded lemon peel mixed with about 1 cup of flour. Position meat fattest side up on a rack in a large open roasting pan and place in oven. After 10 minutes reduce heat to 350° and roast 1½ to 1¾ hours, basting if necessary. Remove from oven, transfer to carving board, and let stand about 15 minutes. Pour surplus fat from pan, slightly brown the pan residues on top of stove, add 1 cup red wine or Madeira plus ½ cup brown stock or bouillon, bring to a boil, stir well, reduce slightly, adjust seasoning, and strain gravy into a sauceboat. To serve, carve both outside and inside slices for each person.

Serve meat with gravy, mashed potatoes with caraway seeds, buttered broccoli or Brussels sprouts, creamed onions, and a California Cabernet Sauvignon.

CROWN ROAST OF PORK

Have a butcher French the bones (cut about 1 inch of meat from end of ribs) and score the fat (diamond shape) on a 9–10 lb. crown of pork, using only the rib ends. Preheat oven to 400° F. Wrap tips of bones in foil, rub meat with sage, thyme, and crushed garlic, and set on a rack in a large open roasting pan. Roast 20 minutes, reduce heat to 325°, and continue roasting 1¼ hours. Remove from oven and fill crown with a savory sausage and prune stuffing. Return to oven and continue roasting 1 hour more, increasing heat to 450° the last 20 minues. Remove from oven, transfer to a round silver serving tray, and remove foil from ends of chops, replacing with decorative paper frills. Pour all but 2 Tb. of fat from roasting pan, sprinkle with 2 Tb. flour, and cook over low heat, stirring, for 2 minutes. Add ½ cup dry white wine, reduce over high heat to about 2 Tb., and add ½ cup chicken stock or broth and 1 cup heavy cream, stirring thoroughly. Over medium heat add 1 Tb. Dijon mustard diluted in 2 Tb. of the sauce, stir well, and adjust seasoning.

Serve with applesauce, peas with tiny onions, and a good Riesling.

LEG OF VEAL

Have butcher remove excess sinew and lightly bard a 15-lb. leg of veal. Preheat oven to 325° F. Bring veal to room temperature and, on the bottom of a large open roasting pan, place 2 finely chopped onions, 2 chopped carrots, 2 ribs celery, 2 crushed cloves garlic, and ½ cup dry white wine. Place veal on a rack in pan, roast 45 minutes, remove from oven, remove barding fat, and let cool slightly. In a bowl mix together 3 Tb. salad oil, 2 Tb. lemon juice, 1 tsp. dill, 1 tsp. chervil, 1 tsp. salt, and ½ tsp. freshly ground pepper. Pat veal dry and rub mixture generously all over the meat, adding any remaining mixture to bottom of roasting pan. Place veal back in oven and continue roasting 1¼ hours longer, basting frequently with pan juices. Remove from oven, transfer to cutting board, and let rest 15 minutes. Pour off surplus fat from pan, strain juices into a saucepan, work vegetables through a fine sieve into juices, and discard solids. Add 1½ cups dry white wine plus 4 Tb. butter, bring to a boil, stirring, adjust seasoning, and strain into a sauceboat.

Serve sauced meat in thin slices with seasoned green noodles or baked yams, sautéed mushroom caps with chives, puree of carrots, and a full-bodied Chardonnay.

BONELESS FULL RACK OF VENISON

Have butcher tie securely and lard two boneless, rolled racks of young venison weighing about 4 lbs. each and measuring about 1½ ft. in length. Prepare the following marinade: 1 bottle dry red wine, ½ cup vegetable oil, 1 large sliced onion, 2 sliced carrots, 1 chopped rib celery, 2 crushed garlic cloves, 2 sprigs parsley, 1 tsp. rosemary, 10 cloves, 2 bay leaves, and 1 tsp. freshly ground pepper. Place venison in marinade and let stand 2 days in refrigerator, turning once or twice a day. Preheat oven to 450° F. Remove meat from marinade, wipe dry, rub with a little oil, and place on a rack in a large open roasting pan (tucking ends around to fit if necessary). Roast 30 minutes, reduce heat to 375°, and continue roasting 30 minutes longer, basting occasionally with a little marinade. Turn off heat, let meat sit in oven 15 minutes, remove and transfer one rack to a serving platter, the other to a carving board. Strain marinade into a large saucepan, discard solids, and reduce liquid over high heat to about 2 cups. Reserve half for future use, add 1 cup beef stock or bouillon to remaining cup, and adjust seasoning. Stir in 1½ tsp. arrowroot mixed with 1 Tb. water and simmer sauce 20 minutes.

Serve sliced venison with sauce, currant jelly, wild rice, puree of chestnuts, pickled peaches, and a sturdy Italian Barolo or California Zinfandel.

LONG LIVE THE COACH HOUSE

•••••••••••••••••••••••••••••••••

THERE ARE few restaurants in this country—indeed, anywhere—whose quality of cooking defies criticism, but even the most prestigious writers and critics in the food world say only good things about The Coach House in New York City. Often called the quintessential American restaurant, The Coach House (originally a carriage stable for the Wanamaker estates) has been going strong in Greenwich Village for over thirty years, the pride and joy of its owner, Leon Lianides, and a gastronomic haven for all who measure the quality of life in terms of what they eat.

Often on a Sunday evening, you will spot James Beard perched at his small corner table, tucking away a bowl of black bean soup and a grilled triple lamb chop. "You just don't find standards like this anymore," insists Craig Claiborne, speaking dreamily about the chocolate cake and dacquoise. "I always feel so safe recommending absolutely anything on the menu," says William Rice, editor of *Food and Wine Magazine* and coauthor of *Where to Eat in America.* "The Coach House is like good comfortable clothes," adds Joe Baum, the entrepreneurial genius who created such legendary New York restaurants as The Four Seasons and Windows on the World. I personally remember evenings when celebrated French chef-restaurateur Jean Troisgros proclaimed The Coach House's pepper steak better than any he'd eaten in France, and Paul Bocuse was so enamored of the restaurant's black bean soup that he made a point of requesting the recipe. As for myself, The Coach House is home.

The restaurant is a visual reflection of its suave owner's taste: brick walls, comfortable red banquettes, neat table linens, a sweeping staircase leading to what was once a hayloft and is now the upstairs dining room, rainbows of fresh flowers, subdued lighting, a highly personal collection of English and American paintings, and displays of both food and the noble French and American wines so loved by Lianides. Its most important distinction, however, stems from the way, over the years, Lianides has drawn on foreign and regional culinary traditions and managed to develop an original, highly refined style of American cookery. At first glance, the menu is deceptively simple: smoked turkey, fresh clams, fresh melon with oysters, prime ribs of beef, rack of lamb. But what clams, what oysters, what an incredible rack of lamb! Striped bass poached in court bouillon and fresh oysters with lump crab meat are as elegant as any dish you'll find anywhere, but there's also a good old American chicken pot pie and chunks of juicy lobster prepared with tangy Greek Feta cheese. On and on the selections run: sausage with cold lentil salad, cold eggplant with tomatoes, currants, and capers, fresh chicken livers sautéed with mushrooms, roast duckling with brandied quince, nuggets of veal fillet with glazed chestnuts, Southern pecan pie, apple tart with fresh whipped cream, and, of course, the restaurant's inimitable seven-rib rack of baby lamb for one. Piping hot corn sticks are served to every diner and, depending on the season or the whims of Lianides, there might also be available the freshest and fattest asparagus, some special variety of oyster, and, a couple of times a year, the famous tripe soup that requires days to prepare and that regulars rush to savor.

But what makes the food at The Coach House so superior to that of similar variety served in thousands of other restaurants throughout the country? Without so much as hesitating to reflect, Lianides sums it up in four words: "Simplicity, quality, timing, and continuity." Pressed to expand on this formula, he continues in his typically analytical fashion: "As I see it, the same principles that apply to producing a fine painting should also apply to food. There must be logic, exposition, and elevation of the idea to a high degree of excellence without destroying the original intention. You know, the most beautiful foods are simple foods: fruit from a tree, a fish fresh from the water, roast baby lamb with no more than a squeeze of lemon, apple pie with fresh whipped cream, homemade pasta with pepper and a touch of good olive oil. But people insist on believing they can improve on nature. Taste comes first from the eye and the brain, meaning that when I see and think 'trout' I don't want that taste altered by an alien lobster sauce. It deceives the senses. Of course, the rage everywhere today is *la nouvelle cuisine* with all its sauces and purees and decorations and so-called simplicity. Well, as far as I'm concerned, *la nouvelle cuisine* is like a confused party in a kindergarten."

While most restaurateurs settle for whatever food supplies the distributors have available, Lianides finds that unacceptable. Every night at midnight he speaks with his two seafood dealers at the Fulton Fish Market to determine what should be delivered the next day; at one in the morning someone on his staff makes the trip to Hunts Point to select fresh fruits and vegetables; fresh eggs from range chickens are brought to the restaurant twice a week by a friend on Long Island; and bread is delivered daily by an Italian baker in the Village. For meat and poultry he deals with two different purveyors ("just to keep them both on their toes"), and to accompany him (as I've done) to a meat market is an experience. He moves slowly from one vast cold locker to the next, feeling huge sides of prime beef, checking the color of veal fat, studying the bones of lamb carcasses, questioning the marbling in steaks. "Mr. Leon is one of the few who select his meat personally," confides a purveyor he has dealt with for years. "He's fussy, demanding, and fastidious, and he couldn't imagine settling for anything but the best—no matter what the cost."

As any serious chef knows, working with the best ingredients means nothing if the preparation of those ingredients is not carried out with intelligence and care, and perhaps where Lianides surpasses others in the business is in his understanding of the chemistry of food. Give him half a chance and he'll go on for hours about how to melt chocolate properly, or why roasting unpeeled onions gives the meat glaze for his pepper steak its distinctive flavor and color. Equally important are temperatures and precise timing, and if some of his techniques appear a bit unorthodox, the results prove that he knows his craft. When a steak at The Coach House is ordered rare, it's cooked for exactly six minutes on each side in smoking-hot rendered beef fat. For corn sticks that are crusty on the outside and soft within, batter is piped into extremely hot greased cast-iron molds and baked no more than fifteen minutes. It's a bit unnerving to realize that a whole rack of lamb or thick triple lamb chop was produced in a very hot oven in no more than twenty minutes. "I've never understood why so many people coat a beautiful piece of lamb with breadcrumb paste," he broods, "and then let it sit in a three-hundred-fifty-degree oven for forty-five minutes to soak up grease. Here we remove almost every ounce of fat, rub the seven-rib rack with a little oil and lemon juice, and sear it quickly.

Pure juicy meat, no fat. I could double my profit by serving a four-rib rack with all its fat, but I wouldn't eat it and what I don't eat my customers don't eat."

Perhaps the two words that best characterize The Coach House are integrity and continuity, subjects about which Lianides speaks passionately. "You know, I'm fully aware that some people talk about my being cold and tyrannical, but they should understand that I'm running a serious restaurant, not a social club. If I hope to continue giving the public the food, service, and atmosphere I've tried to perfect over the years, I have to be tough. I'm not looking for handshakes and back-slaps. My rewards come at the end of the evening when I know I've done my very best, when my customers appear totally satisfied. Then all the neglect of my personal life in favor of this place seems justified."

Dedication is no doubt the secret behind The Coach House's remarkable continuity. Although the restaurant is open only for dinner, Lianides, maître d'hôtel Paul Wilkins, and assistant manager Edna Archer are already busy working by noon, arranging fresh flowers, checking linens and wines, and inspecting food deliveries. (Paul has been with the restaurant for seventeen years, Edna for thirty.) In the kitchen, black bean soup simmers next to a huge stockpot, meringues cool, lamb is being trimmed, and crates of fresh asparagus wait to be opened. For seventeen years Lianides has had Roul Santana as head chef, and underchefs Miguel Peralta and Roosevelt Loften are also longtime employees. Only a team which has been working together in one place for so many years could have performed as they did when I was dining during the great blackout a few years ago. The restaurant was packed when the lights went out. As if they'd been rehearsing for weeks, Lianides and his staff had candles on every table within minutes; cooking with gas continued out back with the aid of flashlights, and not a single customer failed to be served every dish that had been ordered.

Over the years Leon Lianides has seen the famous and powerful at close hand, yet when asked to talk about them, he says, "You want to know who the celebrities are in this place? The celebrities are customers who come in, enjoy their food, and pay the bill."

Coach House Black Bean Soup

2½	cups dried black beans
10	cups water
2	Tb. fat (reserved from Beef Stock*)
1	cup chopped onion
½	cup chopped celery
7	cups Beef Stock*
2	cups water
1	tsp. chopped fresh garlic
¼	cup sherry or Madeira
1	tsp. salt
½	tsp. freshly ground pepper
2	hard-cooked eggs, finely chopped
1 or 2	lemons, thinly sliced and dipped in minced fresh parsley

Soak beans in 10 cups water for at least 12 hours in refrigerator. Drain well. Heat fat in large casserole over medium-high heat, add onions and celery, and sauté till tender. Add beans, stock, 2 cups water, and garlic and simmer uncovered, stirring occasionally and adding water if needed to keep beans covered, until tender—about 2½ hours. Transfer to blender in batches (or work through coarse sieve or food mill) and mix till roughly pureed. Turn into large saucepan and stir in sherry, salt, and pepper. Place over medium heat and bring to serving temperature, stirring occasionally. Gently blend in chopped egg, ladle into serving bowls, and garnish with lemon. SERVES at least 12.

* *BEEF STOCK*

3	lbs. beef bones
3	lbs. ham shank (including bone and rind), meat cut up
¾	lb. meaty beef shinbone
¾	tsp. black peppercorns
3	whole cloves
15	cups water

Combine all ingredients in large pot, bring to boil, reduce heat, cover partially, and simmer 8 to 10 hours. Strain, return to clean pan, and simmer till reduced to about 8 cups.

Let cool, then cover and refrigerate overnight. Remove layer of fat from top (reserve 2 Tb. to use in soup). Makes about 10 cups.

COLD EGGPLANT PROVENÇALE

3   large eggplants, sliced into ½-inch rounds
    Salt
1   cup chopped fresh parsley
2   large onions, thinly sliced
6   large tomatoes, peeled and sliced
2   large garlic cloves, minced
2   celery hearts, finely chopped
2   tsp. black currants
1   tsp. dried basil
1   tsp. crushed black peppercorns
1   tsp. chopped capers
    Salt and freshly ground pepper to taste
1   cup olive oil
    Lemon wedges

Sprinkle eggplant slices generously on both sides with salt. Place in large colander, cover with weight, and let stand about 45 minutes. Rinse thoroughly under cold running water and pat dry with paper towels. Preheat oven to 275° F. Arrange half of eggplant in 11-by-15-inch baking dish and sprinkle with about half the parsley. Arrange onion, tomato, garlic, celery, currants, basil, peppercorns, and capers evenly over top, season to taste with salt and pepper, and sprinkle with remaining parsley. Top with remaining eggplant and pour olive oil evenly over. Cover tightly with foil and bake 4 hours. Remove foil, stir mixture with long fork or spoon, and continue baking 1 hour. Let cool, then chill. Let stand at room temperature 2–3 hours before serving. Garnish with lemon wedges. SERVES 10–14.

GRILLED SHRIMP WITH MUSTARD SAUCE

10–12	large uncooked shrimp, unshelled but slit and deveined
1½	cups dry white wine
	Juice of 1 lemon
10	black peppercorns, crushed
3	shallots, chopped
2	garlic cloves, crushed
1½	Tb. olive oil
	Mustard Sauce*
8 to 10	lemon slices
2	Tb. chopped fresh parsley

Combine all but last 3 ingredients in a medium bowl and stir to coat shrimp thoroughly. Let marinate at room temperature for 2–3 hours. Remove shrimp, reserving marinade, and transfer to a small broiler pan. Broil shrimp just till they turn pink, about 8–10 minutes. Arrange on heated plates, insert lemon slice between each, spoon on mustard sauce, and sprinkle with parsley.

* *MUSTARD SAUCE*

12	oz. light-bodied red wine
1	large onion, sliced
	Reserved marinade from shrimp
5–6	tsp. Dijon mustard
2–3	tsp. Meat Glaze (see Pepper Steak recipe)

Combine wine, onion, and marinade in a 2-quart saucepan, bring to a boil, and cook till liquid is reduced by half. Strain, return to saucepan over low heat, and whisk in mustard and meat glaze. Continue cooking, whisking constantly, till sauce is slightly thickened and coats whisk. Adjust seasoning. SERVES 2.

RACK OF LAMB

1   small rack of lamb (7 ribs)
1   garlic clove, crushed
1   tsp. fresh lemon juice
1   tsp. vegetable oil
    Salt and freshly ground pepper to taste
2   tsp. minced fresh parsley
¼   lemon

Have butcher crack chine bone, remove all fat from meat, and French bones (cut about 1 inch of meat from end of ribs). Preheat oven to 475° F. Rub garlic over bone side of meat and discard garlic. Rub meat with lemon juice, then with oil. Heat skillet over high heat till extremely hot, sear lamb on all sides, transfer to rack in roasting pan, sprinkle with salt and pepper, and rub in parsley. Roast meat-side up 10 minutes, turn meat over, and continue roasting until lamb is well browned on outside but still pink inside, about 10 minutes longer. Place on heated plate, squeeze lemon over meat, and serve. SERVES 1.

STRIPED BASS IN COURT BOUILLON

1	4-lb. striped bass
2½	qts. water
1	cup dry white wine
12	clams, unshucked
2	leeks, chopped
2	onions, chopped
2	bay leaves
4	sprigs parsley
4	cloves garlic, crushed
2	celery ribs, chopped
12	peppercorns
½	tsp. thyme
	Juice of 1 lemon
	Salt to taste
¼	cup olive oil
	Salt and crushed pepper to taste
2	onions, sliced in julienne
2	leeks (white only), sliced in julienne
2	carrots, sliced in julienne
2	celery hearts, sliced in julienne
3	tomatoes, chopped
2	oz. Pernod
2	Tb. chopped parsley

Clean, wash, and fillet the striped bass, reserving head and bones. Place water, white wine, and reserved fish heads and bones in a large pot over high heat. Add clams, leeks, onions, bay leaves, parsley, garlic, celery, peppercorns, thyme, lemon juice, and salt, bring to a boil, lower heat, and simmer, covered, 20 minues. Strain broth through cheesecloth and reserve clams for another use. Pour olive oil into a large kettle, add salt, crushed pepper, and julienne vegetables and sauté till vegetables are soft. Add tomatoes, stir 1 minute, and add fish broth plus Pernod. Bring to boil and simmer 30 minutes. Add fish fillets, cover kettle, poach 10 minutes, and let rest off heat 3 minutes. Sprinkle with chopped parsley and serve fish and broth in soup bowls. SERVES 4.

Pepper Steak

2 18-oz. boneless prime strip sirloin steaks cut 2 inches thick
¼ cup coarsely cracked pepper
¾ cup dry red wine
½ cup Cognac
½ cup Meat Glaze*

Trim excess fat from steaks and render in heavy skillet over high heat. Press pepper onto both sides of meat, remove unrendered fat from skillet, add steaks, and sear 1 minute on each side. Reduce heat and continue cooking, allowing 6 minutes on each side for rare and 10 minutes per side for medium. Transfer meat to heated serving plates and keep warm while preparing sauce. Pour off excess fat in skillet, deglaze pan by adding wine and Cognac, blend in meat glaze, and cook over high heat till sauce thickens. Pour sauce over steaks and serve immediately. Serves 2.

* *MEAT GLAZE*
5 lbs. veal bones, cracked
2 lbs. chicken necks and backs
3 carrots
2 large onions, unpeeled and cut into quarters
2 celery stalks (including leaves), cut coarsely
3 garlic cloves, unpeeled and crushed
2 bay leaves, crushed
2 tsp. salt
1 tsp. black peppercorns, crushed
   Pinch dried thyme
¾ cup all-purpose flour
2 cups dry red wine
3 qts. canned beef broth
2 cups tomato puree
2 leeks (including green part), cut coarsely
3 sprigs Italian parsley

Preheat oven to 475° F. Combine bones, chicken parts, carrots, onions, celery, garlic, bay leaves, salt, peppercorns, and thyme in large shallow roasting pan and roast uncovered for 50 minutes. Remove pan from oven, sprinkle flour over bones, and stir to mix evenly. Return to oven, continue roasting 15–20 minutes, and transfer to stockpot. Set roasting pan over medium heat, add wine, and cook, scraping bottom and sides of pan to loosen browned particles. Add to stockpot along with remaining ingredients. Bring to boil, skimming off foam as it accumulates, then reduce heat and simmer uncovered 3–4 hours, adding more broth or water if necessary. Skim off all fat, remove bones, and carefully strain stock into another large pot. Sauce should be consistency of heavy cream; continue simmering till further reduced if necessary. Store in refrigerator or freezer.

CORN STICKS

4	cups cornmeal
3	cups all-purpose flour
5	Tb. sugar
2	Tb. baking powder
1¼	tsp. salt
4	eggs
3	cups milk
1	cup vegetable shortening, heated but not fully melted

Combine dry ingredients in large bowl and add eggs one at a time, mixing well after each is added. Blend in milk thoroughly, add shortening, mix well, cover, and refrigerate 1 hour. Preheat oven to 500° F. Grease small cast-iron corn stick molds (individual sections should measure 5-by-1½ inches) and set in oven till molds are very hot. Pipe batter into hot molds, bake 10 minutes or till tops are golden brown, and serve immediately.

Sautéed Potatoes

1   stick unsalted butter, room temperature
4   large Idaho potatoes, peeled, sliced paper thin, and patted dry
    Salt and freshly ground pepper

Preheat oven to 425° F. Melt about 2 Tb. butter in a heavy 12-inch ovenproof skillet over medium-high heat. When it begins to sizzle, arrange potatoes loosely on bottom and slightly up sides of pan. Season with salt and pepper and dot with remaining butter. Increase heat to high and sauté potatoes 3 minutes. Transfer to oven and bake about 25 minutes or till golden brown on top. Invert onto heated serving plate and serve immediately. SERVES 4.

Chocolate Cake

Cake

4   cups all-purpose flour
1½   cups (3 sticks) unsalted butter, room temperature
1   lb. bittersweet chocolate
¼   cup water
2   tsp. salt

Filling

1   qt. heavy cream
1½   lbs. bittersweet chocolate
     Powdered sugar and chocolate curls

For Cake: Combine flour and butter in large bowl and mix with fingertips till consistency of coarse oatmeal. Do not allow butter to melt and become oily. Melt chocolate in saucepan over very low heat, add water and salt, and beat till smooth. Make well in flour mixture, pour in chocolate, and mix lightly but thoroughly. Divide into three parts, wrap each in waxed paper, and refrigerate about 20 minutes or till firm. Preheat oven to 350° F. Place one piece of dough between 2 sheets of waxed paper and roll into large circle about ⅛-inch thick. Lift off top sheet of paper and use sharp knife to cut circle 9–10 inches in diameter. Remove excess dough. Carefully invert circle onto ungreased baking sheet, remove remaining paper, and bake 15 to 18 minutes. Working carefully, loosen pastry with spatula and slide onto heavy-duty foil to cool. Repeat with rest of dough.

For Filling: Place cream in large bowl and set in larger bowl or sink on bed of ice. Melt chocolate in heavy saucepan over very low heat or hot water, whip cream till stiff, then fold in chocolate, mixing gently but thoroughly.

To Assemble: Carefully slide one cake layer onto serving plate and spread half of filling over top. Repeat with second layer and remaining filling. Top with last layer. Sprinkle with powdered sugar, garnish with chocolate curls, and refrigerate 2 to 3 hours. Remove cake from refrigerator and slice with a serrated knife. SERVES 16–20.

DACQUOISE

Meringue

5   egg whites, room temperature
⅛   tsp. cream of tartar
1   cup sugar
1   cup plus 1 Tb. ground toasted almonds
3   Tb. cornstarch

Butter cream

½   cup sugar
⅓   cup water
5   egg yolks
2   Tb. Grand Marnier
    Scant ¾ tsp. decaffeinated coffee powder
1   cup (2 sticks) unsalted butter, cut into small pieces
2   Tb. powdered sugar

For Meringue: Position rack in center of oven and preheat to 225° F. Beat egg whites in large bowl till foamy, add cream of tartar, and beat briefly. Gradually add ¾ cup sugar and continue beating till stiff peaks form. Combine remaining ¼ cup sugar with almonds and cornstarch and mix well. Fold into meringue gently but thoroughly. Generously butter large baking sheets and sprinkle with flour, shaking to coat entire surface evenly. Shake off excess. Trace three 9-inch circles on sheets, spoon meringue into pastry bag fitted with ½-inch plain tube, and, starting at center, pipe meringue in spiral to cover circles completely. Bake till meringues are pale brown and have shrunk slightly at edges, about 55 minutes. Gently lift meringues onto racks and let cool completely in draft-free area.

For Butter cream: Combine sugar and water in heavy small saucepan, place over low heat, and let cook without stirring till syrup reaches 234° on candy thermometer (soft-ball stage). Meanwhile, beat yolks with electric mixer till thick, pale yellow and ribbon is formed when dropped from side of spoon. Beating constantly, gradually add syrup in thin steady stream, add Grand Marnier and coffee powder, and mix well. With mixer on high speed, add butter in small pieces and beat till mixture forms smooth peaks. Cover and let cool in refrigerator.

To Assemble: Place one meringue on serving plate and spread some of butter cream evenly over top. Add second meringue, pressing gently into filling, and spread with butter cream. Top with last meringue, pressing gently, and frost top and sides with remaining butter cream. Chill at least 1 hour before serving. Sieve powdered sugar over top and cut into wedges with serrated knife. SERVES 10–12.

BREAD-AND-BUTTER PUDDING

12 or 13	slices French bread cut ½-inch thick, crusts trimmed
3–4	Tb. unsalted butter, room temperature
5	eggs
4	egg yolks
1	cup sugar
⅛	tsp. salt
4	cups milk
1	cup heavy cream
1	tsp. vanilla
	Powdered sugar
	Fresh raspberries, pureed and strained

Preheat oven to 375° F. Butter one side of each slice of bread and set aside. Beat eggs, yolks, sugar, and salt in a large bowl till thoroughly combined and set aside. Combine milk and cream in a saucepan and heat till scalded. Gradually stir into egg mixture, then blend in vanilla. Layer bread buttered-side up in a 2-quart soufflé dish, cutting slices as needed to fit dish and fill spaces evenly. Strain custard over top. Add boiling water to depth of about 1 inch in roasting pan, set soufflé dish in pan, and bake till knife inserted in center comes out clean, about 45 minutes. Remove from roasting pan and sprinkle pudding generously with powdered sugar. Run under broiler till glazed, and serve warm with raspberry sauce. SERVES 10.

A GOURMAND
FIGHTS
BACK

CRY, THE BELOVED COUNTRY HAM

I WANT to tell you now about genuine Southern country ham. No, not a Smithfield or a Suffolk or a Westphalian or any other of those fancy hams often spotted in gourmet shops or propped up elegantly in silver racks at both American and European feasts. Just plain old country ham right off the farm, salt-cured, uncooked, unsmoked, naturally dry-aged with plenty of ugly surface mold, and unforgettably delicious. Unless you were raised in the South or spent lots of time there, I doubt you've ever tasted country ham like this, or any at all. And even if, like myself, you did grow up in the South and did develop from childhood an everlasting passion for the mouth-watering stuff, more than likely most of what you're finding today is that pinkish red, leathery, packaged junk stacked in every Southern supermarket and not the rare type of ham like that I lug out of the Blue Ridge Mountains of North Carolina once a year.

Well, not only are your chances of ever tasting good country ham dwindling day by day, but in all likelihood you won't even be able to find one ten years from now. Some of America's most adept industrial hotshots, namely the technology hucksters, have been putting in overtime during recent years and doing a better job than ever by gradually transforming every nutritious item we put in our mouths, including many of the country's most respected regional products. The exact identity of these culinary wizards is not easy to pinpoint, but you can be sure that among the villains are the food engineers associated with big-league food manufacturers and agricultural "extension services" at major universities, state inspection agencies, and, of course, the officials at the United States Department of Agriculture. Together they help form a conglomerate that not only defies competition but dictates at an ever-increasing rate what we can and cannot eat.

Until fairly recently, the success of this conglomerate has revolved primarily around the technological production of staple foodstuffs. Things like processed meats saturated with preservatives; artifically ripened fruit and uniformly colored vegetables; plastic cheeses; imitation margarines and other nondairy milk products; synthetic seasonings, flavorings, sweeteners; and all the other mess people have been conditioned to eat. A few manufacturers specialize in factory-made food, turning out, in huge quantities, engineered simulations (or "analogues") of chicken, beef chunks, ham, pork sausage, hamburger, and coffee. You'd think there would be a limit to this sort of ingenuity. But just wait. The future promises man-made steaks and mushrooms!

So far I've complained very little about these scientific triumphs. After all, with a good deal of effort I've always been able to locate homemade breads, fresh herbs and spices, naturally aged cheeses, plus any number of delicacies that could be flown in from one place or another. But now, dammit, how dare those megalomaniacs so much as get near my country ham, or any other regional product steeped in sacred tradition! They're simply going too far, and, unless they're stopped, the day will undoubtedly come when they will succeed in transforming and standardizing even the rarest and most remotely located foods indigenous to various areas of the nation. As if the problems were not bad enough already, those of us with any gastronomic pride whatsoever are being asked to tolerate this form of radical, freewheeling exploitation.

So when did all the action start, and how has this particular ham problem gotten out of hand? Back in the forties and early fifties, when small producers were last left alone to raise hogs, process their own meat, then cure and age it according to generations-old practices, we had plenty of good ham. The shanks, tightly sacked and hung up in a smokehouse or basement, were moldy, strangely colored by any number of spices, full of indentions from curing and long natural aging, and by no stretch of the imagination pretty. No one in his right mind ever boiled a properly cured, well-aged ham to get rid of the salty but honest flavor. You just cut off a thick slab for breakfast or supper, threw it in a skillet for a couple of minutes, then made red-eye gravy by adding a little water or coffee to the drippings in the pan. No one ever thought about whether or not this delectable ham had passed rigid inspections; no one to my knowledge ever contracted a case of trichinosis. In fact, the only thing that worried anybody in both urban and rural areas was whether this or that farmer had had the time and money during the preceding year to furnish all his customers with a fifteen- to twenty-pound ham.

By the mid-fifties, what had always been a small business based generally on personal transactions between farmers and regular clients began developing into a multilevel technological enterprise. No doubt you could still find genuine country hams without much trouble, but it became pretty obvious to real ham lovers that the thinly sliced, underaged, processed variety creeping into supermarkets spelled nothing but trouble. Although few people had heard of, much less kept up with, the programs of university food-science departments or the projects of large packing houses, it's for sure that by the early sixties these forces were in full swing, the first trying to teach farmers how to double their volume and reap a sizable profit, and the second capitalizing on whatever increasing demands certain farmers might have been encouraged to make for green (fresh) hams. A few years later, all small producers were hit hard by the passing of the Wholesome Meat Act, designed in 1967 by the sanitation-obsessed Agriculture Department to "protect consumers from contaminated or misbranded meat marketed by plants operating exclusively within the states" and not subject to federal inspection. Although, predictably, this program has proved to have been inefficient, it nevertheless succeeded in placing large, ultramodern meat plants at a clear advantage over the farmer, and it enabled a major company to market and popularize, with minimum interference, more and more streamlined ham—or, according to the package label, "country-style" or "country-brand" ham. It seems that almost everybody had a piece of the action—everybody, that is, except the farmer, who more often than not was in no position to protect either his product or his small-time but respectable business. No one member of the conglomerate was necessarily connected with all the others all the time, but, somehow, all managed to help exploit still another of the nation's gustatory delicacies while, at the same time, reducing the farmer's role.

To get a clearer idea of the conglomerate's power over small food producers, let's consider a few facts. Food scientists at state university extension services claim that their primary function is to help the farmer, or, as one administrative coordinator of the Food Science Extension at North Carolina State University at Raleigh informed me, to help "produce a high-quality product with good consumer acceptance at as low a cost as possible to the consumer" (whatever that means). Perhaps this is true; perhaps their overall intentions are honest, but it so happens that over the past twenty-five years (the period during which such services have been developed) no less than 2 million family farms have disappeared from the face of the nation, while the production costs of those still functioning have risen well over 100 percent. Even more tragic is the assertion by one United States senator that today food manufacturers are driving small farmers out of business at the rate of 1,000 per week, and that the major corporations are in a position to control not only what the farmer produces but also his access to the market and the prices he receives. Add to this the determination of the industry to turn out more and more simulated foods, the willingness of most consumers to be conditioned to any and every marketed item, the tendency of the Agriculture Department to endorse practically any foodstuff that is sanitary and nutritional, and—well, it doesn't take an expert to point out how, before long, corporate industry, aided by governmental authorities, will succeed in wiping out all the little men—and all their genuine country hams.

Old-fashioned production of country ham has always involved not only complex, costly, and time-consuming procedures but heated regional competition into which lots of delightful folklore is blended. Of course there's the never-ending debate in the South over which state or area turns out the finest hams, just as there are daylong gab sessions to determine such crucial matters as what an uncastrated boar should be fed to assure flavorful meat, whether or not to butcher a sow in heat, and why hogs should or should not be killed in the full of the moon. Farmers will argue from sunup to sundown defending their individual convictions, but most are in very serious agreement on two essential points. First, that the texture and flavor of any country ham, no matter whether it's produced in North Carolina, Georgia, Tennessee, Kentucky, or Arkansas, depend on the quality of the green ham, the curing process, and, most important of all, the length of time it's left to age. And second, that the great majority of hams now supplied for commercial sale are a far cry from those few still produced according to family traditions for private consumption or custom orders.

In the old days, the diet of most hogs included plenty of "bran shortening" (a corn product) to insure leanness; milk; and, if possible, peanuts for soft texture, and lots of table scraps for flavor (hence the expression "slopping the hogs"). Depending on location and temperatures, animals were generally butchered during the first cold spell, around the middle of November, but never before. Once processed, the huge hams were hung bone-side down for at least twenty-four hours to allow the meat to drain and cool. If the weather remained cold, fine; if not, the shanks were carefully wrapped in brown paper as protection against flies and their spoilage-causing skippers (eggs). After this initial procedure, the hams were taken down, packed in a salt cure (which might have included any ingredient from sugar to black pepper to mustard) and left for about a month at a temperature ranging from twenty-eight to forty degrees Fahrenheit. Then they were soaked in water, hung up again to dry, rubbed with pepper or borax to assure further protection against vermin and insects, possibly smoked four or five days over slow-burning hickory chips (depending usually on client's orders), sacked, and, finally, left hanging in a barn or storage room to age under natural atmospheric conditions for not less than a year. It was no small production, to say the least, but anyone who has ever tasted ham prepared in this manner knows by its texture and inimitable flavor that there simply can be no shortcuts.

Wilkes County, located in North Carolina's northwest mountainous region, is moonshine territory, although no one has seen a still in years. Nope, no one. The county also produces some of the best country ham in the South, and possibly the best country ham in the county hangs in a storehouse on W. G. Long's property, located at Glendale Springs off Highway 16 about ten miles beyond West Jefferson. At the entrance are two signs, one advertising "Hams for Sale," the other warning "Beware of Dogs." I have the feeling that if you arrive as a customer, the dogs are kept chained, but that if you show up as a state inspector or tax collector snooping around, the beasts are let loose. During my last visit to the farm to buy ham, the whereabouts of Long Senior (or "Mr. G.") was, for some reason, unknown. But his son Clayton, no less an expert on country hams, greeted me cordially (if a bit suspiciously, as always). Entering the cold, dark storehouse, where a few hundred moldy hams were hanging on wooden beams, I asked Clayton how their small business had been affected by state inspection regulations.

"Well," he began, "we never know when the inspectors are gonna show up, but you can bet your bottom dollar that every time they come, we gotta change something in our production. Take this stainless-steel table, for example. Well, for as long as I can remember we had a good old wooden table here, but a couple of years back, in they march and say we gotta use stainless steel. Shortly after that we were told we had to pave the area around the storehouse, then that the iron nails we hung hams on had to be changed to aluminum, that the light bulbs had to be this nonshatter type, and just lately that we have to attach one of these ingredients tags showing what's in the cure on every single ham sold. Always something new, and it's not only costing us more and more money but it's all so unnecessary. One day they'll run us out of business just by making so many demands. And the next thing you know they'll be trying to get us to tear down this old store-house and put up one of those fancy places with air conditioners and heaters."

When I brought up the topic of curing and aging, he pulled down a large ham, slowly twirled an ice pick down through the middle, then held it out for me to sniff. The aroma was luscious. "One day you probably won't be able to smell ham like this. And don't kid yourself, customers who know good ham don't have to do any more than smell this pick to see if we've handled the cure right. We use only salt, sugar, and black pepper—none of that stuff other people use to speed up the process. Until a few years back, we cured at the ratio of about one day per pound, and we rarely lost a ham. Then those fellows from Raleigh came in and said we should keep the meat in cure almost twice that amount of time, no matter what the weight of the ham might be, age it less, and get it on the market. Well, I guess they're trying to help us out, seeing that those big food manufacturers are turning out three hams to our one. But curing a small ham that long just makes it too salty, and you don't need it to kill any live trichinae. On the other hand, unless we age it long enough to make it tender and flavorsome, customers don't come back. Those fellows have lots of textbook learning, but they just don't have the know-how that we got from long, hard experience—like how important it is to age hams under natural weather conditions."

I find it curious (though not surprising) that while we fight for freedom and justice and innumerable personal and social rights, we never do much more than raise our voices slightly over violations committed against something so unimportant as the food we put in our mouths. But I think it's about time for those of us who truly treasure fine food to assert ourselves and express an interest (indeed a deep concern) in helping somebody somewhere to curb the insane undertakings of the technologists. I'm sadly afraid it's too late to stop their work on staple foods, but there is still time to bring a halt to what the conglomerate would do to the speciality items we enjoy. Radical culinary changes are not inevitable, but they are bound to continue as long as those who profit from them receive not only official sanction but official encouragement, and as long as those who oppose them remain isolated and indifferent.

At present there's a serious problem with country ham. But that's just one example, and I wouldn't doubt for a moment that the culprits are already organizing themselves to propose standards for New England apple cider, Louisiana gumbo and jambalaya, Texas chili, Brunswick stew, California cioppino—things people love to eat and which simply cannot be tampered with. So far, most consumers (myself included) have suffered from a chronic affliction of the backbone, and unless we seek a fast remedy we'll be left with the same moans of defeat as those uttered by author John Ciardi not long ago: "We are sheep, alas, and we deserve what we have let ourselves be led to. We have let the technologists talk us into depravity, and we have then let ourselves accept depravity as a norm. Damn technological norms."

I MADE MY OWN WINE

THE DAY I decided to make my own wine was the day I faced up to the realities that I could no longer afford the criminally expensive labels I adore, that I would never become intimate with a Rothschild or a J. Heitz, and that I was no longer on civilized speaking terms with anyone connected with one of those chic wine societies. It was all that simple.

Now, almost everybody has at least heard about the wine-making kits presently being marketed throughout the country, but at first I wasn't about to succumb to such amateurism. No indeed. I fully intended to attempt a top-notch professional job, buy and stomp my own grapes, learn about yeasts, and so forth. (After all, I was no dummy in chem class and I did learn about Pasteur's theory that when yeast attacks the natural sugar of grape juice, carbon dioxide is gradually released and after a while you have vino. All very basic.) Then I began reading about the importance of hydrometers, vinometers, acid-testing kits, sterilizing equipment, and clarifying agents, all of which sounded not only pretty complicated but also dreadfully expensive. What really brought me to my knees, though, was a short article I began studying pertaining to fermentation. Now be honest, would you too not have chickened out when confronted with something like this mess:

> The 3-phosphoglycerate is converted to pyruvate which, in turn, is converted to acetaldehyde. As the acetaldehyde is formed, it becomes a hydrogen acceptor and through enzymic conversion produces the ethanol. This process dominates the rest of the fermentation.

I'd had enough. So began the hassle of choosing what appeared to be the best kit of those widely available on the market. I finally chose one designed to enable epicures to produce five gallons (twenty-five bottles) of Burgundy "equal to the best Europe has to offer at a mere fraction of the cost," and it arrived at my small brownstone apartment exactly three days after it was ordered. The all-inclusive price: $19.95. The parcel, no larger than a hatbox, contained: 1. three quart cans of gourmet-quality superconcentrated (Spanish) grape juice; 2. five-gallon (plastic) fermentation container; 3. bored stopper; 4. (plastic) fermentation air lock; 5. nontoxic (plastic) siphon tubing; 6. wine yeast; 7. wine-yeast nutrient; 8. citric acid; 9. soluble campden (sterilizing) tablets; 10. wine stabilizing tablets; 11. wine-bottle labels and corks. Everything necessary for twenty-five bottles of wine except tap water, five pounds of sugar, and the bottles.

After perusing all the weird-looking packets and gadgets, I turned to the step-by-step instructions of the booklet, concocted as directed a quart of sterilizing fluid in an empty cranberry-juice jar (my prefererd therapeutic beverage, by the way, for a glutted liver), and began the lung-boggling feat of blowing up the inflatable fermentation container until it assumed the shape of a mammoth plastic jug. Totally exhausted, I had to rest before carefully washing, sterilizing, and rinsing every piece of preliminary equipment I saw in the box. (Make note of that important last verb; you'll understand why in a minute.)

Following the directions word for word, I made marks six inches and ten inches up from the bottom of the container, left my well-lighted working area in the kitchenette for my poorly lighted bathroom, stepped inside the bathtub, and proceeded to fill the jug with warm water to the six-inch mark. Back in the kitchenette, I funneled five pounds of white granulated sugar into the container (really about four pounds, twelve ounces, since I got bored and twice overpoured), screwed the cap on, and shook as vigorously and laboriously as I would a two-pound whiskey sour.

After spending a quarter of an hour searching for a church key (that archaic tool which still has its unique value in these twist-off times), I removed the three cans of grape juice from pots of hot water in which the concentrate had been loosening, punched two holes in each top, tasted the glop, gagged, spilled a few indelible drops on my shirt and into the sink, and emptied the cans rather awkwardly into the container. Next the packets of yeast, yeast nutrient (a compound that allegedly gives the yeast an extra kick), and citric acid, then more shaking, then another haul back to the bathrub to fill my plastic incubator to the ten-inch mark. The booklet finally directed that you must once more "invert the fermentation container several times to make sure all the ingredients are mixed." Well, I would defy even a gorilla to try to "invert" what I dragged over the side of the tub! I found the one and only way to wrestle with the weight of that mother was to lie back flat on the floor, roll the flabby container up onto my midsection, clasp it in my arms, and exercise obscene body contortions. The technique worked.

Once I got the container safely balanced on top of a high stool in an appropriately dark area of my hallway, I read that I was to remove the cap, insert the tubular capped air lock in the bored stopper, pour a little water and sterilizing fluid into the network of tubes, fix the apparatus tightly into the neck of the container, and. . . .

Bored stopper? Panic! I didn't remember sterilizing *any* type of stopper or cork with a hole! A thorough search of the kit, the kitchenette, the drain in the sink, the tub, under chairs—everywhere and no bored stopper. Absolutely certain that this essential item had been left out of the kit and that rapid primary (or aerobic) fermentation (the action of which could be properly checked only by observing the speed with which the water moved in the air lock) was already beginning, I had to improvise fast by substituting for the plug a wet rag wrapped around the base of the air lock and crammed as tightly as possible in the neck. It worked, I guess, for, sure enough, the water began going up one tube and down the other.

Afterward I shot to the phone, made contact with the distributor who admitted "such mishaps do occur in packing," and was assured of receiving the bored stopper in one day. It arrived in four, and in the meantime all havoc had broken loose inside that jug. Weird sounds, huge purple bubbles climbing up the sides as oxygen escaped the onslaught of growing yeast, and my entire apartment smelled as if someone had sprayed it with a grape-scented aerosol.

Since I was honestly trying to make my wine in strict accordance with the directions (no matter how simplistic, vague, and, above all, nonexplanatory they were), I was thrilled when the envelope containing the bored stopper finally arrived. Thrilled, that is, until I discovered that the stopper was made of hard plastic and that it wouldn't fit into the neck of the container. Now, believe me, you have never experienced real frustration until you've tried to cut, file, burn, even chisel hard plastic! Knives, razor blades, steel files—you name it, I tried it, and only after going out and buying a pair of authentic surgical scissors did I succeed in crudely reducing the size of that plug. Of course, each time I removed my well-functioning rag contraption to see if the stopper would fit, fresh air (the great enemy of wine) was gushing into the container and the water in the air lock was moving slower and slower. I still don't know how important all this was (very, I should suspect), but by the time I got the hacked-up stopper in place and sealed the miserable object inside the neck with black masking tape, the aqueous life inside the air lock was practically nonexistent. Still, I retained hope that my wine would survive this ludicrous ordeal.

From the moment primary fermentation began till the day—nine weeks later—I siphoned the wine into bottles, just about every procedure required a good deal of imagination and even greater guesswork. What do you do, for example, when the instructions state that the ideal atmosphere should be sixty-five degrees Fahrenheit and the controlled room temperature of your apartment rarely drops below seventy-five during the summer? Easy. You change the location of your window air conditioner, turn all the vents in the direction of the container, keep the unit running full blast day and night, wear a light sweater, and steady yourself when the electric bill arrives. Of course, if you made wine in winter and your apartment had a thermostat, your only problem would be the risk of catching pneumonia. If there were no thermostat (as in my case), you would simply keep opening and closing all the windows, never invite guests in, and risk catching an even worse case of penumonia.

The most irritating of all guesswork throughout the process pertained to interpreting the timing directions. How would you react to such vagaries as "After about eight to fourteen days [do so and so]," or (now get this) "After about four to eight weeks the fermentation should have ceased"? Half by newly acquired instincts, half by a self-invented system of logistics, I learned eventually to approximate the timing of various steps, filling the container with cold water to an indicated level on the tenth day, waiting the necessary nine (not four, not eight!) weeks for the secondary fermentation—without air—to cease (proof: no bubbles). From beginning to end I kept a daily chart, making notations on the brew's colorations, odors, and scum; the water level in the air lock; and when and why I thought (i.e., prayed) the yeast was converting the sugar into alcohol and all that nasty CO_2 was being released. I became more and more fascinated with my living creation, bought more books on wine, read extensively, and would catch myself gawking at the container for a quarter of an hour several times a day, waiting for a bubble to move or pop or mysteriously fade out of sight.

When, after all those pregnant weeks, the concoction displayed no more bubbles or foam, out came the plastic siphon and into boiling water went corks and all the used Sprite, Pepsi, and wine bottles I'd been collecting. As you might have guessed, I'm something less than adept at anything mechanical, so it'll come as no surprise that when I began sterilizing all those bottles in two large roasting pans (still another feature on which the booklet offered no suggestions), I scalded practically every inch of my body not protected by clothing. But it was too late in the game to allow anything like aching flesh to stand in the way of success, so I bravely smeared my pitiful arms with Solarcaine, rushed out and bought an expensive pair of asbestos gloves, picked up my corncob tongs again, and proceeded to sterilize every cork and bottle.

Since the booklet warned against disturbing whatever sediment might have accumulated in the bottom of the container, I got my friendly neighbor to carefully help move big baby and stool from the hallway to the kitchenette. Just as I was about to remove the air lock, I noticed for the first time a tiny speck on top of one tube. Figuring it was no more than a morsel of sediment that had somehow worked its way up into the air lock, I didn't pay it much attention and continued taking out the apparatus. Then, holding the air lock to the light, I became a little more apprehensive and decided to pour the water into my hand to study the foreign object more closely. I touched it, fiddled with it as bit, and. . . . No! It couldn't be! But, by God, it was, because it started to move by itself! Yes, a bug! A detestable reddish bug that after I pounded it dead, displayed two detestable little wings. Now don't ask me where it came from, its genus, how it sneaked down into the capped air lock, or how it survived on top of the water. I don't know and don't want to know and would appreciate not being informed about the disgusting creature. Let's just forget about it.

I was never taught as a youngster to siphon gas from automobiles, but I quickly learned the gravitational principle behind the art while filling my wine bottles. Naturally there were a few initial disasters. Wine spewing in my eyes and all over the floor, permanently stained clothing, and mouthfuls of filthy sediment when I allowed the siphon to drop too near the bottom of the container. But in the long run I perfected the skill, checked each tube carefully to make sure the wine was clear (and bugless!), and tightly corked enough bottles of Burgundy to serve an army. The work was finished. No doubt there had been obstacles, but I'd managed to overcome most and must say I felt the pride of a Burgundian while racking my wine to age in the bottles. Naturally I was anxious to taste properly what I had produced, but, as I said, I did want to give the kit every fair chance and sneaking a taste of the raw wine would have gone against all the rules.

The booklet stated that my gourmet wine could be drunk as shortly as three to four weeks after siphoning. Although I must admit I found the notion rather shocking, I took the company's word and decided to conduct a wine tasting exactly one month after corking. I bought a loaf of French-style bread, a package of imported crisp *biscottes,* and three different varieties of beautifully ripened cheese. I set out my finest crystal goblets, one large, clear decanter, plus a stack of pads on which my very closest of friends could record their reactions. Don't get me wrong. I did have faith—I was determined to have faith—in my thirteen-week-old homemade Burgundy, but my better instincts told me that I would be smart to invite only those honest souls who love me and who, even at the risk of being poisoned, would see me through any crisis.

The moment came. I had uncorked the wine thirty minutes before the tasting, a few people snickered at the Pepsi bottle, but everyone observed carefully as I poured the Burgundy into the decanter. The color did look a little dark, but we could detect no sediment and, thanks be, I saw no bugs. I filled each glass halfway. We swirled, snifted the bouquet, then sipped. No reaction from anyone. More swirling, snifting, sipping, then some began making notes. Intolerable silence, interruped only by a few ummms and ugs and tongue lappings like a dog trying to reach food stuck to his nose.

At first my prejudiced brain convinced me the wine was drinkable, but soon my palate asserted its power, assuring me that what I was sloshing around in my mouth should best be described as a very light grape-flavored Communion wine with a touch of gasoline. I kept quiet. My friends, grabbing for the cheese and bread like dying slaves, tried to be polite—although I did notice they'd quit writing on their pads.

One said the wine was "interesting," another "like nothing I've ever tasted before," while another asked if she could go to the bathroom to cleanse her palate before tasting again. Finally, after thirty minutes of torture, my oldest and dearest and most respected Sybarite placed his glass firmly on the table, looked at me in somewhat of a daze, and candidly announced, "It tastes like absolute hell!"

I was crushed, although I knew he was right. Of course, I was still stubbornly certain that the reason the wine was so dreadful was because it had not had sufficient time to mature in the racks. But what if, after a year or so, it was still glop? Besides all the time and effort I'd spent producing the equivalent of twenty-five bottles, how much had it all cost me? The best I could figure, if what I had to shell out for sugar, telephone and electric bills, masking tape, a Magic Marker, scissors, gloves, a chisel, Solarcaine, three new shirts, bread, and cheese were added to the $19.95 charge for the kit, the total would run to exactly $129.61, or $5.18 per bottle. For that amount, if I purchased by the case immediately, I could probably have stocked up for the next year on plenty of Moulin-à-Vent. On the other hand, there was a principle and a lot of pride involved, and who could say, as the booklet had encourged, that someday I might have found my Burgundy to be one of my most treasured assets.

I didn't have much time to contemplate the alternatives, for within a day or so after the tasting my candid friend sent me a clipping from a back issue of *Playboy* that literally made my knees buckle. Some fellow loner had written to whomever you write at that magazine to inquire about some law governing bachelors making their own wine. The researched response was as follows:

> Federal law states that the head of a household may produce for "food value and medicinal purposes" up to 200 gallons of wine a year without paying taxes on it. He must file Form 1541 with the Bureau of Alcohol, Tobacco, and Firearms to get this exemption. Most bachelors do not qualify as heads of households. Unless you have a legal dependent living with you, you may not make wine tax-free.

I staggered in utter shock and disbelief. There couldn't possibly be such archaic law! But I checked further and, indeed, it's all true; no person or booklet had informed me of this insanity; I had broken the law and the IRS had every right to march into my apartment and confiscate all my Burgundy and maybe even throw me in jail.

Well, that was the final blow. Within minutes I was dumping the contents of my potentially valuable vinaceous asset into the toilet, and, with wrath in my soul, I now challenge any federal inspector to find a trace of homemade wine in my apartment. Most people are in the lucky position to take up legally what is becoming a very popular and tax-free hobby. I can't promise they'll have successful results, but at least they're free to try. Unfortunately, my wine-making days are over—that is, unless my dog develops a demonstrable passion and medically proven need for Burgundy and qualifies as a legal dependent on Form 1541.

CORNFLAKES BE DAMNED!

•••••••••••••••••••••••••••••••••••••

GRADUALLY I'M learning to like, respect, and even trust those who don't share my taste for good Bourbon, thick mutton chops, and genuine country ham, but never, repeat never, could I develop a really meaningful rapport with anyone who doesn't appreciate a wholesome and relaxing breakfast—and I mean the type of breakfast all Americans used to enjoy and not this silly thing called brunch. I love a full hot breakfast more than any meal of the day and refuse to understand why so many other people don't. When I read what our most important political leaders quickly wolf down upon rising, I wonder why the country hasn't fallen apart at the seams. When I run into an acquaintance who doesn't take nourishment before noon and who's miserably choked up with a cold or flu, I express little sympathy. And show me the fool who finds something sensible and dignified about offering plastic cups of instant coffee and a puny piece of bread as an excuse for a business breakfast, and I can only hope that he collapses from lack of adrenaline before the meeting is finished. Call me intolerant, arrogant, eccentric, but when it comes to gastronomic, aesthetic, and nutritional advantages of breakfast, my oriflamme flies high.

"Will you have cornflakes?" the club waiter asked the British army general. "Cornflakes?" snapped the general. "Cornflakes be damned! Bring me a plate of cold, undercooked roast beef and a tankard of ale!" That's the spirit, I say, and even though I've yet to reach the stage where rare meat and ale seem appropriate components of a proper breakfast, a day never passes that I don't tuck away a hearty meal as soon as possible after awakening. Freshly squeezed orange juice, oatmeal with rich cream, eggs, meat, ripe tomatoes, hashed brown potatoes, toast with homemade preserves, seasonal melon, fresh fruits of

almost any variety, milk, chicory coffee—these are but a few of my ordinary early morning staples. Away from home, the possibilities tend
to be a little more exotic, and during the winter months the quantity of
breakfast I consume usually increases. But whatever the circumstances,
I can't imagine not observing that old-fashioned American tradition of
starting every day by stoking my system with delicious food full of natural proteins and vitamins.

Exactly when the demise of the nutritious hot breakfast began in
this country is anybody's guess, but there can be no doubt that today
many Americans would disagree totally with the sagacious Mrs. Beeton, who wrote in her nineteenth-century *Book of Houshold Management*
that "the moral and physical welfare of mankind depends largely on its
breakfasts." It does seem that well into the twentieth century we valued this important meal as much as the English and Scandinavians do
to this day. In fact, breakfast for a true *bon viveur* like the notorious
Diamond Jim Brady consisted of nothing less than eggs, pancakes,
hominy, steak, chops, fried potatoes, corn bread, and muffins, all
washed down with a gallon of orange juice. Of course Diamond Jim
was always a bit excessive in his tastes, but to me even his orgiastic
matinal repasts make a good deal more sense than packaged cereals,
instant liquid breakfasts, frozen waffles, or this anemic modern-day
absurdity known to travelers as the continental breakfast. The continental breakfast is a gastronomic outrage that somehow fascinates
those with certain social pretensions and placates others with a mania
about cholesterol. As far as I'm concerned, it should be banned by the
FDA as a public health hazard.

"But how can you not rhapsodize over those wonderful *petits déjeuners*
and *prime colazioni* in France and Italy?" exclaims an acquaintance.
"Those buttery croissants and brioches, that jam, those huge cups of
café au lait!" Nonsense, I say, having been convinced for years that the
true worth of a croissant is its ability to absorb a runny egg yolk, and
the only merit to European breakfast coffee is the luscious pitcher of
nonhomogenized milk served on the side. Curiously enough, even the
French once honored the type of breakfast the Almighty intended us
all to eat, and I find none so mouth-watering to read about as the one
Brillat-Savarin prepared for friends one morning in the early nineteenth century. To start there were two dozen oysters per person consumed with Sauternes, followed by grilled kidneys on toast, truffled *foie
gras,* and a *fondue* of eggs broiled with cheese. Next came fresh fruit and
sweetmeats, then cups of mocha *à la Dubelloy,* and finally two types of

liqueurs. The legendary gastronome would wince were he to see his cultural descendants dunking croissants and baguettes in their various infusions.

Those of us who do savor a full morning meal day after day, *not* just on weekends, remember and enjoy discussing certain breakfasts the way others like to talk about rare ceremonial dinners. When I return home to the South, for instance, there is nothing I await with more anticipatory delight than the voluptuous breakfasts prepared by my mother: fresh blueberries and peaches in season, platters of slowly stirred cheese and eggs surrounded by fried apples, homemade sausage, salty country ham swimming in red-eye gravy, fresh baking-powder biscuits with any number of homemade preserves, buttery grits, hashed brown potatoes, sliced homegrown tomatoes, fried spots, or Virginia mullets, as these small fish are often called, and even a pitcher of milk punch to get things off to a rosy start.

In New Orleans, it's not unusual for me to stroll down to the French Market at the crack of dawn, order three tiny beignets (doughnuts) and a cup of dark roast chicory coffee, then proceed either to the Acme on Iberville Street for half a dozen or so oysters, or to Vaucresson for an authentic Creole breakfast of banana fritters, rice cakes topped with syrup and confectioners' sugar, and that wonderful local sausage known as *chaurice*. In wintertime, my mind turns instinctively to the fried plantains, fresh pineapple, creamy vegetable omelettes, and Piña Coladas I've enjoyed so often in the Caribbean, and there's hardly a time of the year I wouldn't hop on a plane for Texas just to breakfast on Ruby Red grapefruits, *huevos rancheros,* and roast beef hash sparked with jalapeño peppers.

I can recall beginning the day in Munich with suave goose liver pâté on dark bread at Dallmayr; in Copenhagen with fresh herring, pickled fish, miniature boiled potatoes, and three or four delicate pastries at the venerable Hôtel d'Angleterre; and at Amsterdam's Hotel Amstel, with fresh fruit saturated with rich cream, thin slices of Gouda and Edam on rusks, cold baked ham, and glasses of steaming hot chocolate. France, Italy, and Spain remain never-ending struggles for a passionate American breakfast lover who wishes to rise above the juice-bread-coffee-or-tea syndrome. But that early morning paradise called Great Britain more than makes up for all three with basted farm-fresh eggs served with broiled mushrooms and tomatoes in silver chafing dishes, or thick English bacon and even thicker Scottish porridge, or black pudding and kedgeree, or grilled kidneys and poached finnan haddie in milk, or the myriad of marvelous marmalades and honeys.

I've had memorable breakfasts at the Connaught Hotel, at whiskey distilleries in the Scottish Highlands, and at any number of English country inns, but let me go on record that no breakfast in the world can quite equal the munificent feast in which I indulge myself shamelessly every morning during a transatlantic crossing on the luxury liner *Queen Elizabeth 2.* The options are staggering: six varieties each of juice and fresh fruit, ten cereals, half a dozen egg preparations plus omelettes, two types of bacon and sausage, kippers, grilled lamb chops, sautéed potatoes, a cold buffet with a dozen meats and vegetables, pancakes, countless breads and pastries, an entire trolley of jams, preserves, and honeys, and no less than ten beverages. Of course when I choose to remain in my stateroom for breakfast, freshly squeezed orange juice spiked with champagne, scrambled eggs with caviar, Scotch baps, and a pot of Ceylon tea manage to sustain me until elevenses on deck.

One reason I enjoy breakfast so much on the *QE 2* is because it represents the ultimate opportunity to savor a meal which I'm as accustomed to eating as lunch and dinner. Even when I breakfast alone at home, the occasion assumes the same ritual as a fine dinner, in that the table is set with relatively fine china and silver, attractive stemware, and crisply ironed linen napkins. I deplore the fashionable idea of breakfast in bed. This sort of messy nonsense might be necessary for infants and invalids but not for sensible, healthy adults interested in the art of eating. Also, there was once a time I got a kick out of having my melon with lime, chicken liver omelette, herbed toast, and cold milk rolled ceremoniously into my hotel room by uniformed waiters. Perhaps I began to consider it distasteful to approach a beautiful breakfast in bed clothing, or perhaps I got tired of passing by a table full of dirty dishes, but now I enjoy dressing for breakfast, entering a quiet, well-set hotel dining room or open-air terrace, and either sharing this fine moment with someone pleasant or reading a newspaper while sipping and eating. In many respects, it's the most civilized experience anywhere, one that can't help but add spark to a new day.

Those who eschew a full breakfast to avoid gaining weight are ignorant of nutritional and caloric principles. Nobody has to watch calories more than I, but even when I tone down my eating habits, I never fail to eat a good breakfast. Lunch then becomes a light affair that assures an alert, productive afternoon and, most important, a ravenous appetite in the evening. As a professional gastronome, I've followed this approach to eating for years, and in addition to maintaining reasonably sound health, I've never varied in weight more than five pounds.

The American menus that follow, drawn from regions round the country where breakfast still plays an integral part in the daily lives of people, illustrate how truly exciting and delicious this meal can be with a minimum of effort. Personally, I think nothing of preparing and consuming every item on, say, the Southern and Creole breakfasts, and, indeed, nothing would be more enjoyable than planning a special weekend breakfast for friends and serving all the dishes buffet style. For those who prefer to be more practical, however, three or four selection should make for a nice repast any morning of the week. Most of the dishes require little time to prepare, and once you've grabbed a few good cookbooks and studied the recipes (hint: *The Joy of Cooking* doesn't miss much), you'll be surprised at how many items you can either make ready the night before or cook in a matter of minutes. The important thing is to get into the habit of eating good breakfasts, like those shown here, to warm up the system and to relearn what a gustatory superlative this meal can be when it's approached intelligently. Soon you'll find it virtually impossible to begin a day without this nutritional sustenance, and who knows, eventually you might even find yourself indulging in my own never-ending quest for the quintessential breakfast: a double egg yolk.

SOUTHERN

Oatmeal with Heavy Cream
Honeydew Melon

Cheese and Eggs
Country Ham, Red-Eye Gravy
Buttered Grits

Sliced Tomatoes
Hashed Brown Potatoes
Fried Apple Rings

Baking Powder Biscuits
Peach Preserves

Coffee

CREOLE

Milk Punch
Creole Cream Cheese, Fresh Fruit
Eggs Sardou
Chaurice
Panéed Veal
Banana Fritters
Hot Calas (Rice Cakes), Syrup
Beignets
Pain Perdu
Blackberry Jam
Chicory Coffee
Rosé Wine

TEXAS

Stewed Fruit
Huevos Rancheros
Venison Sausage
Roast Beef Hash with Jalapeño Bits
Chicken-Fried Steak
Nopalito (Cactus)
Corn Muffins
Hominy Bread
Wild Brush Honey, Mayhaw Jelly
Coffee

NEW ENGLAND

Creamed Finnan Haddie
Red-Flannel Hash, Poached Egg
Baked Beans on Toast
Broiled Scrod

Blueberry Pancakes, Maple Syrup
Canadian Bacon
Apple Pandowdy, Thick Cream and Shaved
Maple Sugar
Cranberry-Nut Bread
Beach-Plum Jelly

Hot Chocolate

NEW YORK DELICATESSEN

Fresh Orange Juice

Lox and Eggs
Cream Cheese
White and Black Bagels

Smoked Whitefish
Cold Baked Salmon
Raw Onion Slices

Challah Bread
Danish Pastry
Cherry Preserves

Coffee

BLESSED ARE WE
WHO SERVE

●●

YOU'RE SEATED in a fancy restaurant, and the last thing on your mind is what the captains and waiters are saying to each other—especially the things about you. Right? Well, after my week as an undercover captain in a very fancy French restaurant I now know exactly what is said. For instance:

"Forget the coffee refill on nineteen, ole buddy," directs Paul, another captain who's saucing a rack of veal at the serving table. "And how about cutting me a wagon for the dame on fourteen. For God's sake, don't do anything to raw 'em off. Dig the rock on that fat paw. Her ole man's a mark if I ever saw one—good for maybe twenty-five percent."

I'm worried that the customers might hear the crude language we tend to use among ourselves, possibly as a reaction to all the elegance and display we have to affect for the job. I'm also worried about the coffee for the couple at table nineteen.

"Forget 'em for now," Paul says. "All he cares about is snowing the chick, and besides, you can tell by the wine they're drinking he's no more than a fifteen percenter. Come on, for God's sake, step on it please with that tenderloin. . . . Quick, Jim, behind you on twenty."

I snap around just in time to pull out the table for the lady who is getting up, heading most likely for the john.

"Captain!" This is from table nineteen. "How about a little more coffee over here and a few more of those chocolate things."

I nod, back off, and go across the room to get a busboy to take care of the coffee and chocolate truffles. Then I make tracks for the silver trolley and begin carving three slices of beef. No sooner have I ladled on a bit of Bordelaise sauce and started to wipe dribbles from the edge of the hot plate than Jean-Pierre, the suave maître d'hôtel, passes by taking a new party to their table. He glances down at my handiwork, and, never for an instant losing pace with the two couples, he murmurs, *"Les bouts, n'oublie pas les bouts."* I still haven't gotten it through my thick skull to cover the ends of the meat with sauce.

"Quick, Paul, I need vegetables," I say.

"Yeah, I know, but the bastards didn't send out enough. See if you can grab a kitchenman and. . . . no, forget it. . . . why don't you just run back to the kitchen yourself while I finish up the veal and I'll try to find a cover for the tenderloin. And Jim, while you're back there, for God's sake do something about that sauce on your jacket."

As I break my way through the busy waiters and busboys and pantrymen, slide across the glop in the dishwashing area, grab a wet towel to wipe the Bordelaise off my dinner jacket, and stand puffing frantically on a cigarette while waiting for a chef to spoon out the neglected vegetables, I once again have the feeling I can't make it through the evening. The blood blisters on my left foot, the excruciating pain in my lower back, the dizziness from lack of anything to eat since the cheeseburger in mid-afternoon. So far I've managed to survive this self-inflicted ordeal, and no doubt I'm convinced more than ever before that the project is both noble and constructive. To my knowledge none of us highfalutin, omnipotent, forever-complaining restaurant critics has ever made any effort to experience firsthand the actual running of a great restaurant.

Okay, I know. The customer is shelling out plenty of hard cash, and he shouldn't be expected to understand why a place happens to flop miserably on any given occasion. Correct? For years that was my way of thinking too, until, that is, I began to wonder if there weren't a few hidden facts behind the scenes that could reveal ways whereby I and everybody else just might get better food and service. So I did it, and I learned a lot. Things like this:

• • • You should expect a maître d', captain, or waiter in any first-class restaurant to be able to do anything to enhance your pleasure, but, like it or not, no matter who you are or how fat your wallet, if you don't make some small effort yourself, you'll have a very ordinary experience. You should dress properly, meaning a suit and tie for men, a nice dress for women. Deluxe restaurants have little use for clods. You should ask the captain or waiter his name when he arrives at the table. You should smile from time to time at the people serving you. For heaven's sake, you should say thank you when they do something special. And you're even better off if you can show an intelligent interest in the menu and wine list.

• • • It seriously upsets captains and wine stewards to see guests pouring their own wine. If your glass needs refilling and everyone on the staff is busy, try to be patient a few minutes till someone has time to pour. You shouldn't go thirsty, however, and if you must pour after a short wait, go ahead. But understand that the staff will take this as a complaint. If it's deserved, make it.

• • • Nobody on a restaurant staff is overly fond of couples (deuces), for the simple reason that they require virtually the same amount of time that it takes to serve four, and for half the tips or less. Singles are never loved, contrary to what anybody says. Quite often a maître d' will turn down dozens of same-day requests for deuces in order to hold space for parties of four, six, or eight.

• • • Since those working the floor receive hardly any salary to speak of (union or no union), tips matter more to them than anything else in life. Almost everywhere (except New York City) tips are pooled and distributed after lunch and dinner among either the entire floor staff (as at my restaurant) or those working their separate stations: generally a full cut for captains, waiters, and wine stewards; ¾-cut for kitchenmen; and ½-cut for busboys. Although this means you're really tipping many for a job performed by one or two, don't try to take out your wrath on the system (unless, of course, you found the service rotten). If you automatically stiff the bill thinking the tip is basically impersonal and meaningless, remember you're only decreasing the cut (i.e., livelihood) collected by those who served you well. (Even if you palm a captain, he's expected to contribute that tip to the pool—except in New York City.) Also don't forget that knowledge of your stinginess filters down quickly among the staff, and this could have a disastrous effect on your next visit, no matter who waits on you.

• • • Often the bottle of wine a guest orders is indicative of what the tip will be, but we prayed for 25 percent, were thankful for 20, and said ugly things about those who left only 15 (previously I had rarely tipped over 15 percent in even the finest restaurants).

• • • The best way to tip? Most people simply add a percentage to the credit card slip (either in one lump sum or, say, 15 percent for the waiters and 5 percent for the captain), but nobody impressed us more than those who made the rare gesture of personally handing us the tips while expressing thanks. Does palming a maître d' or captain a five before you sit down guarantee special attention and possibly better food? You can bet your bottom dollar it does!

• • • Nothing irritates a staff so much or causes a greater disruption of service than when customers jump up and leave the table for one reason or another, especially while the main courses are being served.

• • • It hurts when an obviously satisfied customer who's leaving doesn't even have the graciousness to thank those who've provided good service—palmed tip or no palmed tip. This discourtesy is never forgotten.

Before taking on this mission I had no idea what I was getting myself into, but one thing was for sure: the plan was ingenious. Since I was determined to work totally under cover for one week in a deluxe, expensive restaurant and couldn't risk my name or face being recognized in New York, contact was made in Chicago with Jovan Trboyevic, owner of the well-known and highly praised Le Perroquet. Now it so happened that one of Jovan's old friends and colleagues had recently opened a new luxury restaurant in New York, so our story was that the friend was sending this promising waiter by the name of Jim Anderson (my alias) out to Chicago to recieve initial training as a captain by Jovan and his veteran staff. Jovan agreed to all the terms: nobody except Jovan himself was to have an inkling as to what I was about (with the polite understanding that if I suspected betrayal, I'd discontinue the project on the spot); I would stay at the Drake Hotel but there would be a fake address and phone drop elsewhere in case someone wanted to contact me; I would work both lunch and dinner, keeping the same hours as the others; I would be treated by Jovan just like any other employee, even nastily if necessary; and I would turn any and all tips over to the other captains to be included in the normal distribution since, after all, I was there only for the experience. Suffice it to say that the boys bought the story hook, line, and sinker and were convinced from the beginning that this Anderson guy was no more than a New York hashhouse waiter with a sloppy Southern accent who was aspiring to the restaurant big time. How did I happen to know French? By slaving with a bunch of frogs for a year in some French dive on New York's West Side, that's how.

From the moment I showed up for my first lunch it was pretty obvious I was working in a first-class restaurant, one of the best in the country. On the surface Le Perroquet manifests just about what you would expect (and more) of a luxury restaurant in this country: muted mustard and light green murals, red velvet banquettes with appliquéd cushions, starched linen tablecloths, fine etched crystal, silver flatware, small individual table lamps, Lalique flower vases, silver ice buckets, bottles of mineral water on every table, fancy complimentary hors d'oeuvres and chocolate truffles, and so forth. It's all very high class, to say the least, but what was to amaze me continuously during my week there was the assemblage of experts who make the place function so beautifully: three young Americans, no less, holding down the important jobs of head chef, pastry chef, and wine steward; a perfectionist Mexican bartender who has no patience with staffers who don't follow his directions on how to place drink orders; a French maître d'hôtel who can detect (and reject) a slob after ten seconds on the phone; a brigade of American, French, Syrian, Mexican, and Spanish waiters and busboys who don't seem to need to speak much English in order to communicate; and, of course, the dynamic force of Jovan himself, an elegant, proud, often melancholy Yugoslav who is brutally frank in all matters, who proclaims himself a philosophical anarchist in his never-ending struggle against mediocrity and boredom, and who doesn't think twice about throwing out customers who cause unnecesary problems and embarassment.

So there I was that first miserable day, determined to make a go of this thing yet frightened stiff that somebody on the staff (not to mention the customers) would decide there was just something too weird about this fellow. Even the most illiterate, inexperienced greasy-spoon waiter knows how to carry a full tray of drinks, write down an order, and serve food without dumping it in the guy's lap. I didn't, and in case you suffer under the illusion (as I always have) that a captain in a restaurant does no more than smile, take orders, flame an occasional duck, and grab for tips, let me clue you in. In addition to having to execute the most menial tasks, I (like everyone else in Jovan's employ) was expected to be able to cup ashtrays deftly when emptying them, hold lamp wires up with my foot while pulling out tables, pour wine across three bodies when a wall made it impossible to pass behind a customer, gracefully pick up a plate of food and place a clean napkin over a spill without drawing too much attention to the customer's sloppiness, and, of course, prepare and sauce in a matter of seconds an array of exquisite dishes on a flaming hot serving table not much bigger than a TV set.

No task, I was to learn quickly, is too demeaning for any captain who wants things to run smoothly, no matter how proud or experienced he may be. By the same token, it's understood in a great restaurant that regardless of whether you wear a tuxedo or a waiter's white jacket or a kitchenman's lowly black uniform, success (i.e., satisfying customers, keeping your job, and, above all, raking in as much money as possible from the split on tips) is determined by unrelenting teamwork. If a captain sees a dirty dish on a table, he doesn't wait for a busboy to pick it up; if a patron takes a cigarette out, a waiter doesn't hesitate to rush over and light it; and it's nothing extraordinary for a wine steward to fetch a quick pot of coffee, slice a side of smoked salmon, or help a hurried captain dish out at the serving table. As a result of this interchange, a remarkable sense of togetherness develops behind the scenes, an understanding on the part of everyone that if you expect to make a decent livelihood, you'd sure as hell better respect and help the next guy.

By the third day I had the basics pretty well under control, thanks mainly to the sympathetic help of everybody on the staff. I had grasped the technique of referring to tables and customers by number and writing down orders accordingly—vegetable terrine for #2 on table 14, for instance; I reeled off all the specialities with their exotic descriptions, encouraging customers to sample these extraordinary dishes instead of the more standard preparations listed on the menu; I learned how to decant fine red wines at the table and handle dishes and silver and crystal without so much as a tingle; I mastered the delicate art of "pushing" soufflés at dinner by telling customers how delicious they were and reminding them that, of course, these must be ordered in advance. I'd even begun to develop that inimitable look of self-confidence and authority I've always admired in a good captain.

Of course there were disasters, like when I poured '61 Haut Brion into a glass containing humble Beaujolais (the customers were given a new bottle, and I received a blast from Jovan), or when, not having any idea what to do when a slimy *crème caramel* slid off the plate onto a lady's dress, I frantically picked it up from her lap with my fingers, dropped it in a napkin, and inspired something close to hysteria on the part of Madame and staff members alike. I also had to be told constantly by a particularly concerned Mexican waiter always to stand erect when taking orders (Jovan disagreed) and never, but never, to touch the table while talking with a customer. The maître d' had to remind me time and again to be sure to clear away extra place settings, to stand by a table so as not to turn my back to customers, and never, heaven forbid, to serve my dish if the customer happened to be away from the table. These things seemed to work themselves out, however, and I felt that generally I was making fairly good progress.

I gradually became accustomed to much of the same way of life the other guys knew forty-nine weeks out of the year, every day except Saturday lunch and Sunday (when the restaurant was closed). The routine, which is no doubt generally like that in any good restaurant, is deadly and never varies. Around ten-thirty in the morning you show up to analyze the reservations with Jovan and Jean-Pierre, study the special dishes to be offered at lunch, deal with the fresh linen and setting of tables, see that the cold dishes are properly displayed and the sherbet containers spotless, answer the blasting phone and take reservations, on and on, one thing after another. If the laundry isn't delivered, you're sunk and can only pray there's still enough new stock in supply for those tables you can't fake with last night's linen. If a waiter calls in sick, you have to rechart stations and figure out who can best cover for him. If the crayfish pâté looks or tastes wrong, an equally exotic dish must be decided on and prepared in split-second time back in the kitchen. Shortly before noon you change from ratty garb to tux or uniform, exposing holes in T-shirts, pale white skin that's rarely exposed to the sun, a gut bloated from too much wee-hours beer, feet forever swollen from pacing the job some twelve to thirteen hours a day. Soon you hear on the intercom the rugged voice of the off-duty cop downstairs giving the name of the first customer coming up in the elevator. The bowing and scraping and sweeping of arms begins as the mechanics of still another lunchtime are put into motion.

You continue till three, three-fifteen, three-thirty, or till the last guests move toward the elevator. You're anxious to collect your cut of the tips (distributed after every meal around the bar or back in the pantry), and you've had nothing to eat and you're a bit pooped. Instead of sticking around to take chances on what some of the guys who never leave the place are served at four-thirty, you head out for a cheeseburger and fries, dash home, and maybe watch a little TV or soak in a hot tub before heading back to the restaurant around five-fifteen.

Friday night is booked solid, and since there is no reasonable way to turn down anybody who reserved two weeks in advance, you're stuck with far too many deuces to make the evening truly profitable in the way of tips. "Fifty-five dollars, maybe sixty apiece for the captains," guesses Paul, "but then you never know. See those two guys on four?

They're weekend regulars and actually pretty nice and generous. Give 'em plenty of attention and they'll leave a good twenty-five percent. The couple on six is also around about once a week, but remember, the one thing that infuriates that guy is having the menus pushed on him till he asks for them. And the two on twelve—well, I heard those Southern accents when they arrived, and if they're like most Southerners they can't count past fifteen. No offense to you, ole buddy, but Southerners are rotten tippers, the worst."

Enter Tennessee Williams and party of three. The great man himself, and Jovan suggests privately I take on the table in hopes of reaping an interesting scenario ("But no special attention, Jim. He gets no better treatment than any other customer in this restaurant"). Williams smiles, says there'll be no cocktails, and asks what nice dry white wine I'd recommend.

"Sir, would you care to see the wine list?" I answer.

"Naw, I don't feel up to having to wrestle with a long wine list tonight," he drawls, "but you look like the type of captain who'll choose something that's very appropriate for the occasion—hee, hee."

Of course I have no idea what occasion he's talking about or why the giggle, but I nevertheless discuss it with Alain, a wine steward, and together we decide on a fairly rare but reasonably priced Pavillon Blanc du Château Margaux.

"This is superrrb," cries Williams after checking the nose like the old pro he is and taking a huge gulp. "We'll just have to have two bottles, young man, and I'll have an explanation of where you happen to be from with that marrrvelous accent. Now don't tell me. It's Georgia, or maybe South Carolina, but it's *not* Mississippi."

Suddenly I notice the man at the next table reaching for his bottle of wine in the ice bucket, so, leaving Williams's question dangling, I excuse myself momentarily and pour the wine in a flash. I have every intention of returning to Williams's table to absorb every word I can, but no sooner have I placed the bottle back on ice than a waiter who's looking deathly pale asks if I could cover his station and handle serving the soufflés on twelve while he goes to the bathroom. Action is at its peak throughout the restaurant, with not one captain, waiter, or busboy to spare. Held prisoner by two raspberry soufflés that must be spooned out immediately, I'm unable to help poor Roberto, who is struggling with both the pastry wagon and sherbet trolley for the dessert orders on sixteen. Dirty dishes should be cleaned off twenty, but it seems all the busboys are back in the pantry preparing espresso—and besides, though I know my attitude is wrong, I've really lost all desire to try to make things nice for two dolts who've nursed Martinis throughout an entire glorious meal and kept business papers spread out in every direction on the table.

"Hey, captain," I hear behind me, as I feel a hand being placed around my shoulders. "See that cute little thing sitting in front of me over there? Well, I got a big favor to ask of you. See, it's her birthday tonight, and I was just wondering if maybe the restaurant had a little special cake or something. And I was also wondering if later on you could come by and, you know, just give her a little kiss on the cheek and wish her a happy birthday. Really would give her a big thrill, and, don't worry, I'll make it all worth your time—ya know what I mean?"

"Not in this restaurant you don't!" Jovan booms at me. "You inform the guy this place is no playground." Suffice it to say I did a little hand-kissing, then watched the oaf walk out without so much as a fare-thee-well.

As I pass by twenty to check on the wine glasses, I notice the attractive party of three is still seriously involved in their comparative tasting of two first-growth Bordeaux and two fine California Cabernets. One lady, two gentlemen. Like many of the customers, they ordered their food intelligently, asked me the details of each preparation, and, in general, have conducted themselves in such a delightful manner that I find waiting on them an absolute joy. Although Le Perroquet has an exquisite selection of cheeses included in the price of dinner, I've learned not to waste my breath suggesting this course to those who obviously couldn't care less. But for the party at this table, I don't even ask but make the special effort to present the wicker tray, discuss which cheeses I feel would go nicely with the wines, and, although not doubting the ability of the waiter to cut the cheeses properly, choose to serve them myself. And, as I suspected, these sensible souls order no more than a little fresh sherbet for dessert, espresso, and a bit of Cognac. More than likely they'll tip me a ten-in-hand (which it so happens they eventually do), but even if they didn't, I would still consider it a privilege to have served them.

"Jim, do you think you can handle that scene on twenty-one?" whispers Alain.

Rushing up to Williams's table, I see that the drooping head of the guest sitting in front of the playwright is practically touching his salmon steak.

"Excuse me, captain," says Williams calmly, "but it appears that

one of my companions has been stricken by an attack of acute exhaus-
tion necessitating an immediate cup of strong black coffee." (I
jotted down that line the second I got back to the pantry.) Strangely
enough, the other two guests never stop their conversataion or so
much as glance over to see if this guy is alive, and even Mr. Williams
seems too accustomed to his friend's condition to become in any way
alarmed.

It's 12:30 A.M. With only one couple still lingering over coffee, Jean-
Pierre and I stand in the small area behind Gino's bar where throughout the evening we've left cigarettes smoldering in a filthy ashtray.
Although I know some of the boys are back in the pantry snitching
food from the cooler and finishing up whatever was left on the trolleys
and even on plates, I'm too exhausted to be hungry. All I want now is
to go out and get drunk, relax, forget. Returning to check the dining
room, I see Dan, Roberto, Alain, Paul, Zigi, all standing and waiting
and praying it won't be too much longer before they can finish up, collect their tips, and leave.

Finally the time came for Jovan to reveal my cover-up to the staff—I
didn't have the guts to do it myself. All the guests had left, Paul had
just announced that a certain party had tipped exactly $7 on a $410
bill, and a group of us were standing at the bar bemoaning the outcome of the evening's sacred tip sheets.

"And just what do you think of that, Monsieur Villas?" bolted
Jovan, putting his hand on my shoulder.

No reaction from anybody—anybody!

"Gentlemen, look here," he continued. "What would you say if I
told you we've got a phony creep in the group whose name is not
Anderson?"

Jean-Pierre raised his eyes, glanced at Jovan, then at me, then back
to Jovan. As the explanation continued, a formidable silence came
over the rather frightened men as they all glared at me in disbelief.
Feeling more and more rotten, I could find nothing to say but "I'm
sorry," and I was sorry, for the noble project now seemed a little distasteful. These guys had become my friends. Then Gino smiled politely
for the first time and Paul offered to light my cigarette and nobody re-
minded me it would be my turn to buy the beer. I knew a unique experience was over.

So the week came to an end. Physically, I ached and had lost five
pounds; spiritually, I'd gained invaluable insight into the special world
I write about. Perhaps the most important lesson I learned at Le Per-

roquet is that the public is dealing with pros who, if treated right, can and will move mountains to make people feel special.

But my experience in Chicago has made me ever less tolerant of those in the business who're quite obviously out to con the public. Shortly after my arrival back in New York, for instance, I had occasion to dine for the first time in one of the city's more fashionable restaurants. At the very beginning, I attempted to establish a rapport with the captain by asking his name, soliciting his opinions on the menu, taking his wine recommendation, and generally making him feel we needed and trusted him. Nothing worked. The food was garbage, the service shoddy, and the captain totally indifferent. He never supervised anything we were served, he allowed us to pour our own wine throughout the meal, he stood chatting casually with the haughty maître d'hôtel while I motioned for him. When I finally managed to wave him over to complain that my companion's calf's liver was tough as leather, he merely shrugged and suggested that perhaps she just didn't like liver. He was hopeless and should have been jobless. When time came to pay the bill, naturally he was there, hovering, pampering, eyeing. To the amount of the bill I begrudgingly added 10 percent for the incompetent waiter only because he might have been inexperienced or sick or in love.

"Did Monsieur not enjoy his meal?" questioned the captain as we brushed by, still hoping I'd palm him a bill.

"No, Monsieur did not enjoy his meal," I snapped, "and I'd like to add that the service was inexcusable."

"But Monsieur, you don't understand. Tonight was exceptionally busy, and if you could put yourself in my place, having to take care of this many people, maybe you'd understand."

Staring him straight in the eye, I was almost tempted. Then I turned, took the lady's arm, and walked out.

WHEN LUCULLUS
DINES WITH
LUCULLUS

●●●

At 8:20 P.M. in New York, a middle-aged American executive in town on business approaches the stone-faced maître d' at a luxury restaurant, twenty minutes late for his reservation. He is alone. He wears a beige lightweight suit, carries a newspaper under his arm, and looks a bit lost. It is suggested he have a drink at the bar while his table is prepared. He finds the bar and orders a drink. Thirty minutes later he's shown to a table near the entrance to the pantry. He sits. Flagging down the first waiter he sees, he asks for another Scotch and water, opens his newspaper, and begins to read nervously. The captain passes by, leaves a menu on the table, and returns almost immediately to take the order. Rather than struggle with the French or risk embarrassment by asking the captain foolish questions, he settles for *la vichyssoise* and *le filet mignon,* followed by cheese—any cheese. Would Monsieur care to see the wine card? No need. A bottle of red wine will be just fine.

Finished with the newspaper and the cocktail, he sits, waiting, wishing the food and wine would arrive, tearing off morsels of the little roll that won't be replaced, staring into space, uncomfortable. At one point he suspects a party across the room might be feeling sorry for him, and fidgeting with the silverware, he begins to wonder what the hell he's doing here. It's getting late. The soup finally arrives as well as a bottle of claret, still corked and price unknown. Unable to attract the attention of the captain, he grabs his waiter and asks him to open the bottle. Next comes the steak, which he finds too rare. He says nothing but pours himself another glass of wine. And so it will go, through the cheese, maybe some salad and dessert, the coffee, right up to the miserable last moment when, half-smashed, he'll wish he'd taken time to notice at the bottom of the menu the warning that the restaurant accepts no credit cards.

This poor fellow serves to illustrate my point: When it comes to the problem of having to dine out alone, Europeans generally carry it off very well. Americans do it badly, in fact, horribly. Everywhere—New York, Kansas City, Seattle—it's the same embarassing story: Americans are either frightened to death to dine out by themselves in good restaurants or, if they decide to risk it, they're generally treated like dogs.

God knows, there aren't many people who ever actually choose to savor a great meal all alone, but sometimes you're forced to consider the possibility—if, that is, you care anything about good food and wine. You could be traveling to meet someone or attending a convention or just stuck away somewhere on business. Tomorrow's a busy day, so your first inclination might be simply to call room service or wander out like a coward to some safe hash house or fast-food joint. Then you think how nice it would be to go to a truly fine restaurant, relax, be waited on in style, and order a couple of those fancy dishes you don't get back home. You think again. Forget it, you say, and face reality: Most restaurants hate singles, male and female, for singles waste space and look strange and aren't worth as much in tips as a couple. It's too much of an ordeal.

Well, all I can say is that anybody who refuses to confront this problem head-on is a damn fool, for as one who spends more time dining out alone than I care to relate, I'm happy to report I've not only become a master of the art but have actually learned to enjoy the occasion. A few years back it was a nightmare, to be sure, but not anymore. I learned the ropes, and I must say that now I conduct myself with great aplomb. I don't think twice about booking a table for one in even the snootiest restaurants, and I defy any maître d' or captain or waiter to treat me with anything less than total respect—even friendship. No doubt it often takes plenty of guts, but believe me, in the long run it pays off. If, for instance, a maître d' tries to direct me to an objectionable table, I reply that if there's not another one available, I'll wait—and not necessarily at the bar but right there beside him at the busy entrance. If a wine steward or captain allows a bottle of white wine to remain in the ice bucket too long, I display indignation and direct that it be placed on the table. And what about a waiter who from the start tends to give me as little time and service as possible? Simple. When he serves the first course, I look him straight in the eye, get his name, smile, and ask if he's new in the place. It works.

If all this sounds uppity, even a bit militant, let me assure you it's the only way if you ever hope to develop the skills that will enable you to walk confidently into any fine restaurant, let them know who's boss, and, above all, make dining alone a pleasant and enriching experience. I see it as the ultimate test of character, an occasion wherein you're forced not only to come to grips with a form of psychological uncertainty but also to look upon food and drink in a truly serious manner (perhaps for the first time ever). In the presence of one or more persons, the normal tendency (or requirement) is to indulge fully in polite conversation, debate, business, passion, what have you. But when alone at table, you're automatically relieved of such distractions, and this should enable you to calm down, contemplate, and devote yourself completely to the pleasures of gastronomy. Now you have the opportunity really to taste food, discuss its preparation with an enthusiastic captain or waiter, and perhaps learn something important. With other people around there's never adequate time to analyze properly a wine card, but alone you can spend a good thirty minutes studying the listings, asking the wine steward questions, making a few notes on labels and vintages you're unfamiliar with, and, eventually, choosing the exact bottles you'd like to try and possibly share with the sommelier. Best of all, should you feel like swirling wine around in your mouth, "chewing" it, and making all those gurgling sounds that you've always been afraid might offend unenlightened table mates, you're free as an eagle.

Of course, every professional loner has his or her opinions on the best ways to attack the problem and I've known a few who can still teach even me a point or two. Take, for example, a high-powered public relations woman in New York who's forced to face knife and fork alone time and again throughout the world. Maybe it's true that women have to confront more obstacles than men, but for her, meeting the challenge is as much a part of her hectic schedule as trying to hold down accounts.

"Sure it can be a bug," she says, "but if you insist—as I do—on dining well when you happen to be alone, you must learn not only to take the bull by the horns and assert yourself but also demonstrate some degree of knowledge about food and wine. Any woman—or man, for that matter—who commands respect but can't handle a menu and wine card intelligently deserves the treatment she or he gets. I mean, just go into '21' in New York and watch all the single ladies ordering scrambled eggs and bacon instead of something more interesting, or look around in any fine Italian restaurant at the singles rushing through a plate of spaghetti washed down with a cocktail. No wonder they're treated like peasants! It's sad, but they just don't seem to know any better. Either that, or they're terrified to experiment on their own."

How does she command respect?

"I'll give you a perfect example. A year or so ago I was shown to a rear table in the elegant dining room of the Palace Hotel in St. Moritz. Noticing the table hadn't been cleaned, I turned to the majordomo, told him I refused to sit down till the table was ready, and stalked back to the entrance. Later, when the captain left on the table a corked bottle of Bordeaux I'd chosen for my main course, I signaled him back and politely asked if he didn't think it would be a good idea to open the wine immediately, pour a glassful, and let it breathe. Well, suffice it to say that after a few more such episodes, I had everybody in the place jumping, and when I returned a few nights later I not only got the best table in the restaurant but was sent a Cognac compliments of the house."

Next is the young female art director of a major national magazine who'd just returned from assignment in Paris. Before she left, I'd given her the names of a few classic restaurants and insisted she try them. "But I can't imagine dining out alone in fancy restaurants," she'd cried.

"Nonsense," I countered. "You love good food, you always dress attractively, so get the concierge at the hotel to book you a reservation [the quickest and easiest way to get a table in many great European restaurants], drum up your courage, and do it."

The results?

"A fabulous revelation," she began. "Oh, at one place they put me at a middle table in the back room, but that really didn't bother me since, after all, we were late making the reservation and the restaurant was full. I did take a book along, as you suggested, but you know, I think that's bad, a real insult to the restaurant. Besides, I could never really figure out where to place it! What impressed me most was that I never really understood menus or noticed food more than when I was forced to go it alone. Nobody to order for me, nobody to make the wine decision, nobody with whom I was obliged to keep a conversation going while trying to eat and taste. Sure, there was one bad scene when a waiter announced I'd have to hurry through the cheese since my lemon soufflé was ready. He meant well, I suppose, but you know what I told him? 'I'm not finished, so let it wait—and at these prices it had better be good!' It was delicious, and he got a fat tip."

Myself excepted, I know of nobody who has to dine out alone any more than a certain former executive of the Cunard Line in London who's now a peripatetic business consultant in the United States. A shameless gourmand in his own right, he allows absolutely nothing to interfere with his passion for food and wine, and he's completely intolerant of those who don't seem to understand all the virtues of occasionally being by oneself in a restaurant.

"It's the ultimate Sybaritic experience," he says, "for you can do exactly as you please. The problem with most single diners is that they're so insecure they don't know how to create their own excitement. They allow restaurant personnel to make them feel embarrassed about taking up a table (forgetting, after all, that even the haughtiest captain is still there to serve); they're intimidated by those around them; and they need something to do so desperately they bring along diversions like books and newspapers. Ridiculous. For me, dining out alone provides a wonderful chance to reflect calmly, explore, experiment with unusual dishes and wines, and even meet new people. Why, I could spend hours studying the decor of a fine restaurant, discussing (and, mind you, learning more about) wines with a knowledgeable wine steward, and simply creating fantasies about those around me. You know, when I'm eating alone I become so aware of the fact that for the first time in a long while I'm observing people dispassionately, my fellow human beings, and I can't help but feel this benefits me and my work somehow. Singles in this country always seem to be worried that others are staring at or feeling sorry for them. Well, that's sheer paranoia! And to be quite frank, I've discovered that if people do glance over from time to time, it's usually because they're curious about what *I* have ordered. Not long ago, in fact, one gentleman left his party for a moment, came over to my table, and asked point-blank what I was eating. And later he invited me to join them for coffee and brandy. Now that's what I mean when I say dining alone can be very exciting."

While I know a few restaurants that have proved they have the best interests of the single diner at heart, these are no doubt few and far between, and you're crazy to take chances when you're shelling out plenty of hard cash for what is supposed to be a real treat. So maintain a defensive attitude no matter where you go, dress properly, leave the newspapers and novels back in the room, sit at the table with authority, handle the menu and wine card intelligently, and tip a hardworking, friendly captain and waiter well. Above all, remember that this is your evening, and you're entitled to enjoy it in any manner you like without criticism from anybody. If you want two Martinis before dinner, order them; if you prefer to spend twenty minutes musing over a menu, announce your intentions firmly to the captain; if your fish is overcooked, send it back in a flash; and if you crave a cigarette after the main course, by God, light one up. It's all a matter of self-confidence and style, and who knows, before long you probably won't give so much as a second thought to tasting sauces with your fingertips or sloshing wine around in your mouth or sucking on a frog's leg.

GAMES RESTAURANTS
PLAY

●●●

WITHOUT FAIL it happens every time you sit down in a fancy restaurant—as well as in a few not so fancy joints. You and your companion study the menu and wine list, and while trying to decide what you'd like to order, that little calculator in your brain starts clicking away automatically. In the past you've always been stung when the final bill arrives, but this time, damn it, you're determined to beat the rap by analyzing carefully every single charge that could conceivably be made. Appetizers, main courses, maybe a small salad and side vegetable for two, wine, tax, tip—you quickly consider everything and come up with a figure that not only fits your budget but can't possibly be off by more than a dollar or two. Right? Wrong, for when the bill is presented you suddenly realize your nice well-planned $60-dinner has somehow soared to a grand total of $100. You think about haggling with the captain, but in the long run you simply sit there, shell out, and admit once again to being taken.

Unfortunately it's not very likely that any of us will ever become absolute masters at the art of assessing correctly the costs of such first-class experiences for the simple reason that swanky restaurant owners (not all, but most) make up one of the shrewdest breeds in creation when it comes to reaping that extra buck. Needless to say, it's bad enough that so many get by with palming off margarine for butter, soy patties for milk-fed veal, and pork shoulder picnic for Virginia ham, but their degree of expertise at making out tricky menus and formulating all sorts of legitimate extra charges is downright frightening. I think it's safe to say that anyone who dines out more or less regularly is accustomed to coping with the additional cost of such obvious items as cocktails, coffee, and those maddening dishes with supplemental prices tacked on, but what really can make a disaster of the bill are literally dozens of other charges that you have no sane reason to suspect but which are as carefully manipulated by owners, captains, and waiters as the amount of caviar spooned from a tin.

Heaven knows, even I who spend most of my waking hours restaurant-hopping have never once managed to pinpoint a bill, but, unlike most people in this overly polite society, I don't hesitate for one minute to challenge overtly the system every time I dine out. No doubt lots of embarrassed table companions and enraged restaurant personnel make ugly comments about me behind my back (cheap, paranoid, ungracious—things like that), but as a result of my perseverance, I've learned quite a bit that might not only help save you lots of money but, in the long run, will most likely bring you the respect from others you deserve. If you're the type who barely looks at a menu or who frowns upon the sensible practice of checking and, if necessary, questioning a bill, you might as well stop reading here. If, on the other hand, you're truly serious about dining out and entertaining in fine restaurants, take note:

• • • First and foremost, learn to scan a menu (especially the big elaborate ones) with the exact alertness you exercise when examining a medical insurance policy. Quite often those extra charges that end up on the bill are indicated somewhere: the Roquefort salad dressing your waiter recommends over the house dressing, the mushroom sauce that does not come automatically with the London broil, the baked Alaska that runs a dollar more if it's flambéed, and the "tureen" of soup which is more expensive than the "bowl." It's also by carefully studying a menu that you run across the sleazy notice in fine print that "all prices are subject to change." If you disregard this warning or fail to ask if it applies to what you're ordering, you could be in big trouble.

• • • The only thing that incurs my wrath and indignation more in certain American restaurants than that abominable and outdated practice of adding an automatic cover charge or "bread & butter" to the bill (even the French abolished the custom in 1967) is when the charge is displayed sneakily on the menu. At one celebrated place I know, this extra charge, listed as "B & B Cover," is wickedly camouflaged among the appetizers; at another it is graphically indistinguishable from the potatoes; and at still another it shows up in miniscule italics in a remote bottom corner of a mind-boggling menu listing no less than two hundred items. On even the most streamlined menus search carefully for this item that can set you back as much as $2.75 per person, and remember that if you're really adamant about not having to tolerate this rip-off, simply send away the bread, butter, olives, celery, or whatever is placed automatically on the table and refuse resolutely to pay the cover when the bill arrives. Contrary to popular belief, you do not legally have to pay for anything you don't order.

· · · Another hidden cost you're by no means obliged to pay is a service charge added automatically to the bill—an infuriating European custom that now seems to be catching on in fancy American restaurants. I don't suppose I really object that much to a sensible 15-percent gratuity charged at places that are consistently respectable and where management at least has the decency to warn you on the menu, but you should not tolerate highfalutin restaurants that slap an unannounced 20-percent "service" on an already outrageous bill unless the action happens to be justified by absolutely flawless food and service. If and when you run into this sort of problem, and have good reason not to tip what the restaurant tries to force you to tip, simply tell the owner or maître d' to call in the police.

· · · Beware particularly of *table d'hôte* menus, few of which hold up to the pitch that "the price of the main course includes the full dinner." Usually this setup includes not one morsel more than an appetizer, main course, and dessert, meaning that if you fail to notice the dangerous word *or* between the multiple appetizer and soup listings, the salads and vegetables, and the cheeses and desserts, you could get clipped. Remember also that few *table d'hôte* menus include things like Roquefort dressing, cheese, and coffee, and I've yet to see one in this country that allowed for so much as a glass of jug wine. If you have any doubts about this type of menu, look boldly at the captain or waiter and ask if so-and-so is included on the fixed-price dinner.

· · · Nowhere are you conned with more cunning than in high-class Italian and Chinese restaurants, most of which make their fortunes either by constantly suggesting specially prepared dishes not on the menu or charging extra for any item divided by two or more persons. A platter of fried zucchini (currently so in vogue) is indeed pleasant to have while you're sipping cocktails, and what better recommendation from your captain than an attractive assortment of *antipasti* or hot Szechuan appetizers for everyone to taste? Nice, yes, but unless you have the gall to ask what the cost will be, prepare to pay whatever the management decides to charge. As for splitting pasta dishes as a possible first or second course, occasionally you'll be advised in fine print on the menu that these orders "will be charged at our discretion," but generally no such indication is made and you're at the mercy of a tip-hungry staff. To come out on top financially in any Italian or Chinese restaurant, the best rule to follow is never, repeat, *never* order anything that's not priced clearly on the menu, and never allow a dish to be divided.

· · · If the Italians and Chinese are experts at the "specially prepared" and "split dish" routines, nobody can outwit the French when it comes to the "special of the day" and what I call the "friendly tasting" bits. In a more honest day, specials were always spelled out and priced in longhand on menus, and generally they were the least expensive items. Today in most lavish French restaurants, however, the gimmick is to have the captain or waiter simply recite the specials in glowing terms, never mention a price, and charge what can be astronomically more than for any dish on the menu. In the same vein there's no better way to pull in extra cash than to find a customer who can't decide, say, whether he wants as an appetizer the *terrine de ris de veau*, the *pâté maison*, or the *mousse de poissons*. Solution? It's suggested you be served a little of each "just to taste," which is fine and dandy except for the probability you'll be charged a supplement. Again, speak up when that smiling face serving you asks if you'd like to sample both the *milles-feuilles* and the fresh raspberries.

· · · A most lucrative convention in the luxury restaurant business is first not indicating on menus that main courses are appropriately garnished, then allowing customers to order extra vegetables à la carte without so much as a mention of what comes with the dinner. Believe it or not, restaurant personnel don't necessarily think twice about serving both a dish garnished with boiled potatoes and an à la carte side order of *gratin dauphinois,* and believe it or not, when this stunt is pulled I don't think twice about refusing to accept the two-dollar side order.

· · · The only question uttered by captains and waiters that is more lethal than the innocent-sounding "And would you care for a nice salad?" is the even more deadly "And would you care for a nice Caesar salad?" Of course these questions are *never* asked till the customers' minds have been made up, the orders taken, and the menus collected, the psychology being that although Americans are the world's greatest salad lovers, in fine restaurants they would rarely consider paying extra for a fairly common item they're accustomed to being served free elsewhere. No big deal, you say? Maybe not, but when that bill arrives and you notice that each person at the table has been charged a whopping $3.50 for a few lettuce leaves (I know one restaurant that gets $7.75 for Bibb and watercress), you have only yourself to blame.

• • • One of the biggest tests of anybody's character is the all-American steak house which follows that nefarious practice of providing no menu and having waiters recite what's available without mentioning prices. Today most people eating in these blue-chip emporia take for granted that a prime sirloin or filet is going to set them back $19.00 or $20, but what they're rarely led to suspect is that a substitute of hashed browns, cottage fries, onion rings, or salad for the traditionally complimentary baked potato could cost as much as $3.50 extra apiece. Nor are most customers aware that having even a giant porterhouse divided for two will often bring a supplementary charge of about $4. Sure, it takes nerve to get all this straight when ordering, but in the long run you'll be proud of your business acuity.

• • • It should be no news to anybody that most snazzy restaurants collect their greatest profits by chargin, hefty prices for cocktails, wines, digestives, and now, heaven forbid, imported mineral water. To maintain standards they have to, so you shouldn't begrudge paying $3.50 for a Manhattan and you should learn to tolerate those insane 200- to 300-percent markups on wine lists. Beware, on the other hand, of corkage charges in those restaurants that allow customers to bring their own wine. Normally the fee (which is never indicated on menus and wine lists) for opening and serving brown-bag wine is about $1 a bottle, but show up with an impressive magnum of '61 La Tâche or those two bottles of '64 Lafite-Rothschild you were told to hold for a special occasion and you could be charged as much as $5.00 a bottle (especially if the wine is decanted) unless you've settled the matter beforehand on the phone. Another problem that could result in a considerable addition to the bill is when the captain or waiter announces that the vintage you ordered is temporarily out of stock but somehow fails to inform you that the substitute he suggests runs $10 more. And still another travesty could arise should you prefer a little postprandial Cognac and allow yourself to be served something like Martell Cordon d'Argent at $10 a shot. Believe me, this sort of monkey business does exist in even the most reputable establishments, so unless you want to be played for a real sucker when it comes to ordering wines and digestives, either start reading carefully Lichine's *Wines & Spirits* or learn to quiz those who serve you on every recommendation they make.

I know all this might sound both defensive and a bit distasteful, but in this day the outlandish cost of dining out in style simply demands that we meet certain problems head-on if we hope to get a square deal. Confronting hucksters is never easy or pleasant, but not till you begin demonstrating a little prowess about clout will that blessed evening finally arrive when the bill at least comes close to your approximation. Then the only jolt left is being told "Sorry, this restaurant takes no credit cards."

A POSTSCRIPT

"BUT WHY AREN'T YOU FAT!"

● ●

ONCE, TWICE, three times a week I'm hit with the same irritating question: "But why aren't you fat! If you're such a gourmand, how in this world do you stay in good shape?" For a while I found it embarrassing to give a proper answer; then I just pretended not to hear; and now, without absolutely no modesty and even less patience, I blurt out the same response: "Because I eat *correctly,* that's why!"

If the truth must be known, I consider myself a far cry from being in ideal physical condition, a near impossibility for any Sybarite who recoils at the very idea of strenuous exercise (calisthentics, yes, but never rough workouts, jogging, and all that), who spends the better part of life sedentarily folded up in a writing chair or perched in ecstasy on restaurant banquettes, and who must subject the body inordinately to never-ending gustatory risks (bad wine, food poisoning, unavoidable bouts with gastritis). But, generally, I am healthy, energetic, and in complete control of my weight. I eat three wholesome meals every day of the year, I dine out in restaurants at least half a dozen times a week, I never "diet" in the more perverse sense of the word, and I don't think much about my intake of cholesterol, sodium, saturated fats, and starches for the simple reason that these nutritives which inspire such panic in others figure automatically and logically in the natural scheme of my eating habits. For those who might conclude that I'm one of those blessed souls who simply has never had a tendency to gain weight, let it be known that twenty years ago I topped off at a cool 215 pounds, 5 feet 10½ inches. After a radical change in eating habits, I eventually settled at a more sensible 170 pounds, and since then my weight has never varied more than 5 pounds. It never will.

Call me antisocial, snobbish, eccentric, but, to put it mildly, I really don't understand, much less communicate with, anyone who doesn't love food passionately and who doesn't at least try to develop respect for everything they put in their mouths. Obviously I'm more sensitive than most toward the gastronomic makeup of American life, but when, day after day, I witness all the dietary abuse not only blindly practiced by the vast majority but blatantly promoted by hucksters in the advertising media, I shiver. Mornings, I watch the masses choking down their sweet rolls and countless cups of coffee, hopeless time-clock victims who've apparently forgotten what a civilized, leisurely breakfast of bacon and eggs is all about. In offices I cringe when I see everyone from secretaries to top executives dash to the concession cart for stale bologna sandwiches, packaged cookies, and, of course, more hot caffeine instead of *automatically* making it a point to go out, relax, and enjoy a decent lunch.

Often I have occasion to glance into home refrigerators, and what I usually see makes my temperature rise; gallons of cola, frozen vegetables, pizzas and TV dinners, pounds of processed cheese in individual plastic wraps, boxes of disgusting breakfast cakes and rolls, and packages of those processed meats I wouldn't even feed my beagle. At movies I'm dumbfounded at the amount of popcorn, candy, and sweet drinks that is consumed (when and where *do* those people eat dinner?). Once in a while I'll literally stop in my tracks before a fast-food joint, peer with amazement through the window, and try to comprehend how the mobs can so casually swallow all those hamburger buns, fries, and shakes. I stand in disbelief as a friend tells about a bulimarexic female executive who goes on a starvation diet, then, to maintain the desired weight while satisfying hunger, gorges herself with enough food to induce vomiting. And, in the evening, I watch night after night as customers come into restaurants, order without hardly glancing at (much less studying) the menu and wine list, exchange little conversation, gulp down instinctively whatever is placed in front of them, and get out. As to what the budding palates of our youngsters are exposed to on the TV screen, I refuse even to comment.

Nerves wracked, metabolism shot, and overweight, much of this same society (roughly 20 percent of the American population at any given time) eventually reaches out for any means possible to correct the damage. And the possibilities are limitless: drugstores full of diet pills, diuretics, and vitamins (and plenty of doctors all too ready to write out plenty of prescriptions); sporting-goods emporia making a killing on jogging outfits; supermarkets literally overflowing with yogurt, cottage cheese, and special low-calorie foods; magazines creating every diet fad imaginable; TV commercials advertising expensive "sauna suits"; and, to be sure, the ever-understanding, ever-successful, and ever-expanding Pritikin Better Health Program, Nutri/System, and Weight Watchers International (which services no less than 550,000 fatties a week around the globe).

All of this sickens me, no matter what the so-called pros say about the so-called need today to reshape the public's eating habits, to teach what they call "behavior modification techniques" in nutrition education, and to resolve the gap between the sedentary individual and his "food-laden environment"—whatever that means. If, I ask, the large majority of us who live by the knife and fork somehow manage to eat well continually and still maintain a healthy weight level, why, in heaven's name, can't other intelligent beings do the same without resorting to what amounts to commercial swindle? Basically people know that the answers to good health and weight control ultimately come from no other source than plain old common sense, but big business stands steadfast. "The will to be cheated," Lucius Beebe commented some years ago, "is, apparently, a deep-rooted and inherent American instinct, but it seems a pity when it leads to the rejection of the all-too-infrequent natural pleasures that make life bearable at all. As someone once remarked, the customers at diet-fad groceries always seem to look as though they got there ten years too late."

While it seems that for most Americans the consumption of food is undertaken either as a necessary function of survival, a casual social diversion, or a reaction to serious psychological problems, for me eating is a sensual ritual, a highy refined art capable of enhancing life immeasurably. Whether it be fresh sturgeon caviar or sea urchin or a juicy hamburger, I hold almost all that I ingest sacred, to such an extent that no matter how urgent a business, financial, or social problem might be, I never allow it to affect when and what I eat. The ideas of not indulging in a wholesome breakfast, of ordering lunch at a plastic counter or from a coffee cart, of so much as purchasing a frozen TV dinner, or of consuming the glop served aboard airborne stockyards are as foreign to my way of life as double-knit polyester garments. I do not eat fast foods, processed meats and cheeses, packaged cookies, sugar and salt substitutes, canned fruits and vegetables, frozen French fries, MSG, synthetic bacon and hamburger, pizza, or so-called health food, and I do not drink domestic beer, decaffeinated coffee, or cheap wine. I do eat butter, olive oil, eggs, fresh vegetables, prime beef, natural cheeses and peanut butter, goose liver, fried country ham with red-eye gravy, and fresh cookies, and I do drink Manhattans, milk, fine wines, and lots of city tap water. I literally cannot remember when I did not sit down to three meals a day (including rare periods of illness), and I cannot recall eating without a proper table setting (including the times I dine alone at home) or rushing through a meal. I love a few salted peanuts with cocktails at a bar, but I rarely touch food served on buffets and at cocktail parties. I'm always hungry, I think about food incessantly, but, perhaps most important, when time comes to eat, I actually taste more than I consume—especially in the company of those who enjoy stimulating conversation. I never count calories consciously, though I could quote the caloric content of almost any food or beverage in question. If my clothes tell me I've gained a couple of pounds (I never step on a scale), I simply watch carefully what I eat and cut down on booze for a day or so. It always works for me.

It goes without saying that the big problem with most Americans is not losing pounds but maintaining a desirable weight, and rest assured that the diet cultists, doctors, and nutritionists have every secret imaginable to assure success. Well, at least as far as I'm concerned, healthy weight control is no more problematic than brushing teeth or walking the dog or preparing breakfast, meaning that what might appear to be a boring chore can, through habit, be transformed into a very enjoyable experience. When I wake up in the morning (even with a hangover), I know almost exactly where and what type of food I'll be eating throughout the day and night—and, despite inevitable worries and miscalculated work loads, the anticipation nears being erotic. If I'm entertaining at home or eating alone, the menu is as much on my mind as the writing deadline I'm struggling to meet; if I'm to dine out in public, I might spend an hour thinking about and discussing with others just which restaurant would be right; and if I'm invited to someone's home for dinner, I don't hesitate a moment to inquire the day before what is being served (often with the excuse that I'd like to bring some wine). An obsession, you say? You're right. But, as a result, I also remain in the euphoric position whereby I eat anything and everything my metabolism will allow without too much fear of affecting my health and waistline.

Many enlightened souls throughout the centuries have championed gourmandism as one of life's more civilized pleasures, but surely none stated the case more colorfully than the composer Rossini: "Aside from doing nothing, I know of no more delightful occupation for myself than eating—eating, that is, properly. What love is to the heart, appe-

tite is to the stomach. The stomach is the chapel master which acti-
vates and directs the great orchestra of our passions. An empty stomach represents the bassoon or piccolo, one groaning out dissatisfaction,
the other yelping for contentment. A full stomach, on the other hand,
is the triangle of pleasure, the tympani of joy."

INDEX OF RECIPES

●●